Arnold S. Wood

Martingale Asset Management

Behavioral
Finance and
Investment
Management

RESEARCH FOUNDATION

OF CFA INSTITUTE

Statement of Purpose

The Research Foundation of CFA Institute is a not-for-profit organization established to promote the development and dissemination of relevant research for investment practitioners worldwide.

ISBN 978-1-934667-34-7

17 December 2010

Editorial Staff

Maryann Dupes
Book Editor

Mary-Kate Brissett
Assistant Editor

Cindy Maisannes
Publishing Technology Specialist

Lois Carrier
Production Specialist

Contents

CFA Institute
CE Qualified Activity

This publication qualifies for 5 CE credits under the guidelines of the CFA Institute Continuing Education Program.

Editor's Preface

Behavioral Finance and Investment Management is about how and why we make the decisions we do. It is intended as an enlightenment piece. It is meant to increase our awareness of the simple mental faux pas and misjudgments we make every day, every minute. It is about us, our clients, everyone—no exceptions.

This book is a portfolio of different insights by different authors—all intended to help us make better choices. Each piece in some way touches on our biases, our embedded beliefs, and considers how these biases and beliefs can help as well as hinder our decisions. We make choices based on what we see, what we hear, and what preconceived notions and oh-so-natural reactions we have accumulated and demonstrated over our lifetimes. Our world is a mostly subjective one in which formulas are rarely the way to a solution. We seldom know what the outcomes of our decisions will be. We do know, however, that risky judgments dominate our lives, our livelihoods, and others around us. Although decisions that are expected to have a high probability of delivering positive outcomes may commonly prevail, the possibility of unexpected, negative consequences can have an indelible impact on how we treat similar choices under similar circumstances.

It is scary out there, so hopefully this book will provide a thoughtful handbook for improvement and for recognition of false confidence. That's the motive: better choices through awareness.

The River

Behavioral finance sits at the point where three tributaries combine to form a broad river.[1] Each tributary can take on varying importance, and the tributaries are not independent of one another but, rather, are sourced from different disciplines and thought patterns. Each source helps us understand just how complex this subject is and how important it is to get an overarching understanding.

---

[1]My description of behavioral finance engages in oversimplification because the division of the topic into tributaries makes what could otherwise be a confusing book more palatable, less overbearing, and more practical.

The first tributary is psychology, a science that focuses on individual behavior. It is this tributary that provides a litany of mental traps that regularly bedevil us. Red cars go fast! True or false? Or is it just an impression? The stock market is a mess today; does that make you less likely or more likely to increase your stock allocation?

The second tributary is social psychology. Perhaps an oversimplification to the precise mind of a scientist, social psychology is the study of how we behave and, in particular, how we make decisions in the presence of others. Group or committee behavior is, and has long been, a veritable petri dish for social psychologists. A committee chair who commits to a decision before the discussion begins, the domineering expert who "just knows" what to do, and the clarity of hindsight—all are well-known characteristics of group behavior.

The third tributary, where research has been ramped up dramatically over the past five years, is the anatomy, mechanics, and functioning of the brain, so-called neurofinance. Who could even conceive of pronouncing "amygdala" or knowing where the prefrontal cortex is located three years ago? Who is Phineas Gage, and what did the iron pole exploding through his head end up telling us about the geography of the brain?

Combined, these three tributaries of research help us understand how and why we make choices. They provide a framework to evaluate the origins of behavioral insights and their potential validity. But no matter how much we learn, no matter how introspective we become, ours is the business of dealing with uncertainty. At the same time, it is a business about the future, and how much influence the past will have is a matter of endless contention. Experts inevitably get tripped up; what looks risky may not be; and although clients justifiably expect performance, it can be a frustrating weight. This is why, to a great extent, indexing is a viable alternative. We are often our own worst enemy. This book is intended to help defeat the enemy.

The Tipping Point

The origins of behavioral finance date back to the very first financial choice made. But for me, the tipping point for the discipline occurred on 10 October 2002. I remember it very clearly.

That morning the phone rang as soon as I walked into my office. It was my wife. She sounded panicky. "Where is Oskar?" Oskar is our standard poodle and like a fourth child. Each morning before I go to work, I let Oskar out, and while he does what dogs do, I scan the headlines of the *New York Times* and the *Boston Globe*. That day, below the fold of the *Times'* first page, was an announcement. It was not just any announcement. The article title read, "A Nobel That Bridges Economics and Psychology."

Daniel Kahneman and Vernon Smith had won Nobel Prizes for their research and insights into why and how we make economic and financial decisions. The article went on:

> Two Americans have won this year's Nobel award in economics for trying to explain idiosyncrasies in people's ways of making decisions, research that has helped incorporate insights from psychology into the discipline of economics. . . . Their work shed light on strategies for explaining everything from stock market bubbles to regulating utilities and countless other economic activities. . . . Though the two winners will now inevitably be grouped together, they approached their field from very different backgrounds. "Kahneman's a psychologist—he's interested in how your brain works, how you make decisions," said Alvin E. Roth, an economist at Harvard who specializes in experimental methods. "Smith is an economist. He's interested in how markets work."[2]

After reading that headline, it did not dawn on me to let Oskar back in—a routine I had been doing faithfully for years. I was so excited by the news that I jumped in my car and drove to work, completely taken by the announcement. Some of us in the investment business, although not many back then, were sparked by the research of people like these two Nobel Prize winners. We had an unyielding curiosity as to why well-educated, well-incentivized investment practitioners behaved the way they did; yet we realized that our enthusiasm was not particularly widely shared. The Nobel Prize was the proverbial "tipping point" for an appreciation of what these two researchers, and others following similar paths, were bringing to the forefront of our business.

Today, Oskar's routine has not changed, but the investment management business and its clientele have. The surge of research, the proliferation of academic and practitioner papers, and the appearance of several best-sellers have turned our industry into a Garden of Eden for behavioral insights. When behavioral finance and behavioral economics were a loose and easily maligned collection of hypotheses on the scientific frontier, the evidence was everywhere—an irresistible laboratory. Today, the discipline has achieved respect, and this book gives recognition to a few of the people who have enriched all of us with their research and determination to know what makes us tick.

The Secret

It may be convenient to think that behavioral finance is about how other investors, managers, analysts, and so on behave—not about how we behave. But that is far from the case. Behavioral finance is intensely personal. No one is beyond its reach or its impact.

---

[2]Daniel Altman, "A Nobel That Bridges Economics and Psychology," *New York Times* (10 October 2002).

Among other accomplishments, Aristotle Onassis is famous for saying, "The secret of business is to know something that nobody else knows." One must ask oneself, "What is it that I know that nobody else knows as well as I do?" The answer is yourself. This is not just a matter of casual introspection, nor is it a useless existential thought. It is a practical answer.

In a world that is focused on governance, the way we behave and the choices we make deserve attention at least equal to what the more obvious questions of organizational or structural governance get. Is auditing your cognitive processes not a key governance responsibility? We are accountable for our decisions. So, knowing about ourselves in a way that nobody else does makes it incumbent that we monitor and adjust our own cognitive processes and emotions with the clear mission of making better decisions.

Summary

Once again, this book is about us, about how and why we make the decisions we do. After reading its many insights, you will be equipped with a useful mirror into your choices and will have a better measure of their effectiveness. It is about us, our clients, everyone—no exceptions, no excuses.

Arnold S. Wood
Partner, President, and CEO
Martingale Asset Management

What Is Behavioral Finance?

Meir Statman

Standard finance, also known as *modern portfolio theory*, has four foundation blocks: (1) investors are rational; (2) markets are efficient; (3) investors should design their portfolios according to the rules of mean-variance portfolio theory and, in reality, do so; and (4) expected returns are a function of risk and risk alone. Modern portfolio theory is no longer very modern, dating back to the late 1950s and early 1960s. Merton Miller and Franco Modigliani described investors as rational in 1961. Eugene Fama described markets as efficient in 1965. Harry Markowitz prescribed *mean-variance portfolio theory* in its early form in 1952 and in its full form in 1959. William Sharpe adopted mean-variance portfolio theory as a description of investor behavior and in 1964 introduced the capital asset pricing theory (CAPM). According to this theory, differences in expected returns are determined only by differences in risk, and beta is the measure of risk.

Behavioral finance offers an alternative block for each of the foundation blocks of standard finance. According to behavioral finance, investors are "normal," not rational. Markets are not efficient, even if they are difficult to beat. Investors design portfolios according to the rules of behavioral portfolio theory, not mean-variance portfolio theory. And expected returns follow behavioral asset pricing theory, in which risk is not measured by beta and expected returns are determined by more than risk. In this chapter, I describe each of these building blocks of behavioral finance.

Putting It in Context

What triggered you to write this piece? And how do you think it should be helpful to professional investment practitioners?

What we know today as behavioral finance was initiated some three decades ago by a small number of people who asked questions seldom asked before and offered answers not offered before. Today, many people are engaged in behavioral finance, and there is wide disagreement about its boundaries and frontiers. Many see behavioral finance mainly as a refutation of the efficient market hypothesis and as a tool to beat the market. This, I believe, is a mistake. I was motivated to write my article to correct that mistake.

Behavioral finance is an attempt to understand investors and the reflection of their interactions in financial markets. Such understanding can, for example, help investment professionals tamp down the overconfidence of investors in their ability to beat the market. Or it can help investment professionals cater to this overconfidence.

"Normal" Investors and Rational Ones

The reluctance to realize losses is one of many examples of the differences between *rational investors* and *normal investors*. That reluctance is puzzling to rational investors since, as Miller and Modigliani (1961) wrote, rational investors care only about the substance of their wealth, not its form. In the absence of transaction costs and taxes, paper losses are different from realized losses only in form, not in substance. Moreover, tax considerations give an edge to realized losses over paper losses because realized losses reduce taxes while paper losses do not.

Normal investors are you and me, and even wealthy and famous people, such as Martha Stewart. We are not stupid, but neither are we rational by Miller and Modigliani's definition. Evidence presented at Martha Stewart's trial highlights her reluctance to realize losses. "Just took lots of huge losses to offset sonic gains," Ms. Stewart wrote in an e-mail to Mark Goldstein, a friend, on December 22, 2001, "made my stomach turn." If Ms. Stewart were rational, she would have felt her stomach turn when the prices of her stocks declined and she incurred her "paper" losses, but not when she realized her losses, since transaction costs associated with the realization of losses were likely small relative to its tax benefits.

Shefrin and Statman (1985) presented the reluctance to realize losses in a behavioral framework. They argue that the reluctance stems from a combination of two cognitive biases and an emotion. One cognitive bias is faulty framing, where normal investors fail to mark their stocks to market prices. Investors open mental accounts when they buy stocks and continue to mark their value to purchase prices even after market prices have changed. They mark stocks to market only when they sell their stocks and close their mental accounts. Normal investors do not acknowledge paper losses because open accounts keep alive the hope that stock prices will rise and losses will turn into gains. But hope dies when stocks are sold and losses are realized.

The second cognitive bias that plays a role in the reluctance to realize losses is hindsight bias, which misleads investors into thinking that what is clear in hindsight was equally clear in foresight. Hindsight bias misleads investors into thinking that they could have seen losing stocks in foresight, not only in hindsight, and avoided them. The cognitive bias of hindsight is linked to the emotion of regret. Realization of losses brings the pain of regret when investors find, in hindsight, that they would have had happier outcomes if only they had avoided buying the losing stocks.

Postponing the realization of losses until December is one defense against regret. Normal investors tend to realize losses in December, and Ms. Stewart followed that practice when she realized her losses in December 2001. There is nothing rational in the role that December plays in the realization of losses.

Investors get no more tax benefits from the realization of losses in December than in November or any other month. Indeed, Shefrin and Statman (1985) showed that it makes rational sense to realize losses when they occur rather than wait until December. The real advantage of December is the behavioral advantage. What is framed as an investment loss in November is framed as a tax deduction in December.

Behavioral Portfolio Theory

Behavioral portfolio theory, introduced by Shefrin and Statman (2000), is a goal-based theory. In that theory, investors divide their money into many mental account layers of a portfolio pyramid corresponding to goals such as having a secure retirement, paying for a college education, or being rich enough to hop on a cruise ship whenever they please.

The road to behavioral portfolio theory started more than 60 years ago when Friedman and Savage (1948) noted that hope for riches and protection from poverty share roles in our behavior; people who buy lottery tickets often buy insurance policies as well. So, people are risk-seeking enough to buy lottery tickets while they are risk-averse enough to buy insurance. Four years later, Markowitz wrote two papers that reflect two very different views of behavior. In one (Markowitz 1952a), he created mean-variance theory, based on expected utility theory; in the other (Markowitz 1952b), he extended Friedman and Savage's insurance-lottery framework. People in mean-variance theory, unlike people in the insurance-lottery framework, never buy lottery tickets; they are always risk averse, never risk seeking.

Friedman and Savage (1948) observed that people buy lottery tickets because they aspire to reach higher social classes, whereas they buy insurance as protection against falling into lower social classes. Markowitz (1952b) clarified the observation of Friedman and Savage by noting that people aspire to move up from their current social class or "customary wealth." So, people with $10,000 might accept lottery-like odds in the hope of winning $1 million, and people with $1 million might accept lottery-like odds in the hope of winning $100 million. Kahneman and Tversky (1979) extended the work of Markowitz (1952b) into prospect theory. Prospect theory describes the behavior of people who accept lottery-like odds when they are below their levels of aspiration but reject such odds when they are above their levels of aspiration.

A central feature in behavioral portfolio theory is the observation that investors view their portfolios not as a whole, as prescribed by mean-variance portfolio theory, but as distinct mental account layers in a pyramid of assets, where mental account layers are associated with particular goals and where attitudes toward risk vary across layers. One mental account layer might be a "downside protection" layer, designed to protect investors from being poor.

Another might be an "upside potential" layer, designed to give investors a chance at being rich. Investors might behave as if they hate risk in the downside protection layer, while they behave as if they love risk in the upside potential layer. These are normal, familiar investors, investors who are animated by aspirations, not attitudes toward risk.

In 2002, *Wall Street Journal* writer Mylene Mangalindan told the story of David Callisch, a man who bet on one stock. When Callisch joined Altheon WebSystems, Inc., in 1997, he asked his wife "to give him four years and they would score big," and his "bet seemed to pay off when Altheon went public." By 2000, Callisch's Altheon shares were worth $10 million. "He remembers making plans to retire, to go back to school, to spend more time with his three sons. His relatives, his colleagues, and his broker all told him to diversify his holdings. He didn't." Unfortunately, Callisch's lottery ticket turned out to be a loser.

Callisch's aspirations are common, shared by the many who gamble on individual stocks and lottery tickets. Most lose, but some win. One lottery winner, a clerk in the New York subway system, said "I was able to retire from my job after 31 years. My wife was able to quit her job and stay home to raise our daughter. We are able to travel whenever we want to. We were able to buy a co-op, which before we could not afford." Investors such as Mr. Callisch and lottery buyers such as the New York subway clerk aspire to retire, buy houses, travel, and spend time with their children. They buy bonds in the hope of protection from poverty, stock mutual funds in the hope of moderate riches, and individual stocks and lottery tickets in the hope of great riches.

Mean-variance portfolio theory and behavioral portfolio theory were combined recently as mental accounting portfolio theory by Das, Markowitz, Scheid, and Statman (2010). Investors begin by allocating their wealth across goals into mental account layers, say 70 percent to retirement income, 20 percent to college funds, and 10 percent to being rich enough to hop on a cruise ship whenever they please. Next, investors specify the desired probability of reaching the threshold of each goal, say 99 percent for retirement income, 60 percent for college funds, and 20 percent for getting rich. Each mental account is now optimized as a sub-portfolio by the rules of mean-variance theory, and each feasible goal is achieved with a combination of assets. For example, the retirement goal is likely to be achieved in a sub-portfolio with a combination weighted toward bonds, the college goal is likely to be achieved in a sub-portfolio with a balanced combination of stocks and bonds, and the getting rich goal is likely to be achieved in a sub-portfolio with a combination weighted toward stocks, perhaps with some options and lottery tickets thrown in. The overall portfolio is the sum of the mental account sub-portfolios, and it, like the mental account sub-portfolios, lies on the mean-variance efficient frontier.

Behavioral Asset Pricing Model

Stripped to their basics, all asset pricing models are versions of the old reliable supply-and-demand model of introductory economics. The benefits that determine demand vary from product to product, but they can be classified into three groups: utilitarian, expressive, and emotional. The utilitarian benefits of a car include good gas mileage and reliability. Expressive benefits are those that enable us to signal to ourselves or others our values, social class, and tastes. Expressive characteristics include style (e.g., the style of a Jaguar) and social responsibility (e.g., the environmental responsibility of a Prius). Emotional benefits include pride (e.g., "having arrived" with a Rolls Royce) and exhilaration (e.g., BMW as the "ultimate driving machine").

In the investment context, utilitarian benefits are often labeled "fundamental," and expressive and emotional benefits are often labeled "sentiment." High expected returns and low risk are utilitarian benefits of a stock, and those who restrict the demand function to it are considered rational. The rubric of rationality is not so easily extended to expressive and emotional benefits, such as the display of social responsibility in a socially responsible mutual fund, the display of wealth in a hedge fund, or the excitement of an initial public offering.

What characteristics do stock buyers like? Investors like stocks with low volatility in prices and earnings. They also like stocks with large capitalization, high price-to-book ratios, high price-to-earnings ratios, low leverage, and more. Stocks with desirable characteristics fetch higher prices, and higher prices correspond to lower expected returns. Stocks with low book-to-market ratios (growth stocks) and large-cap stocks have low expected returns. In the *behavioral asset pricing model* (BAPM) (Shefrin and Statman 1994, Statman 1999), stocks with desirable characteristics have low expected returns.

The asset pricing model of standard finance is moving away from the *capital asset pricing model* (CAPM)—in which beta is the only characteristic that determines expected stock returns—toward a model that is similar to the BAPM. For instance, the *three-factor model* formulated by Fama and French (1992), popular in standard finance, adds market capitalization and book-to-market ratio to beta as characteristics that affect expected returns. One difference between this three-factor model of standard finance and the BAPM is in the interpretation of these characteristics. In standard finance, market capitalization and book-to-market ratios are interpreted as measures of risk; small-cap stocks and stocks with high book-to-market ratios (value stocks) are considered high-risk stocks, and the high risk justifies high expected returns.

In contrast, in *behavioral asset pricing theory*, the same characteristics are interpreted as reflections of affect, an emotion, and representativeness, a cognitive bias. Both lead investors to identify good stocks as stocks of good companies. Small-cap stocks and stocks with high book-to-market ratios (value stocks) are stocks of "bad" companies (e.g., bank stocks in 2008). These companies have negative affect, so investors shun them, depressing their prices and pushing up their expected returns. Statman, Fisher, and Anginer (2008) find that respondents in the *Fortune* surveys of admired companies consider stocks of small-cap, high book-to-market companies as unattractive investments, yet stocks of admired companies yielded lower returns, on average, than stocks of spurned companies.

Still, the road from the preferences of normal investors to security returns is not straightforward, as explained by Shefrin and Statman (1994) and more recently by Pontiff (2006). Suppose that most investors are indeed normal investors who believe, erroneously, that good stocks are stocks of good companies. But surely not all investors commit that error. Some investors are rational, investors aware of the biases of normal investors and seeking to capitalize on them favoring stocks of "bad" companies. Would rational investors not nullify any effect of normal investors on security prices through arbitrage? If the effects of normal investors on stock returns are nullified, risk-adjusted expected returns to stocks of good companies will be no different from risk-adjusted expected returns to stocks of bad companies. However, if arbitrage is incomplete, risk-adjusted expected returns to stocks of bad companies will exceed risk-adjusted expected returns to stocks of good companies.

As we consider arbitrage and the likelihood that it would nullify the effects of the preferences of normal investors on stock price, note that no perfect (risk-free) arbitrage is possible here. To see the implications of imperfect arbitrage, imagine rational investors who receive reliable, but not perfect, information about the expected return of a particular stock. Imagine also that the nature of the information is such that the expected return of the stock as assessed by rational investors is higher than the expected return as reflected in the current price of the stock. It is optimal for rational investors to increase their holdings of the particular stock, but as the amount devoted to the stock increases, their portfolios become less diversified as they take on more idiosyncratic risk. The increase in risk leads rational investors to limit the amount allocated to the stock, and with it, limit their effect on its price.

So, what does the BAPM look like?

The CAPM is expressed as an equation where:

Expected return of a stock $= f$ (market factor).

The three-factor model is expressed as an equation where:

Expected return of a stock $= f$ (market factor, book-to-market factor, market cap factor).

Similarly, the BAPM is expressed as:

Expected return of a stock = f (market factor, book-to-market factor, market cap factor, momentum, affect factor, social responsibility factor, status factor, and more).

Market Efficiency

Fama (1991) noted long ago that market efficiency per se is not testable. Market efficiency must be tested jointly with an asset pricing model, such as the CAPM or the three-factor model. For example, the excess returns relative to the CAPM of small-cap stocks and stocks with high book-to-market ratios might indicate that the market is not efficient or that the CAPM is a bad model of expected returns.

The definition of "market efficiency" says that a market for a stock is efficient if the price of a stock is always equal to its fundamental value. A stock's fundamental value is the present value of cash flows the stock can reasonably be expected to generate, such as dividends. Over the years, the definition of "market efficiency" became confused with the notion that a market is efficient when you cannot beat it by earning excess returns (or positive "alpha"). To earn excess returns, you must identify deviations of price from fundamental value and then buy undervalued securities and sell overvalued ones. Logically, a market that is efficient in terms of the price-equals-fundamental value definition is also a market that cannot be beaten, but a market that cannot be beaten is not necessarily efficient. For example, think of a market in which price deviates greatly from fundamental value, such as during a bubble. Still, you cannot beat the market unless you have a way to take advantage of differences between price and value, and that's not always possible. Plenty of investors believed that the stock market was experiencing a bubble in 1998, yet plenty of them lost much money by shorting stocks in 1999.

We have much evidence that stock prices regularly deviate from fundamental value, so we know that markets for stocks are not always efficient. Richard Roll (1988) found that only 20 percent of changes in stock prices can be attributed to changes in fundamental value, and Ray Fair (2002) found that many changes in the S&P 500 Index occur with no change in fundamental value. The stock market crash of 1987 stands out as an example of deviation from market efficiency. The U.S. stock market dropped more than 20 percent in one day, October 19, 1987 (popularly referred to as "Black Monday"). No one has been able to identify any change in the fundamental value of U.S. stocks that day that might come close to 20 percent.

The problem of joint testing makes much of the debate on market efficiency futile. Proponents of standard finance regard market efficiency as fact and challenge anomalies that are inconsistent with it. For their part, investment professionals who claim that they can beat the market regard market efficiency as false and delight in anomalies that are inconsistent with it. Standard finance proponents were happy with the CAPM as its asset pricing model as long as it served to show that markets are efficient, but they abandoned the CAPM in favor of the three-factor model when the CAPM produced anomalies inconsistent with market efficiency. The problem of jointly testing market efficiency and asset pricing models dooms us to attempt to determine two variables with only one equation. Instead, we can assume market efficiency and explore the characteristics that make an asset pricing model, or we can assume an asset pricing model and test market efficiency. I am inclined toward the former. When we see a Toyota automobile in a showroom with one price tag side by side with a Lexus with a higher price tag, we are inclined to look to the automobile asset pricing model for reasons for the price difference rather than conclude that the automobile market is inefficient. Does the Lexus have leather seats while the Toyota's seats are upholstered in cloth? Does the Lexus nameplate convey higher status than the Toyota nameplate? The same is true when we see Stock A with an expected return of 8 percent and Stock B with an expected return of 6 percent.

Elegant Theories and Testable Hypotheses

The statement that behavioral finance is an interesting collection of stories but does not offer the equivalent of the comprehensive theory and rigorous tests of standard finance is as common as it is wrong. When people think about standard finance, they usually think about the CAPM and mean-variance portfolio theory. These two models are elegant, but few use them in their elegant form. The elegant CAPM has been replaced as standard finance's asset pricing model by the messy three-factor model, which claims that expected return is a function of equity market capitalization and the ratio of book value to market value in addition to beta. In turn, the three-factor model has become the four-factor model with the addition of momentum and the five-factor model with the addition of liquidity. The list is likely to grow. Similarly, few apply mean-variance theory or its optimizer in their elegant forms. Instead, it is mostly constraints on the optimizer that determine mean-variance optimal portfolios, and these constraints are often rooted in behavioral consideration. A constraint on the proportion allocated to foreign stocks is one example, driven by "home bias." But we don't need elegant models; we need models that describe real people in real markets. These are the models of behavioral finance.

Behavioral finance offers behavioral asset pricing theory and behavioral portfolio theory, which are no less elegant than the models of standard finance and are much closer to reality. Moreover, behavioral finance offers testable hypotheses and empirical assessments that can reject these hypotheses if they deserve to be rejected. For example, Shefrin and Statman (1985) offered the testable "disposition" hypothesis that investors are disposed to hold on to losing stocks. This hypothesis can be rejected by empirical evidence that investors are quick to realize losses. But the evidence among many types of investors in many countries supports the hypothesis.

Summary

Standard finance, introduced in the late 1950s and early 1960s, was preceded by what I call *proto-behavioral finance* and followed, beginning in the early 1980s, by behavioral finance. Proto-behavioral finance and behavioral finance are populated by normal people, while standard finance is populated by rational people. Rational people always prefer more wealth to less and are never confused by the form of wealth. In contrast, normal people, affected by cognitive biases and emotions, are often confused by the form of wealth, and while they always prefer more to less, it is not always wealth they want more of. Sometimes normal people want more status or more social responsibility and are willing to sacrifice wealth for them.

The distinction between rational and normal underlies other differences between standard finance and behavioral finance, including those related to answers to portfolio theory, asset pricing theory, and market efficiency theory. I described the path from proto-behavioral finance to standard finance and to behavioral finance in Statman (2005).

Finance was in its proto-behavioral era in 1957 when Howard Snyder (1957) taught normal investors "how to take a loss and like it" in an article by that name. "There is no loss without collateral compensation," he wrote, explaining that realizing losses increases wealth by reducing taxes. Yet he went on to note that normal investors are reluctant to realize losses. "Human nature being what it is, we are loath to take a loss until we are forced into it. Too often, we believe that by ignoring a loss we will someday glance at the asset to find it has not only recovered its original value but has shown some appreciation" (p. 116). Snyder's observation about the reluctance of normal investors to realize losses more than a half a century ago was reintroduced by Shefrin and Statman as the "disposition effect" in 1985, the early period of behavioral finance.

Proto-behavioral finance was the obese era of finance. It described normal human behavior, encompassed many human concerns, and recognized many human proclivities, but it was unstructured and unfit, often going straight from anecdote to conjecture and to general conclusion.

Standard finance ruled in the anorexic era of finance. Its narrowing focus is illustrated by the common standard finance refrain: "Yes, but what does it have to do with asset prices?" Proponents of standard finance were busy excluding questions from its domain rather than answering them. As Merton Miller (1986) wrote in response to Shefrin and Statman's (1984) article on dividends ". . . stocks are usually more than just the abstract 'bundles of return' of our economic models. Behind each holding may be a story of family business, family quarrels, legacies received, divorce settlement, and a host of other considerations almost totally irrelevant to our theories of portfolio selection. That we abstract from all these stories in building our models is not because the stories are uninteresting but because they may be too interesting and thereby distract us from the pervasive market forces that should be our principal concern" (p. S467).

Behavioral finance is the era that strives for a muscular and fit finance. Behavioral finance describes normal people in many settings, including those that Merton Miller preferred to exclude. It includes explorations into why people trade, why they consume more from dividend dollars than from capital dollars, and why they prefer to invest in socially responsible companies, or eager to invest in hedge funds.

Behavioral finance owes much to standard finance. Standard finance introduced into finance the exacting rules of science, where theory leads to hypotheses and to empirical evidence that can support the hypotheses or reject them. Behavioral finance will never abandon the scientific method. For example, the disposition hypothesis predicts that people will realize gains in haste but procrastinate in the realization of losses. The hypothesis can be rejected by analysis of data. But it has been overwhelmingly supported by many empirical studies.

Meir Statman is the Glenn Klimek Professor of Finance at Santa Clara University, Santa Clara, California, and a visiting professor of finance at Tilburg University, Tilburg, the Netherlands.

REFERENCES

Das, S., H. Markowitz, J. Scheid, and M. Statman. 2010. "Portfolio Optimization with Mental Accounts." *Journal of Financial and Quantitative Analysis*, vol. 45, no. 2 (April):311–334.

Fama, E.F. 1991. "Efficient Capital Markets: II." *Journal of Finance*, vol. 46, no. 5 (December): 1575–1617.

———. 1965. "Random Walks in Stock Market Prices." *Financial Analysts Journal*, vol. 21, no. 5 (September/October):55–59.

Fama, E.F., and K. French. 1992. "The Cross-Section of Expected Stock Returns." *Journal of Finance*, vol. 47, no. 2 (June):427–465.

Fair, R. 2002. "The Events That Shook the Market." *Journal of Business*, vol. 75, no. 4 (October):713–731.

Friedman, M., and L. Savage. 1948. "The Utility Analysis of Choices Involving Risk." *Journal of Political Economy*, vol. 56, no. 4 (August):279–304.

Kahneman, D., and A. Tversky. 1979. "Prospect Theory: An Analysis of Decision under Risk." *Econometrica*, vol. 47, no. 2 (March):263–291.

Mangalindan, M. 2002. "Hoping Is Hard in Silicon Valley." *Wall Street Journal* (July 15): Cl.

Markowitz, H.M. 1952a. "Portfolio Selection." *Journal of Finance*, vol. 7, no. 1 (March):77–91.

———. 1952b. "The Utility of Wealth." *Journal of Political Economy*, vol. 60, no. 2 (April): 151–158.

———. 1959. *Portfolio Selection: Diversification of Investments*. New York: John Wiley & Sons.

———. 1999. "The Early History of Portfolio Theory: 1600–1960." *Financial Analysts Journal*, vol. 55, no. 4 (July/August):5–15.

Miller, M.H. 1986. "Behavioral Rationality in Finance: The Case of Dividends." *Journal of Business*, vol. 59, no. 4 (October):S451–S468.

Miller, M., and F. Modigliani. 1961. "Dividend Policy, Growth, and the Valuation of Shares." *Journal of Business*, vol. 34, no. 4 (October):411–433.

Pontiff, J. 2006. "Costly Arbitrage and the Myth of Idiosyncratic Risk." *Journal of Accounting and Economics*, vol. 42, no. 1–2 (October):35–52.

Roll, R.R. 1988. "R^2." *Journal of Finance*, vol. 43, no. 3 (July):541–566.

Sharpe, W.F. 1964. "Capital Asset Prices: A Theory of Market Equilibrium under Conditions of Risk." *Journal of Finance*, vol. 19, no. 3 (September):425–442.

Shefrin, H.M., and M. Statman. 1984. "Explaining Investor Preference for Cash Dividends." *Journal of Financial Economics*, vol. 13, no. 2 (June):253–282.

———. 1985. "The Disposition to Sell Winners Too Early and Ride Losers Too Long: Theory and Evidence." *Journal of Finance*, vol. 40, no. 3 (July):777–790.

————. 1994. "Behavioral Capital Asset Pricing Theory." *Journal of Financial and Quantitative Analysis*, vol. 29, no. 3 (September):323–349.

————. 2000. "Behavioral Portfolio Theory." *Journal of Financial and Quantitative Analysis*, vol. 35, no. 2 (June):127–151.

Snyder, W.H.T. 1957. "How to Take a Loss and Like It." *Financial Analysts Journal*, vol. 13, no. 2 (May):115–116.

Statman, M. 1999. "Behavioral Finance: Past Battles and Future Engagements." *Financial Analysts Journal*, vol. 55, no. 6 (November/December):18–27.

————. 2005. "Martha Stewart's Lessons in Behavioral Finance." *Journal of Investment Consulting*, vol. 7, no. 2 (Winter):52–60.

Statman, M., K.L. Fisher, and D. Anginer. 2008. "Affect in a Behavioral Asset-Pricing Model." *Financial Analysts Journal*, vol. 64, no. 2 (March/April):20–29.

The End of Behavioral Finance

Richard H. Thaler

In 1985, Werner De Bondt and I published an article that asked the question: "Does the stock market overreact?" The article was controversial because it gave evidence to support the hypothesis that a cognitive bias (investor overreaction to a long series of bad news) could produce predictable mispricing of stocks traded on the NYSE. Although this idea was hardly shocking to practitioners, the conventional wisdom among finance academics was that we must have made a mistake somewhere.

The academic community considered several possibilities to explain our results: We made a programming error; the results were correctly measured but explainable by chance variation (data mining); the results were correct and robust (no data mining), but rather than discovering mispricing caused by cognitive errors, we discovered some new risk factor. The possibility that we had both the facts and the explanation right was thought by many academics to be a logical impossibility, and the demise of behavioral finance was considered a sure bet.

Fifteen years later, many respectable financial economists work in the field called behavioral finance.[1] I believe the area no longer merits the adjective "controversial." Indeed, behavioral finance is simply a moderate, agnostic approach to studying financial markets. Nevertheless, I too predict the end of the behavioral finance field, although not for the reasons originally proposed.

To understand what behavioral finance is and why it was originally thought to be a fleeting heresy, one must first understand the standard approach to financial economics and why those who used this approach believed, on theoretical grounds, that cognitive biases could not affect asset prices.

Why Behavioral Finance Cannot Be Dismissed

Modern financial economic theory is based on the assumption that the "representative agent" in the economy is rational in two ways: The representative agent (1) makes decisions according to the axioms of expected utility theory and (2) makes unbiased forecasts about the future. An extreme version of this theory assumes that every agent behaves in accordance with these assumptions. Most

---

[1] For surveys of behavioral finance, see De Bondt and Thaler (1995), Shefrin (2000), and Shleifer (2000).

economists recognize this extreme version as unrealistic; they concede that many of their relatives and acquaintances—spouses, students, deans, government leaders, and so on—are hopeless decision makers. Still, defenders of the tradi-tional model argue that it is not a problem for some agents in the economy to make suboptimal decisions as long as the "marginal investor," that is, the investor who is making the specific investment decision at hand, is rational.

The argument that asset prices are set by rational investors is part of the grand oral tradition in economics and is often attributed to Milton Friedman, one of the greatest economists of the century and one of the greatest debaters of all time. But the argument has two fundamental problems. First, even if asset prices were set only by rational investors in the aggregate, knowing what individual investors are doing might still be of interest. Second, although the argument is intuitively appealing and reassuring, its adherents have rarely spelled it out carefully.

Suppose a market has two kinds of investors: rational investors (rationals), who behave like agents in economics textbooks, and quasi-rational investors (quasi's), people who are trying as hard as they can to make good investment decisions but make predictable mistakes. Suppose also that two assets in this market, X and Y, are objectively worth the same amount but cannot be transformed from one into the other. Finally, assume that the quasi's think X is worth more than Y, an opinion that could change (quasi's often change their minds) while the rationals know that X and Y are worth the same. What conditions are necessary to assure that the prices of X and Y will be the same, as they would be in a world with only rational investors?

This question is complex, but some of the essential conditions are the following. First, in dollar-weighted terms, such a market cannot have too many quasi's (in order for the rational investors to be marginal). Second, the market must allow costless short selling (so that if prices get too high, the rationals can drive them down). Third, only rational investors can sell short; otherwise, the quasi's will short Y when the two prices are the same because they believe X is worth more than Y. The result would be no equilibrium. Fourth, at some date *T*, the true relationship between X and Y must become clear to all investors. Fifth, the rationals must have long horizons, long enough to include date *T*. These conditions are tough to meet.

Consider the example of the Royal Dutch/Shell Group, as documented in Rosenthal and Young (1990) and Froot and Dabora (1999). Royal Dutch Petroleum and Shell Transport are independently incorporated in, respectively, the Netherlands and England. The current company emerged from a 1907 alliance between Royal Dutch and Shell Transport in which the two companies agreed to merge their interests on a 60/40 basis. Royal Dutch trades primarily in the United States and the Netherlands and is part of the S&P 500 Index; Shell trades primarily in London and is part of the Financial Times Stock Exchange Index. According to any rational model, the shares of these two components (after adjusting for foreign exchange) should trade in a 60–40 ratio. They do not; the actual price ratio has deviated from the expected one by more than 35 percent. Simple explanations, such as taxes and transaction costs, cannot explain the disparity.[2]

Why don't rational investors intervene to force the shares of Royal Dutch/ Shell back to their rational 60–40 ratio? The answer is that hedge funds do make investments based on this disparity: They buy the cheaper stock and short the more expensive one. Indeed, Royal Dutch/Shell is one of many such investments Long-Term Capital Management had in place in the summer of 1998. In August 1998, when things started to unravel for LTCM, the Royal Dutch/Shell disparity was relatively large, so at a time when LTCM might have chosen to increase the money it was willing to bet on this anomaly, it had to cut back instead. Shleifer and Vishny (1997) envisioned this scenario in their article explaining the "Limits of Arbitrage."

The lesson from this example is that even when the relationship between two prices is easy to calculate and fixed by charter, prices can diverge and arbitrageurs are limited in their ability to restore the prices to parity. What, then, are the prospects for prices to be rational in more-complex settings? Take the case of Internet stocks. Many, if not most, professional analysts believe that the valuations of Internet stocks are too high. In surveys of professional investors that I conducted in the spring of 1999, the median respondent thought that the intrinsic value of a portfolio of five Internet stocks (America Online, Amazon.com, eBay, Priceline.com, and Yahoo!) was 50 percent of the market price. Suppose the "professionals" are right and these multibillion dollar companies are worth only half of their current prices. Suppose further that this valuation is the consensus of Wall Street experts. How can such a situation exist? The answer is that it may be an equilibrium (although not a "rational equilibrium") as long as the Wall Street experts are not the marginal investors in these stocks. If Internet stocks are primarily owned by individual investors, Wall Street pessimism will not drive the price down because the supply of short sellers will then be too limited. Although some hedge funds are willing to bet on convergence for the Royal Dutch/Shell disparity, few are willing to bet on the demise of the Internet frenzy, or at least too few to cause it to happen.

---

[2]See Froot and Dabora, who also studied the similar cases of Unilever N.V./PLC and SmithKline Beecham.

The analysis of Internet stocks applies with even greater force to the current level of the U.S. stock market. The consensus on Wall Street (and on similar streets around the world) is that the U.S. stock market is 20–30 percent overvalued; yet, prices can continue to increase because the investors who are willing to bet on a decline have too few dollars to prevail. First, in the U.S. market, the largest investors—pension funds, endowments, and wealthy individuals—typically use some rule of thumb for asset allocation, such as 60 percent in equities, and are thus relatively insensitive to the level of asset prices. Second, such insensitivity is even more characteristic of individual investors in 401(k) plans, who rarely rebalance their portfolios.

Evidence That Should Worry Efficient Market Advocates

The previous section showed that the premise of behavioral finance—that cognitive biases may influence asset prices—is at least theoretically possible. But is it worth the trouble? What is the evidence that existing models cannot do the job? Surely the Royal Dutch/Shell example, although striking, is not by itself enough to undermine the rational efficient market paradigm that has served the field well for so long. I will briefly discuss five areas in which behavior in the real world seems most at odds with the theories in textbooks.

Volume. Standard models of asset markets predict that participants will trade very little. The reason is that in a world where everyone knows that traders are rational (I know that you are rational, you know that I am rational, and I know that you know that I am rational), if I am offering to buy some shares of IBM Corporation and you are offering to sell them, I have to wonder what information you have that I do not. Of course, pinning down exactly how little volume should be expected in this world is difficult, because in the real world people have liquidity and rebalancing needs, but it seems safe to say that 700 million shares a day on the NYSE is much more trading than standard market models would expect. Similarly, the standard approach would not expect mutual fund managers to turn over their portfolios once a year.

Volatility. In a rational world, prices change only when news arrives. Since Robert Shiller's early work was published in 1981, economists have realized that aggregate stock prices appear to move much more than can be justified by changes in intrinsic value (as measured by, say, the present value of future dividends). Although Shiller's work generated long and complex controversy, his conclusion is generally thought to be correct: Stock and bond prices are more volatile than advocates of rational efficient market theory would predict.

Dividends. Modigliani and Miller (1958) showed that in an efficient market with no taxes, dividend policy is irrelevant. Under the U.S. tax system, however, dividends are taxed at a higher rate than capital gains and companies can make their taxpaying shareholders better off by repurchasing shares rather than paying dividends.[3] This logic leaves us with two major puzzles, one about company behavior and the other about asset prices. Why do most large companies pay cash dividends? And why do stock prices rise when dividends are initiated or increased? Neither question has any satisfactory rational answer.[4]

The Equity Premium Puzzle. Historically, the equity premium in the United States and elsewhere has been huge. For example, a dollar invested in U.S. T-bills on January 1, 1926, would now be worth about $14; a dollar invested in large-cap U.S. stocks on the same date would now be worth more than $2,000. Although one would expect returns on equities to be higher, because they are riskier than T-bills, the return differential of 7 percent a year is much too great to be explained by risk alone (Mehra and Prescott 1985).

Predictability. In an efficient market, future returns cannot be predicted on the basis of existing information. Thirty years ago, financial economists thought this most basic assumption of the efficient market hypothesis was true (Fama 1970). Now, everyone agrees that stock prices are at least partly predictable (see, for example, Fama 1991) on the basis of past returns, such measures of value as price-to-earnings or price-to-book ratios, company announcements of earnings, dividend changes, and share repurchases and seasoned equity offerings.[5] Although considerable controversy remains about whether the observed predictability is best explained by mispricing or risk, no one has been able to specify an observable, as opposed to theoretical or metaphysical, risk measure that can explain the existing data pattern (see, for example, Lakonishok, Shleifer, and Vishny 1994). Furthermore, the charge that these studies are the inevitable result of data mining is belied by the fact that the authors have covered every important corporate announcement that a company can make. Academics have not selectively studied a few obscure situations and published only those results. Rather, it seems closer to the truth to say that virtually every possible trigger produces apparent excess returns.

---

[3] See Miller (1986) for a convincing summary of this argument.

[4] The argument is sometimes made that prices increase when dividends increase because companies are using a change in dividend to signal something. Benartzi, Michaely, and Thaler (1997) found no evidence, however, that increases in dividends provide any information about future changes in earnings.

[5] For a sampling of the empirical literature, see De Bondt and Thaler (1987), Lakonishok, Shleifer, and Vishny (1994), Bernard (1992), Michaely, Thaler, and Womack (1995), and Ikenberry, Lakonishok, and Vermaelen (1995). For an alternative interpretation of this literature, see Fama (1998).

What should one conclude from these and other empirical facts? On one side of the coin is my own conclusion: In many important ways, real financial markets do not resemble the ones we would imagine if we only read finance textbooks. On the other side of the coin is the compelling evidence that markets are efficient: the performance of active fund managers. Many studies have documented the underperformance of mutual fund managers and pension fund managers relative to passive investment strategies (see, for example, Malkiel 1995). Furthermore, although there are always some good performers, good performance this year fails to predict good performance the following year, on average (see, for example, Carhart 1997). These cold facts should be kept firmly in mind when evaluating market efficiency. Regardless of the results of academic studies reporting apparently successful trading rules, real-world portfolio managers apparently have no easy time beating the market.

This brief discussion of some of the empirical literature should leave the reader with a mixed impression. Market behavior often diverges from what we would expect in a rational efficient market, but these anomalies do not create such large profit opportunities that active fund managers as a group earn abnormal returns. No inherent contradiction exists in this combination of facts, although economists have often been confused on this point. A drunk walking through a field can create a random walk, despite the fact that no one would call his choice of direction rational. Still, if asset prices depended on the path the drunk adopted, it would be a good idea to study how drunks navigate.

What We Have Learned

So far, I have been considering whether behavioral finance is a worthy endeavor on a priori grounds. My conclusion, unsurprising given the source, is that we can enrich our understanding of financial markets by adding a human element. Some researchers have been at this task for quite a while, however, so it is reasonable to ask whether any real progress has been made.

Perhaps the most important contribution of behavioral finance on the theory side is the careful investigation of the role of markets in aggregating a variety of behaviors. The second generation of this kind of theorizing has recently begun. Three teams of authors (Barberis, Shleifer, and Vishny 1998; Daniel, Hirshleifer, and Subrahmanyam 1998; Hong and Stein 1999) have undertaken the task of generating asset-pricing models to explain the puzzling pattern of empirical results from the last decade—in particular, returns that exhibit underreaction in the short run and overreaction in the long run.[6] All three studies draw on results from psychology to motivate the behavior of the agents in their models. At the very least, these works serve as "existence proofs"

---

[6]That is, short-run positive serial correlation and long-term mean reversion. See the three papers cited in the text for summaries of the empirical facts and see Fama (1998) for another interpretation.

for behavioral finance theorizing. That is, they show that it is possible to create a coherent theoretical model, one grounded in solid psychology *and* economics, that can explain a complex pattern of empirical results. At the moment, no rival nonbehavioral model can say the same.

Progress has also been made in understanding the equity premium puzzle by using psychological concepts. Benartzi and I (1995) argued that the equity premium can be explained by a combination of behaviors called "myopic loss aversion." Loss aversion refers to the observed tendency for decision makers to weigh losses more heavily than gains; losses hurt roughly twice as much as gains feel good. We added the adjective "myopic" because even investors with long-term horizons appear to care about short-term gains and losses. We found that if investors evaluate their portfolios once a year, loss aversion can explain much of the equity premium.

Barberis, Huang, and Santos (1999) extended this idea in an ambitious new approach. They tried to explain the equity premium within a full equilibrium model that incorporates consumption as well as returns. They could do so only by adding another behavioral factor: the "house money effect." The house money effect captures the intuition that when gamblers are ahead (playing with what they refer to as the "house's money"), they become less loss averse and more willing to take risks. Similarly, investors who have recently earned high returns will be less risk averse.

On the empirical side, much of the effort of behavioral researchers has been in uncovering new anomalies that cause us to think hard about market efficiency. Of course, these studies also create controversy because the implications of the results are subject to interpretation.

One branch of empirical behavioral research should be uncontroversial: the investigation of what individual investors do with their money. Even if individuals' actions have no effect on prices, understanding how well individuals manage their portfolios is certainly useful to investors and investment professionals. Because data about individual behavior are hard to come by, such research is less common than the usual tape-spinning exercises with CRSP and Compustat, but some data are starting to emerge. Terrance Odean has managed to get a data set of trades made by some customers of one large discount brokerage firm. His research so far has shown that important behavior documented by psychologists in the lab, such as overconfidence and loss aversion, is also displayed by individuals managing their portfolios. Odean found that individuals trade too much (overconfidently thinking that they can pick winners, whereas the stocks they buy do worse than the stocks they sell) and are reluctant to sell losers (and mentally "declare" the loss), even though tax considerations should make them prefer selling a loser to selling a winner (Odean 1998).

Another important set of individual investors, in addition to those studied by Odean, is those who invest in 401(k) plans where they work. A large and rapidly growing pot of money is being managed by individuals who, for the most part, have little or no knowledge about investing. Benartzi and I (2000) have recently studied one aspect of this group's decision making—diversification strategies. We found that many 401(k) investors appear to use simple rules of thumb to invest their money, including what we refer to as the "$1/n$ heuristic": If a plan contains n funds, allocate contributions evenly among the n funds. We found that when plans add a stock fund, allocation to equities rises. As the public debates the pros and cons of privatizing some or all of the U.S. Social Security system, we will need to know more about how participants will take on the task of investing their retirement savings.

What's Next: A Wish List

Forecasting the future is always difficult, and the only prediction in which I have complete confidence is that behavioral finance will be dominated by young scholars who are not burdened with large investments in the old paradigm (even economists have trouble ignoring sunk costs). So, instead of predicting what kinds of research will appear in the next decade, I offer a wish list of topics that I would like to see studied.

First, I would like to see the theory papers discussed previously come to grips with institutions. Most of the anomalies that receive attention in the academic literature are stronger for small- and mid-cap stocks than for large-cap stocks. For large-cap stocks, there seem to be more anomalies on the short side than on the long side. Why? I believe that the answer depends on limits-of-arbitrage arguments, but some of the institutional barriers, such as those regarding short selling, may also have behavioral explanations. Bringing institutions more directly into the behavioral model and applying the behavioral model to institutions will be hard but worth doing.

Second, I would like to see more behavioral finance research in the field of corporate finance. Most of the research so far has been in the field of asset pricing; much less has been done on corporate finance—at least recently. My favorite corporate finance paper is John Lintner's 1956 study of dividend policy. Lintner took an unusual tack for an academic—talking to executives about how they set dividend policy. After listening, he composed a very simple model in which companies move their dividends toward a desired payout ratio while being careful to avoid the necessity of ever cutting the dividend. To this day, his model remains an accurate description of dividend policy. One example of the kind of research that it might be possible to do in the realm of behavioral corporate finance is Jeremy Stein's (1996) article "Rational Capital Budgeting in an Irrational World." Stein ponders how companies should make investment decisions if asset prices are not set rationally. Many other papers, both theoretical and empirical, are waiting to be written in this important area.

Finally, I wish for more data on individual investors to become available. I hope someday soon a scholar will acquire a data set for online traders and day traders. Until such data become available, we will never fully understand what I think will become known as the Great Internet Stock Bubble. Similarly, tracking the behavior of investors in 401(k)-type pension plans is of growing importance. Benartzi and I have been hampered in our studies by the absence of longitudinal data for plan participants. For both cases, the data exist in the files of private firms. I am hopeful that some firms will see the benefit of sharing such data with researchers; for sharing to become a reality, confidentiality will have to be adequately protected—confidentiality of the source of the data and of the identities of the individual investors.

The End of Behavioral Finance

Behavioral finance is no longer as controversial a subject as it once was. As financial economists become accustomed to thinking about the role of human behavior in driving stock prices, people will look back at the articles published in the past 15 years and wonder what the fuss was about. I predict that in the not-too-distant future, the term "behavioral finance" will be correctly viewed as a redundant phrase. What other kind of finance is there? In their enlightenment, economists will routinely incorporate as much "behavior" into their models as they observe in the real world. After all, to do otherwise would be irrational.

Richard H. Thaler is the Robert P. Gwinn Professor of Behavioral Science at the University of Chicago Booth School of Business, Chicago.

REFERENCES

Barberis, N., M. Huang, and T. Santos. 1999. "Prospect Theory and Asset Prices." Mimeo. University of Chicago.

Barberis, N., A. Shleifer, and R. Vishny. 1998. "A Model of Investor Sentiment." *Journal of Financial Economics*, vol. 49, no. 3 (September):307–343.

Benartzi, S., and R.H. Thaler. 1995. "Myopic Loss Aversion and the Equity Premium Puzzle." *Quarterly Journal of Economics*, vol. 110, no. 1 (February):73–92.

———. 2000. "Naive Diversification Strategies in Defined Contribution Savings Plans." *American Economic Review*.

Benartzi, S., R. Michaely, and R.H. Thaler. 1997. "Do Changes in Dividends Signal the Future or the Past?" *Journal of Finance*, vol. 52, no. 3 (July):1007–1034.

Bernard, V. 1992. "Stock Price Reactions to Earnings Announcements." In *Advances in Behavioral Finance*. Edited by R.H. Thaler. New York: Russell Sage Foundation.

Carhart, M.M. 1997. "On Persistence in Mutual Fund Performance." *Journal of Finance*, vol. 52, no. 1 (March):57–82.

Daniel, K.D., D. Hirshleifer, and A. Subrahmanyam. 1998. "Investor Psychology and Security Market Under- and Overreactions." *Journal of Finance*, vol. 53, no. 6 (December):1839–1885.

De Bondt, W.F.M., and R.H. Thaler. 1985. "Does the Stock Market Overreact?" *Journal of Finance*, vol. 40, no. 3 (July):793–808.

———. 1987. "Further Evidence on Investor Overreaction and Stock Market Seasonality." *Journal of Finance*, vol. 42, no. 3 (July):557–581.

———. 1995. "Financial Decision-Making in Markets and Firms: A Behavioral Perspective." In *Handbooks in Operations Research and Management Science: Finance*. Edited by R.A. Jarrow, V. Maksimovic, and W.T. Ziemba. San Diego, CA: Elsevier (385–410).

DeLong, J.B., A. Shleifer, L.H. Summers, and R.J. Waldmann. 1990. "Noise Trader Risk in Financial Markets." *Journal of Political Economy*, vol. 98, no. 4 (January):703–738.

Fama, E.F. 1970. "Efficient Capital Markets: A Review of Theory and Empirical Work." *Journal of Finance*, vol. 25, no. 2 (May):383–417.

———. 1991. "Efficient Capital Markets: II." *Journal of Finance*, vol. 46, no. 5 (December): 1575–1617.

———. 1998. "Market Efficiency, Long-Term Returns, and Behavioral Finance." *Journal of Financial Economics*, vol. 49, no. 3 (September):283–306.

Froot, K.A., and E.M. Dabora. 1999. "How Are Stock Prices Affected by the Location of Trade?" *Journal of Financial Economics*, vol. 53, no. 2 (August):189–216.

Hong, H., and J. Stein. 1999. "A Unified Theory of Underreaction, Momentum Trading, and Overreaction in Asset Markets." *Journal of Finance*, vol. 54, no. 6 (December):2143–2184.

Ikenberry, D., J. Lakonishok, and T. Vermaelen. 1995. "Market Underreaction to Open Market Share Repurchases." *Journal of Financial Economics*, vol. 39, no. 2–3 (October):181–208.

Lakonishok, J., A. Shleifer, and R.W. Vishny. 1994. "Contrarian Investment, Extrapolation, and Risk." *Journal of Finance*, vol. 49, no. 5 (December):1541–1578.

Lintner, J. 1956. "Distribution of Incomes of Corporations among Dividends, Retained Earnings, and Taxes." *American Economic Review*, vol. 46, no. 2 (May):97–113.

Malkiel, B.G. 1995. "Returns from Investing in Equity Mutual Funds 1971 to 1991." *Journal of Finance*, vol. 50, no. 2 (June):549–572.

Mehra, R., and E.C. Prescott. 1985. "The Equity Premium: A Puzzle." *Journal of Monetary Economics*, vol. 15, no. 2 (March):145–161.

Michaely, R., R.H. Thaler, and K.L. Womack. 1995. "Price Reactions to Dividend Initiations and Omissions: Overreaction or Drift?" *Journal of Finance*, vol. 50, no. 2 (June):573–608.

Miller, M.H. 1986. "Behavioral Rationality in Finance: The Case of Dividends." *Journal of Business*, vol. 59, no. S4 (October):S451–S468.

Modigliani, F., and M.H. Miller. 1958. "The Cost of Capital, Corporate Finance and the Theory of Investment." *American Economic Review*, vol. 48, no. 3 (June):261–297.

Odean, T. 1998. "Are Investors Reluctant to Realize Their Losses?" *Journal of Finance*, vol. 53, no. 5 (October):1775–1798.

———. 1999. "Do Investors Trade Too Much?" *American Economic Review*, vol. 89, no. 5 (December):1279–1298.

Rosenthal, L., and C. Young. 1990. "The Seemingly Anomalous Price Behavior of Royal Dutch/Shell and Unilever N.V./PLC." *Journal of Financial Economics*, vol. 26, no. 1 (October): 123–141.

Russell, T., and R.H. Thaler. 1985. "The Relevance of Quasi Rationality in Competitive Markets." *American Economic Review*, vol. 75, no. 5 (December):1071–1082.

Shefrin, H. 2000. *Beyond Greed and Fear: Understanding Behavioral Finance and the Psychology of Investing*. Boston, MA: Harvard Business School Press.

Shiller, R. 1981. "Do Stock Prices Move Too Much to Be Justified by Subsequent Changes in Dividends?" *American Economic Review*, vol. 71, no. 3 (June):421–436.

Shleifer, A. 2000. *Inefficient Markets: An Introduction to Behavioral Finance*. New York: Oxford University Press.

Shleifer, A., and R.W. Vishny. 1997. "The Limits of Arbitrage." *Journal of Finance*, vol. 52, no. 1 (March):35–55.

Stein, J.C. 1996. "Rational Capital Budgeting in an Irrational World." *Journal of Business*, vol. 69, no. 4 (October):429–455.

Fear

Jason Zweig

Neither a man nor a crowd nor a nation can be trusted to act humanely or think sanely under the influence of a great fear. . . . To conquer fear is the beginning of wisdom.

—Bertrand Russell[1]

What Are You Afraid Of?

Here are a few questions that might, at first, seem silly.

- Which is riskier: nuclear reactors or sunlight?
- Which animal is responsible for the greatest number of human deaths in the U.S.?
  — Alligator
  — Bear
  — Deer
  — Shark
  — Snake
- Match the causes of death (on the left) with the number of annual fatalities worldwide (on the right):

  1. War   a. 310,000

  2. Suicide   b. 815,000

  3. Homicide   c. 520,000

Now let's look at the answers.

The worst nuclear accident in history occurred when the reactor at Chernobyl, Ukraine, melted down in 1986. According to early estimates, tens of thousands of people might be killed by radiation poisoning. By 2006, however,

Putting It in Context

What triggered you to write this piece? And how do you think it should be helpful to professional investment practitioners?

Folk wisdom on Wall Street has long held that the two emotional extremes of investing are fear and greed. It just so happens that neuroscientists have made significant discoveries in recent years about how fear is generated in the human brain. They have also explored how it shapes memory, changes judgments about risk and time, and skews behavior.

As Benjamin Graham understood and Warren Buffett has also exemplified, investing is above all about self-control. You stand no chance of making sense out of the markets if you cannot govern your own emotions. One of the central lessons both of behavioral finance and of neuroeconomics is that we are often in the grip of emotions without even realizing it. I hope this article enables investment professionals to recognize the importance of thinking more deeply about the hidden forces that can drive our decisions.

---

[1] Bertrand Russell. "An Outline of Intellectual Rubbish" (1943): www.solstice.us/russell/intellectual_rubbish.html.

fewer than 100 had died. Meanwhile, nearly 8,000 Americans are killed every year by skin cancer, which is most commonly caused by overexposure to the sun.[2]

In the typical year, deer are responsible for roughly 130 human fatalities—seven times more than alligators, bears, sharks, and snakes combined. How could gentle Bambi cause such bloodshed? Unlike those other, much more fearsome animals, deer don't attack with teeth or claw. Instead, they step in front of speeding cars, causing deadly collisions.

Finally, most people think war takes more lives than homicide—which they believe kills more people than suicide. In fact, in most years, war kills fewer people than conventional homicides do, and the number of people who take their own lives is almost twice the number of those who are murdered. (In the list on the previous page, the causes and the number of deaths that result from them are already matched correctly.) Homicide seems more common than suicide because it's a lot easier to imagine someone else dying than it is to imagine killing yourself.

None of this means that nuclear radiation is good for you, that rattle-snakes are harmless, or that the evils of war are overblown. What it does mean is that we are often most afraid of the least likely dangers, and frequently not worried enough about the risks that have the greatest chances of coming home to roost. It also reminds us that much of the world's misfortune is caused not by the things we are afraid of, but by being afraid. The most terrible devastation wrought by Chernobyl, for example, did not come out of its nuclear reactors. Instead, it came from the human mind. As panicky business owners fled the area, unemployment and poverty soared. Anxiety, depression, alcoholism, and suicide ran rampant among the residents who could not afford to leave. Fearing that their unborn babies had been poisoned, expectant mothers had more than 100,000 unnecessary abortions. The

---

[2]Mark Peplow, "Counting the Dead," *Nature*, vol. 440, no. 7087 (20 April 2006):982–983; Dillwyn Williams and Keith Baverstock, "Chernobyl and the Future: Too Soon for a Final Diagnosis," *Nature*, vol. 440, no. 7087 (20 April 2006):993–994 (www.nature.com/news/2005/050905/full/437181b.html; www.who.int/mediacentre/news/releases/2005/pr38/en/index.html); seer.cancer.gov/statfacts.html/melan.html. Roughly 4,000 cases of thyroid cancer resulted from the Chernobyl accident: so far, 15 have been fatal. While the U.N.'s worst-case estimate is that more than 9,000 people may eventually die as a result of Chernobyl, nearly all the potential victims remain alive two decades after the accident.

damage from radiation was dwarfed by the damage from the fear of radiation, as imaginary terrors led to real tragedies on a massive scale.[3]

We're no different when it comes to money. Every investor's worst nightmare is a stock market collapse like the Crash of 1929 that ushered in the Great Depression. According to a recent survey of 1,000 investors, there's a 51 percent chance that in any given year, the U.S. stock market might drop by one-third. And yet, based on history, the odds that U.S. stocks will lose a third of their value in a given year are only around 2 percent. The real risk is not that the stock market will have a meltdown, but that inflation will raise your cost of living and erode your savings. Yet only 31 percent of the people surveyed were worried that they might run out of money during their first ten years of retirement. Riveted by the vivid fear of a market Chernobyl, they overlooked the more subtle but severe damage that can be dealt by the silent killer of inflation.[4]

If we were strictly logical, we would judge the odds of a risk by asking how often something bad has actually happened under similar circumstances in the past. Instead, explains psychologist Daniel Kahneman, "we tend to judge the probability of an event by the ease with which we can call it to mind." The more recently an event has occurred, or the more vivid our memory of something like it in the past, the more "available" an event will be in our minds—and the more probable it will seem to happen again. But that's not the right way to assess risk. An event does not become more likely to recur merely because its last occurrence was recent or memorable.[5]

Just say these words aloud: *airplane crash*. What do you see in your mind's eye? Chances are, you imagine a smoky cabin filling with screams, a bone-shattering crunch, a giant fireball pinwheeling down a runway. In principle, says Paul Slovic, a psychologist at the University of Oregon, "risk is brewed from an equal dose of two ingredients—probabilities and consequences." But

---

[3] *NYT* (12 November 2002):F4; www.flmnh.ufl.edu/fish/sharks/attacks/relariskanimal.htm; Ricky L. Langley, "Alligator Attacks on Humans in the United States," *Wilderness and Environment Medicine*, vol. 16, no. 3 (September 2005):119–124; www.natural-resources.wsu.edu/research/bear-center/bear-people.htm; www.cdc.gov/nasd; *World Report on Violence and Health*, U.N. World Health Organization (2002):10 (www.who.int/violence_injury_prevention/violence/world_report/en); UNDP and UNICEF, "The Human Consequences of the Chernobyl Nuclear Accident," United Nations Development Programme (25 January 2002): www.undp.org; Douglas Chapin et al., "Nuclear Safety: Nuclear Power Plants and Their Fuel as Terrorist Targets," *Science*, vol. 297, no. 5589 (20 September 2002):1997–1999. These data are for calendar year 2000, but even the war in Iraq has not changed the numbers enough to alter the order they are listed in.

[4] John Ameriks, Robert D. Nestor, and Stephen P. Utkus, "Expectations for Retirement," Vanguard Center for Retirement Research (November 2004):12–14.

[5] Jason Zweig and Malcolm Fitch, "When the Stock Market Plunges, Will You Be Brave or Will You Cave?" *Money Magazine*, vol. 26, no. 1 (January 1997):104.

in practice, when we perceive the risks around us, the doses of those two ingredients are not always equal. Since the consequences of a crash can be so horrific, while the probabilities of a crash evoke no imagery at all, we get zero comfort from the fact that the odds against dying in a U.S. plane crash are roughly 6,000,000 to one. Those images of death are scary, while "6,000,000 to one" is an abstraction that conveys no feeling at all. ("I don't have a fear of flying," the basketball player Toni Kukoc once said, "I have a fear of crashing.") Once again, the emotional force of the reflexive brain overwhelms the analytical powers of the reflective brain.

On the other hand, we feel perfectly safe—if not immortal—when we're behind the wheel of our own car. Many travelers think nothing of having a couple of beers, then climbing into their car and driving to the airport with a cell phone in one hand and a cigarette in the other. Many of them even worry about whether their plane might crash—and remain utterly blind to the ways their own behavior is riddled with risk. The numbers tell the story: Only 24 people died on commercial aircraft in the U.S. in 2003, while 42,643 people were killed in car accidents. Adjusting for the distance traveled, you're about 65 times more likely to die in your own car than in a plane. And yet it's air travel that frightens us. Over the twelve months after the terrorist attacks of September 11, 2001, the fear of flying put far more people onto U.S. roads, causing an estimated 1,500 extra deaths in car crashes.[6]

The more vivid and easily imaginable a risk is, the scarier it feels. People will pay twice as much for an insurance policy that covers hospitalization for "any disease" than one that covers hospitalization for "any reason." Of course, by definition, "any reason" includes all diseases. But "any reason" is vague, while "any disease" is vivid. That vividness fills us with a fear that makes no economic sense. However, it makes perfect emotional sense.[7]

---

[6]Paul Slovic, "Informing and Educating the Public about Risk," *Risk Analysis*, vol. 6, no. 4 (December 1986):403–415; www.planecrashinnfo.com/cause.htm; Kukoc, *Sports Illustrated* (24 February 24):46; *National Transportation Statistics 2005*, U.S. Department of Transportation (December 2005):Table 2–1 (www.bts.gov/publications/national_transportation_statistics/ 2005/index.html); Michael Sivak and Michael J. Flannagan, "Flying and Driving after the September 11 Attacks," *American Scientist*, vol. 91, no. 1 (January–February 2003):1 (http:// american.scientist.org/template/AssetDetail/assetid/16237); Gerd Gigerenzer, "Out of the Frying Pan into the Fire: Behavioral Reactions to Terrorist Attacks," *Risk Analysis*, vol. 26, no. 2 (April 2006):347–351.

[7]Eric J. Johnson, John Hershey, Jacqueline Meszaros, and Howard Kunreuther, "Framing, Probability Distortions, and Insurance Decisions," in *Choices, Values, and Frames*, edited by Daniel Kahneman and Amos Tversky (New York: Cambridge University Press, 2000):224–240.

The emotion generated in our reflexive system can shove our analytical abilities aside, so the presence of one risk can make other things seem riskier, too. In the wake of September 11, for example, the Conference Board's Consumer Confidence Index, a measure of how Americans feel about the economic outlook, slumped by 25 percent. And the number of people who said they planned to buy a car, a home, or a major appliance in the coming six months dropped by 10 percent.

When an intangible feeling of risk fills the air, you can catch other people's emotions as easily as you can catch a cold. Merely reading a brief newspaper story about crime or depression is enough to prompt people into more than doubling their estimates of the likelihood of unrelated risks like divorce, stroke, or exposure to toxic chemicals. Just as when you have a hangover the slightest sound can seem deafening, an upsetting bit of news can make you hypersensitive to anything else that reminds you of risk. As is so often the case with the reflexive brain, you may not realize that your decisions are driven by your feelings. Roughly 50 percent of people can recognize when they have been disturbed by a bit of negative news, but only 3 percent admit that being upset may influence how they react to other risks.[8]

Our intuitive sense of risk is driven up or down by what Paul Slovic calls "dread" and "knowability." Those two factors, he explains, "infuse risk with feelings."

- Dread is determined by how vivid, controllable, or potentially catastrophic a risk seems to be. Repeated surveys have found that people consider handguns a bigger risk than smoking. Because we can choose not to smoke (or choose to quit if we do), the hazards of smoking seem to be under our control. But there's not much you can do to prevent some thug from putting a bullet through your head at any moment, and TV cop shows pump your living room full of gunshots every night—so handguns seem scarier. Yet smoking kills hundreds more people than handguns do.

- The "knowability" of a risk depends on how immediate, specific, or certain the consequences appear to be. Fast and finite dangers (fireworks, skydiving, train crashes, etc.) feel more "knowable" (and less worrisome) than vague, open-ended risks like genetically modified foods or global warming. Americans rate tornadoes as a much more frequent killer than asthma. Because asthma moves slowly and many of its victims survive, it seems less dangerous, even though it kills many more people. If the consequences of

---

[8] Consumer confidence data courtesy of the Conference Board's Carol Courter, e-mail to JZ (14 March 2006). Eric J. Johnson and Amos Tversky, "Affect, Generalization, and the Perception of Risk," *Journal of Personality and Social Psychology*, vol. 45, no. 1 (1983):20–31; Eric Johnson, interview by JZ via e-mail (14 February 2006).

a risk are highly uncertain and poorly understood, any perceived problem can trigger a frenzy of publicity. Thus hedge funds, those giant investment pools that operate in almost complete secrecy, become front-page news whenever they lose money.[9]

Dread and knowability come together to twist our perceptions of the world around us: We underestimate the likelihood and severity of common risks, and we overestimate the likelihood and severity of rare risks—especially if we have never personally experienced them. When we feel we are in charge and we understand the consequences, risks will seem lower than they truly are. When a risk feels out of our hands and less comprehensible, it will feel more dangerous than it actually is. It's as if we see the world through warped binoculars that not only magnify whatever is remote but shrink whatever is near.

That's why so many people buy flight insurance at the airport: The chance of dying in a plane crash is almost zero, and most passengers are already covered by life insurance anyway, but air travel still *feels* risky. Meanwhile, roughly three-quarters of all Americans living in vulnerable areas have no flood insurance. Because homeowners can readily see how high the water has risen in the past, and because they can easily invest in drainage systems and other techniques that seem to control the risk of flooding, they feel safer than they really are. Hurricane Katrina exposed how dangerous this feeling of safety can be.[10]

In the stock market, these quirks of risk perception can be a big distraction. On March 22, 2005, a woman named Anna Ayala was eating at a Wendy's restaurant in San Jose, California. She spooned a helping of chili into her mouth, started to chew, and then spat out a human finger. When the news broke, Wendy's stock fell 1 percent on heavy trading volume, and by April 15, 2.4 percent had been chopped off the market value of the stock. Customers turned away, costing the company an estimated $10 million in revenues. But investigators soon found that Ayala had planted the finger (which one of her husband's coworkers had lost in an industrial accident) in the bowl of chili

---

[9]Sarah Lichtenstein et al., "Judged Frequency of Lethal Events," *Journal of Experimental Psychology: Human Learning and Memory*, vol. 4, no. 6 (November 1978):551–578; Paul Slovic, "Perception of Risk," *Science*, vol. 236, no. 4799 (17 April 1987):280–285; Paul Slovic and Ellen Peters, interview by JZ via e-mail (29 June 2005). Besides dread and knowability, there is a third factor—how many people are exposed to the risk—but it appears to play a less significant role.
[10]www.floodsmart.gov; Mark J. Browne and Robert E. Hoyt, "The Demand for Flood Insurance: Empirical Evidence," *Journal of Risk and Uncertainty*, vol. 20, no. 3 (May 2000):291–306; Howard Kunreuther, "Has the Time Come for Comprehensive Natural Disaster Insurance?" in *On Risk and Disaster*, edited by Ronald J. Daniels, Donald F. Kettl, and Howard Kunreuther (Philadelphia: University of Pennsylvania Press, 2006):175–202.

herself. Wendy's business recovered steadily, and anyone who sold the stock in the initial panic was left feeling like somebody with ten thumbs, as it nearly doubled over the coming year.[11]

Much the same thing happened in June 1999, when eBay's website crashed and "went dark" for 22 hours. Trading in Beanie Babies and G.I. Joes ground to a halt, costing eBay about $4 million in lost fees and causing consternation among thousands of buyers and sellers. Over the next three trading days, eBay's shares fell 26 percent, a loss of more than $4 billion in market value. Because the internet was still relatively young, many investors had no idea when eBay could fix the problem—so the consequences seemed highly uncertain, arousing enormous fear. But eBay's site was soon running smoothly, and the stock almost tripled over the next five years.

In short, overreacting to raw feelings—"blinking" in the face of risk—is often one of the riskiest things an investor can do.

The Hot Button of the Brain

Deep in your brain, level with the top of your ears, lies a small, almond-shaped knob of tissue called the amygdala. When you confront a potential risk, this part of your reflexive brain acts as an alarm system—generating hot, fast emotions like fear and anger that it shoots up to the reflective brain like warning flares. (There are actually two amygdalae, one on the left side of your brain and one on the right, just as office elevators often have one panic button on either side of the door.)

The amygdala helps focus your attention, in a flash, on anything that's new, out of place, changing fast, or just plain scary. That helps explain why we overreact to rare but vivid risks. After all, in the presence of danger, he who hesitates is lost; a fraction of a second can make the difference between life and death. Step near a snake, spot a spider, see a sharp object flying toward your face, and your amygdala will jolt you into jumping, ducking, or taking whatever evasive action should get you out of trouble in the least amount of time. This same fear reaction is triggered by losing money—or believing that you might.

While other parts of your brain also generate fear, the amygdala's role is probably the best understood so far. While it can fire up around pleasant stimuli, too, it seems to be custom-fit for fear. The amygdala links directly to areas that manipulate your facial muscles, control your breathing, and regulate your heart rate. Fibers emanating from the amygdala also signal other parts of the brain to release norepinephrine, a kind of starter fluid that prepares the delivery of

---

11 Wendy's, press release, Wendy's International Inc. (7 July 2005); Wendy's, 10-Q report (11 August 2005); www.cnn.com/2005/LAW/09/09/wendys.finger.ap; stock data from http://finance.yahoo.com; Patricia Sellers, "eBay's Secret," *Fortune*, vol. 150, no. 8 (18 October 2004):160–178 (www.forbes.com/forbes/1999/0726/6402238a.html).

energy to your muscles for instant action. And the amygdala helps infuse your bloodstream with corticosterone, a stress hormone that assists the body in responding to an emergency.

Remarkably, the amygdala can flood your body with fear signals before you are consciously aware of being afraid. If you smell smoke in your home or office, your heart will hammer and your feet will start flying well before any fire alarm goes off. In the presence of real or potential danger, the amygdala waits for nothing. "You don't need to fall off a ten-story building in order to be afraid of falling off it," says neuroscientist Antoine Bechara of the University of Southern California. "Your brain doesn't need actual experience."[12]

A rat born and bred in a laboratory, where it has never seen a cat, will nevertheless freeze instantly if it encounters one. The rat's amygdala senses danger and triggers an automatic fear response—even though the rat has no idea what a cat is. A rat with an injured amygdala, however, will not freeze; instead, it will scamper up to the cat, climb on its back, even nibble on its ear. (Fortunately for the rats, in these experiments the cat has been sedated.) When the amygdala is damaged, the sense of fear is broken.

"Emotion can be beneficial when it is triggered by a chain of prior experiences," explains Bechara. "Otherwise, you would take forever to decide." In speeches to investors, I sometimes reach into a sealed bag, pull out a rattlesnake, and throw it into the audience. In theory, "rational" people should sit there while the snake flies through the air. They should take a few moments to decide whether it's worth causing a ruckus by scrambling out of the way, and to calculate the odds that a writer would throw a live snake at them during a speech. Having weighed the potential costs against the possible benefits, "rational" people should conclude that there's no cause for alarm. Instead, they scream and bolt out of the chair. (Needless to say, the snake isn't real; it's a rubber toy.)

Does this lightning response of the amygdala make us "irrational"? Of course not. As it helped our remote ancestors survive, the fear reflex remains a vital survival tool in daily life today: It makes you look both ways before you cross the street and reminds you to hold the railing on high balconies. However,

---

[12]Antonio R. Damasio, *Descartes' Error: Emotion, Reason, and the Human Brain* (New York: Penguin, 1994); Joseph LeDoux, *The Emotional Brain: The Mysterious Underpinnings of Emotional Life* (New York: Simon & Schuster, 1996); Andrew J. Calder, Andrew D. Lawrence, and Andrew W. Young, "Neuropsychology of Fear and Loathing," *Nature Reviews Neuroscience*, vol. 2 (May 2001):352–363; K. Luan Phan et al., "Functional Neuroanatomy of Emotion," *NeuroImage*, vol. 16, no. 2 (June 2002):331–348; M. Davis and P. J. Whalen, "The Amygdala: Vigilance and Emotion," *Molecular Psychiatry*, vol. 6, no. 1 (January 2001):13–34; Nathan J. Emery and David G. Amaral, "The Role of the Amygdala in Primate Social Cognition," in *Cognitive Neuroscience of Emotion*, edited by Richard D. Lane and Lynn Nadel (New York: Oxford University Press, 2000):156–191; Antoine Bechara, interview by JZ (2 April 2002); D. Caroline Blanchard and Robert J. Blanchard, "Innate and Conditioned Reactions to Threat in Rats with Amygdaloid Lesions," *Journal of Comparative and Physiological Psychology*, vol. 81, no. 2 (1972):281–290.

when a potential threat is financial instead of physical, reflexive fear will put you in danger more often than it will get you out of it. Selling your investments every time they take a sudden drop will make your broker rich, but it will just make you poor and jittery.

Social signals can set off the hot button of your brain as easily as physical dangers can. When photographs of fearful faces are flashed for 33 one-thousandths of a second—and immediately followed by longer exposures of emotionally neutral faces—your reflective mind has no time to become aware that you saw anything scary. But your reflexive brain will "know" it with lightning speed. The exposure to a fearful face for just a thirtieth of a second is enough to spark intense activation in the amygdala, priming your body for action just in case this subliminal threat turns out to be real.[13]

The amygdala also enables us to spot fearful body language in a split second: The mere glimpse of someone standing hands-up makes us expect a mugging, and a hunched and cowering figure makes us anticipate a beating. If you were exposed for just a third of a second to images of anonymous actors making agitated gestures, your amygdala would instantly "catch" their fear, alerting the stress systems throughout your body in a flash.

Finally, the amygdala is sensitive to that uniquely human way of conveying threats—through language. Brain scans show that your amygdala will fire more intensely in response to words like *kill, danger, knife,* or *torture,* than to words like *towel, formation, number,* or *pen.* Researchers in France have recently shown that a frightening word can make you break out in a sweat even if it appears for only 12 one-thousandths of a second—roughly 25 times faster than the blink of a human eye! (No wonder you cringe when someone says, "I got killed on that fund" or "Buying that stock would be like trying to catch a falling knife.")[14]

An alarming word or two can even be powerful enough to transform your memories. In a classic experiment by psychologist Elizabeth Loftus, people viewed video footage of car accidents. Some of the viewers were asked how fast the cars were going when "they hit each other." Others were asked how fast the cars were going when "they smashed into each other." Even though both groups

---

13 Paul J. Whalen et al., "Masked Presentation of Emotional Facial Expressions Modulate Amygdala Activity without Explicit Knowledge," *Journal of Neuroscience,* vol. 18, no. 1 (1 January 1998):411–418; Beatrice de Gelder, "Towards the Neurobiology of Emotional Body Language," *Nature Reviews Neuroscience,* vol. 7 (March 2006):242–249; Beatrice de Gelder et al., "Fear Fosters Flight," *PNAS,* vol. 101, no. 47 (23 November 2004):16701–16706.

14 N. Isenberg et al., "Linguistic Threat Activates the Human Amydala," *Proceedings of the National Academy of Sciences of the United States of America,* vol. 96, no. 18 (31 August 1999):10456–10459; Laetitia Silvert et al., "Autonomic Responding to Aversive Words without Conscious Valence Discrimination," *International Journal of Psychophysiology,* vol. 53, no. 2 (July 2004):135–145; Elizabeth L. Loftus and John C. Palmer, "Reconstruction of Automobile Destruction: An Example of the Interaction between Language and Memory," *Journal of Verbal Learning and Verbal Behavior,* vol. 13, no. 5 (October 1974):585–589. A normal eyeblink lasts about 320 milliseconds (e-mail from SUNY Stony Brook neurobiologist Craig Evinger to JZ, 23 March 2006).

saw the same videos, the people who were prompted by the words "smashed into" estimated that the cars were going 19 percent faster. "Hit" may not sound very scary, but "smashed into" does. That evidently switches on the amygdala, splashing emotion back onto your memory and changing your perceptions of the past.

What does all this tell us about investing? Humans are reflexively afraid not just of physical dangers, but also of any social signal that transmits an alarm. A television broadcast from the floor of the stock exchange on a bad trading day, for example, combines a multitude of cues that can fire up the amygdala: flashing lights, clanging bells, hollering voices, alarming words, people gesturing wildly. In a split second, you break out in a sweat, your breathing picks up, your heart races. This primal part of your brain is bracing you for a "fight or flight" response before you can even figure out whether you have lost any money yourself.

Both actual and imagined losses can flip this switch. Using brain scans, one study found that the more frequently people were told they were losing money, the more active the amygdala became. Other scanning experiments have shown that even the expectation of financial losses can switch on this fear center. Traumatic experiences activate genes in the amygdala, stimulating the production of proteins that strengthen the cells where memories are stored in several areas of the brain. A surge of signals from the amygdala can also trigger the release of adrenaline and other stress hormones, which have been found to "fuse" memories, making them more indelible. And an upsetting event can shock neurons in the amygdala into firing in synch for hours—even during sleep. (It is literally true that we can relive our financial losses in our nightmares.) Brain scans have shown that when you are on a financial losing streak, each new loss heats up the hippocampus, the memory bank near the amygdala that helps store your experiences of fear and anxiety.[15]

---

[15]Tiziana Zalla et al., "Differential Amygdala Responses to Winning and Losing: A Functional Magnetic Resonance Imaging Study in Humans," *European Journal of Neuroscience*, vol. 12, no. 5 (May 2000):1764–1770; Grafman, interview by JZ (6 March 2002); Hans C. Breiter et al., "Functional Imaging of Neural Responses to Expectancy and Experience of Monetary Gains and Losses," *Neuron*, vol. 30, no. 2 (May 2001):619–639; Gleb P. Shumyatsky et al., "Stathmin, a Gene Enriched in the Amygdala, Controls Both Learned and Innate Fear," *Cell*, vol. 123, no. 4 (18 November 2005):697–709; R. Douglas Fields, "Making Memories Stick," *Scientific American*, vol. 292, no. 2 (February 2005):75–81; Karim Nader, Glenn E. Schafe, and Joseph E. Le Doux, "Fear Memories Require Protein Synthesis in the Amygdala for Reconsolidation after Retrieval," *Nature*, vol. 406 (17 August 2000):722–726; James L. McGaugh, "Memory—A Century of Consolidation," *Science*, vol. 287, no. 5451 (14 January 2000):248–251; B. A. Strange and R. J. Dolan, "β-Adrenergic Modulation of Emotional Memory-Evoked Human Amygdala and Hippocampal Responses," *Proceedings of the National Academy of Sciences of the United States of America*, vol. 101, no. 31 (3 August 2004):11454–11458; James L. McGaugh et al., "Modulation of Memory Storage by Stress Hormones and the Amygdaloid Complex," in *Modulation of Memory Storage by Stress Hormones and the Amygdaloid Complex*, edited by Michael Gazzaniga (Cambridge, MA: MIT Press, 2000):1081–1098; Joe Guillaume Pelletier et al., "Lasting Increases in Basolateral Amygdala Activity after Emotional Arousal," *Learning and Memory*, vol. 12 (2005):96–102; Rebecca Elliott et al., "Dissociable Neural Responses in Human Reward Systems," *Journal of Neuroscience*, vol. 20, no. 16 (15 August 2000):6159–6165. "Adrenaline" is the common term for epinephrine.

What's so bad about that? A moment of panic can wreak havoc on your investing strategy. Because the amygdala is so attuned to big changes, a sudden drop in the market tends to be more upsetting than a longer, slower—or even a much bigger—decline. On October 19, 1987, the U.S. stock market plunged 23 percent—a deeper one-day drop than the Crash of 1929 that ushered in the Great Depression. Big, sudden, and inexplicable, the Crash of 1987 was exactly the kind of event that sparks the amygdala into flashing fear throughout every investor's brain and body. The memory was hard to erase: In 1988, U.S. investors sold $15 billion more shares in stock mutual funds than they bought, and their net purchases of stock funds did not recover to precrash levels until 1991. The "experts" were just as shell-shocked: The managers of stock funds kept at least 10 percent of their total assets in the safety of cash almost every month through the end of 1990, while the value of seats on the New York Stock Exchange did not regain their precrash level until 1994. A single drop in the stock market on one Monday in autumn disrupted the investing behavior of millions of people for at least the next three years.[16]

The philosopher William James wrote that "an impression may be so exciting emotionally as almost to leave a *scar* upon the cerebral tissues." The amygdala seems to act like a branding iron that burns the memory of financial loss into your brain. That may help explain why a market crash, which makes stocks cheaper, also makes investors less willing to buy them for a long time to come.

Fright Makes Right

I learned how my own amygdala reacts to risk when I participated in an experiment at the University of Iowa. First I was wired up with electrodes and other monitoring devices—on my chest, my palms, my face—to track my breathing, heartbeat, perspiration, and muscle activity. Then I played a computer game designed by neuroscientists Antoine Bechara and Antonio Damasio. Starting with $2,000 in play money, I clicked a mouse to select a card from one of four decks displayed on the computer monitor in front of me. Each "draw" of a card made me either "richer" or "poorer." I soon learned that the two left decks were more likely to produce big gains but even bigger losses, while the two right decks blended more frequent but smaller gains with a lower chance of big losses. (The left decks were the rough equivalent of an aggressive growth fund that invests in risky small stocks, while the right decks resembled

---

[16]ICI, *2005 Investment Company Fact Book* (Washington, DC: Investment Company Institute, 2005):77; ICI, *1996 Mutual Fund Fact Book* (Washington, DC: Investment Company Institute, 1996):125; Donald B. Keim and Ananth Madhavan, "The Relation between Stock Market Movements and NYSE Seat Prices," *Journal of Finance*, vol. 55, no. 6 (December 2000):2817–2840; William James, *The Principles of Psychology, volume 1* (New York: Henry Holt, 1890), reprinted (Mineola, NY: Dover Press, 1980):670. (Italics in original.)

a balanced fund that mixes stocks and bonds for a smoother return.) Gradually, I began picking most of my cards from the decks on the right; by the end of the experiment I had drawn 24 cards in a row from those safer decks.[17]

Afterward, I looked over the printout of my bodily responses with a profound sense of wonder. I could see that the paper was covered with jagged lines that traced my spiking heartbeat and panting breath as the red alert of risk swept through my body. But the reflective areas of my brain never had a clue that I was on edge. So far as I "knew," I was doing nothing more than calmly trying to make a few bucks by picking cards.

At first, the printout showed, my skin would sweat, my breath quicken, my heart race, and my facial muscles furrow immediately after I clicked on any card that cost me money. Early on, when I drew one card that lost me $1,140, my pulse rate shot from 75 to 145 in a split second. After three or four bad losses from the risky decks, my bodily responses began surging before I selected a card from either of those piles. Merely moving the cursor over the riskier decks, without even clicking on them, was enough to make my physiological functions go haywire—as if I had stepped toward a snarling lion. It took only a handful of losses for my amygdala to create an emotional memory that made my body tingle with apprehension at the very thought of losing money again.

My decisions, I now could see, had been driven by a subliminal fear that I sensed with my body even though the "thinking" part of my mind had no idea I was afraid. As anyone who has ever come upon a sudden danger knows, it's often only after the fact that you realize how keyed up you were in your moment of peril. My brain handled this danger the same way, even though it was a financial, not a physical, risk and even though it involved only play money, not real cash.

At least in the developed world, money has become an inherently desirable object. Current social pressures—plus centuries of tradition—lead us to equate money with safety and comfort. (Ironically, we even call stocks, bonds, and

---

[17]JZ participated in the Iowa Gambling Task (and interviewed Antoine Bechara and Antonio Damasio) at the University of Iowa, 2 April 2002. The experiment is also described in Antonio Damasio, *Descartes' Error: Emotion, Reasons, and the Human Brain* (New York: Penguin, 1994):212–222; Antonio R. Damasio, "The Somatic Marker Hypothesis and the Possible Functions of the Prefrontal Cortex," *Philosophical Transactions of the Royal Society of London Series B, Biological Sciences*, vol. 351, no. 1346 (October 1996):1413–1420; Antoine Bechara et al., "Different Contributions of the Human Amygdala and Ventromedial Prefrontal Cortex to Decision-Making," *Journal of Neuroscience*, vol. 19, no. 13 (1 July 1999):5473–5481; Antoine Bechara, D. Tranel, and A.R. Damasio, "The Somatic Marker Hypothesis and Decision-Making," in *Handbook of Neuropsychology, volume 7: The Frontal Lobes*, 2nd edition, edited by Jordan Grafman (London: Elsevier, 2002):117–143. For a divergent view, see Alan G. Sanfey and Jonathan D. Cohen, "Is Knowing Always Feeling?" *Proceedings of the National Academy of Sciences in the United States of America*, vol. 101, no. 48 (30 November 2004):16709–16710, and Tiago V. Maia and James L. McClelland, "A Reexamination of the Evidence for the Somatic Marker Hypothesis," *Proceedings of the National Academy of Sciences in the United States of America*, vol. 101, no. 45 (9 November 2004):16075–16080.

other investments "securities"!) So a financial loss or shortfall is a painful punishment that arouses an almost primitive fear. "Money is a symbolic token of the problem of life," says neuroscientist Antonio Damasio. "Money represents the means of maintaining life and sustaining us as organisms in our world." Seen in this light, it's not surprising that losing money can ignite the same fundamental fears you would feel if you encountered a charging tiger, got caught in a burning forest, or stood on the crumbling edge of a cliff.

Ironically, this highly emotional part of our brain can sometimes help us act more rationally. When Bechara and Damasio run their card-picking game with people whose amygdalas have been injured, they find that these patients never learn to avoid choosing from the riskier decks. If amygdala patients are told that they have just lost money, their pulse, breathing, and other bodily responses show no change. With the amygdala knocked out, a financial loss no longer hurts.

The result is what Bechara calls "a disease of decision-making." With no emotional signal from the amygdala to alert the prefrontal cortex about how bad it will feel to lose money, these people sample cards from all the decks—good and bad—until they end up going broke. Normally, the amygdala plays a vital role as the alarm that signals "Don't go there!" But once the reflexive brain is impaired, then the reflective areas say, "Hmm, maybe I should try that one." Without the saving grace of fear, the analytical parts of the brain will keep trying to outsmart the odds, with disastrous results. "The process of deciding advantageously," says Damasio, "is not just logical but also emotional."

A team of researchers designed an even simpler game to test how fear affects our financial decisions. Starting off with $20, you could then risk $1 on a coin flip (or pass and risk nothing). If the coin came up heads, you would lose your $1; if it came up tails, you would win $2.50. The game ran for 20 rounds. The researchers tried the experiment on two groups: people with intact brains (or "normals") and people with injuries to emotional centers of the brain like the amygdala and the insula ("patients").[18]

The "normals" were reluctant to bet. They gambled in only 58 percent of all the rounds (even though, on average, they could have come out ahead just by betting on every flip). And they proved the proverb "Once burned, twice shy": Immediately after a loss, the normals would bet only 41 percent of the time. The pain of losing $1 discouraged the normals from trying to win $2.50.

The people with damaged emotional circuits behaved very differently. They bet their dollar, on average, in 84 percent of all the rounds—and, even when the previous flip had lost them $1, the patients took the next bet 85 percent of the time. That's not all. The longer they played, the more willing the patients became to flip the coin again—regardless of how much they had

---

[18]Baba Shiv et al., "Investment Behavior and the Negative Side of Emotion," *Psychological Science,* vol. 16, no. 6 (June 2005):435–439.

lost. In their case, it's as if the pain circuits in the brain had been anesthetized, making it impossible for the patients to feel the anguish of loss. Therefore, they bet with abandon: Damn the consequences, full speed ahead!

The result? The people with emotionally impaired brains earned 13 percent more money than those whose brains were undamaged. With their fear circuits knocked offline, these people take chances that the rest of us are too scared to touch.

The lesson? It's not that you could raise your investing returns by whacking yourself upside the head with a hammer. It's that the fear of financial loss *always* lurks within the normal investing brain. When the market is flat or rising, your sense of fear may go into deep hibernation. But believing that you are fearless is very different from being fearless. During the peak of the bull market, investors bragged that they didn't mind taking big risks in the pursuit of bigger gains. But most of these people had never suffered a major financial loss—and the meltdown in the amygdala that goes along with it. That led all too many investors to the mistaken conclusion that big losses wouldn't bother them.

But you can't change the biological facts. Imagining that you can shrug off setbacks before you've ever suffered any is a disastrous delusion, since it leads you to take such high risks that huge losses become inevitable. When the bull market of the 1990s died, people lost trillions of dollars on stocks they never should have owned in the first place. These people paid a terrible price for their poor self-knowledge.

Is There Safety in Numbers?

Nowadays, investment herds often form in online chat rooms where intense peer pressure pulls each visitor toward the views of the most vocal and charismatic members. You look around and find a large support group all expressing similar views—so you feel "there's safety in numbers."[19]

But groups of animals, points out University of California, Los Angeles, ecologist Daniel Blumstein, "have more eyes, ears, and noses with which to detect predators." In general, animals in groups are *more* sensitive to risk than

---

[19]Luc-Alain Giraldeau, "The Ecology of Information Use," in *Behavioural Ecology: An Evolutionary Approach*, 4th edition, edited by John R. Krebs and Nicholas B. Davies (Oxford: Blackwell, 1997):42–68; Isabelle Coolen et al., "Species Difference in Adaptive Use of Public Information in Sticklebacks," *Proceedings: Biological Sciences,* vol. 270, no. 1531 (22 November 2003):2413–2419; Theodore Stankowich and Daniel T. Blumstein, "Fear in Animals: A Meta-Analysis and Review of Risk Assessment," *Proceedings of the Royal Society of London, Series B, Biological Sciences,* vol. 272, no. 1581 (22 December 2005):2627–2634; Blumstein, interview by JZ via e-mail (6 March 2006). The science and mathematical laws of herding are explored in depth in Luc-Alain Giraldeau and Thomas Caraco, *Social Foraging Theory* (Princeton, NJ: Princeton University Press, 2000).

they are in isolation. The larger the group in which animals gather together, the sooner and faster they will tend to flee from danger. So there's safety in numbers only when there's nothing to be afraid of. The comfort of being part of the crowd can disappear in a heartbeat.

Of course, anyone who has ever been a teenager knows that peer pressure can make you do things as part of a group that you might never do on your own. But do you make a conscious choice to conform, or does the herd exert an automatic, almost magnetic, force? People were recently asked to judge whether three-dimensional objects were the same or different. Sometimes the folks being tested made these choices in isolation. Other times, they first saw the responses of either four "peers" or four computers. (The "peers" were, in fact, colluding with the researchers conducting the study.) When people made their own choices, they were right 84 percent of the time. When all four computers gave the wrong answer, people's accuracy dropped to 68 percent. But when the peer group all made the wrong choice, the individuals being tested chose correctly just 59 percent of the time. Brain scans showed that when people followed along with the peer group, activation in parts of their frontal cortex decreased, as if social pressure was somehow overpowering the reflective brain.[20]

When people did take an independent view and guessed against the consensus of their peers, brain scans found intense firing in the amygdala. (There was no such pattern when they guessed independently of the computers, showing that it is human peer pressure that makes it so hard for us to think for ourselves.) Neuroeconomist Gregory Berns, who led the study, calls this flare-up in the amygdala a sign of "the emotional load associated with standing up for one's belief." Social isolation activates some of the same areas in the brain that are triggered by physical pain. In short, you go along with the herd not because you consciously choose to do so, but because it hurts not to.

Once you join the crowd, your feelings are no longer unique. A team of neuroscientists scanned the brains of people watching the classic spaghetti western *The Good, the Bad and the Ugly*, leaving the viewers free to daydream, get caught up in Ennio Morricone's eerie music, or wonder why Clint Eastwood can't stop squinting. Even so, a third of the surface of each viewer's cerebral cortex lit up in lockstep with the other viewers' brains—a striking phenomenon that the researchers call "ticking together." People's brains were especially prone to tick together at the most obvious turning points in the movie, like gunshots,

---

[20]Gregory S. Berns et al., "Neurobiological Correlates of Social Conformity and Independence during Mental Rotation," *Biological Psychiatry*, vol. 58, no. 3 (1 August 2005):245–253; Jaak Panksepp, "Feeling the Pain of Social Loss," *Science*, vol. 302, no. 5643 (10 October 2003):237–239; Naomi I. Eisenberger, Matthew D. Lieberman, and Kipling D. Williams, "Does Rejection Hurt?" *Science*, vol. 302, no. 5643 (10 October 2003):290–292.

explosions, or sudden plot twists. When emotions run high, individual brains converge to think almost as one. (If you have a DVD of *The Good, the Bad and the Ugly*, you can follow along on your computer, matching the footage of the movie with other people's brain activation patterns, at www.weizmann.ac.il/neurobiology/labs/malach/brainshow/.)[21]

"Ticking together" suggests that our own emotions tend to peak in synch with other people's reactions to the same stimuli. We move in herds partly because, although we are all individuals, our brains respond in common to common circumstances. When we face the same conditions, "ticking together" leads many of us to share the same emotions. If the financial news makes you feel anxious or afraid, surprised or elated, the chances are high that many other investors feel the same way.

Being part of a larger group of investors can make you feel safer when everything is going great. But once risk rears its ugly head, there is no safety in numbers: You may find that everyone in the herd is dumping your favorite stock and, in effect, running for their lives. One burst of bad news, and the support group can become a stampede. You will suddenly be all alone, just when nothing feels safe anymore.

When Nobody Knows the Odds

Military-intelligence scholar Daniel Ellsberg helped to bring down the presidency of Richard Nixon when, in 1971, he leaked the Pentagon Papers to the *New York Times*. That top-secret report documented systematic flaws of decision-making in the Vietnam War. Ellsberg was no stranger to the notion that people don't always have good judgment. A decade earlier, as an experimental psychologist at Harvard, he had published the results of a mind-bending little discovery that became known as the Ellsberg Paradox. Here's how it works. Imagine that you have two urns in front of you. They are open at the top so you can reach in, but you cannot see what is inside. The first—call it Urn A—contains exactly 50 red balls and 50 black balls. Urn B also contains exactly 100 balls; some are red and some are black, but you do not know how many there are of each. You will win $100 if you draw a red ball from either urn.[22]

[21]Uri Hasson et al., "Intersubject Synchronization of Cortical Activity during Natural Vision," *Science*, vol. 303, no. 5664 (12 March 2004):1634–1640; Luiz Pessoa, "Seeing the World in the Same Way," *Science*, vol. 303, no. 5664 (12 March 2004):1617–1618.

[22]Ellsberg's biography and his classic article "Risk, Ambiguity, and the Savage Axioms" (*Quarterly Journal of Economics*, vol. 75, no. 4 [November 1961]:643–669) are available at www.ellsberg.net. The Ellsberg Paradox has been replicated in many subsequent experiments; see Colin Camerer and Martin Weber, "Recent Developments in Modeling Preferences: Uncertainty and Ambiguity," *Journal of Risk and Uncertainty*, vol. 5, no. 4 (October 1992):325–370, and Catrin Rode et al., "When and Why Do People Avoid Unknown Probabilities in Decisions Under Uncertainty?" *Cognition*, vol. 72, no. 3 (26 October 1999):269–304. Rumsfeld, remarks at news briefing, Department of Defense (12 February 2002).

Which urn would you pick from? If you're like most people, you prefer Urn A.

Now let's repeat the game, but change the rules: This time, you win $100 if you draw a *black* ball from either urn. Which urn would you pick from now? Most people stick with Urn A. But that makes no logical sense! If you went with Urn A the first time, you obviously acted as if it contained more red balls than Urn B. Since you know Urn A has 50 red balls, your first choice implies that Urn B contains fewer than 50 red balls. Therefore, you should conclude that more than 50 balls in Urn B are black. Now that you are trying to draw a black ball, you should pick from Urn B.

Why, then, do people prefer Urn A in both the first and second rounds? In a press conference in 2002, U.S. Secretary of Defense Donald Rumsfeld made a widely mocked distinction between what he called "known knowns," "known unknowns," and "unknown unknowns." But—although he has less in common with Ellsberg than almost anyone else alive—Rumsfeld was right. "Known knowns," Rumsfeld explained, "are things we know that we know." In the case of known unknowns, he continued, "we know there are some things we do not know."

In those terms, Ellsberg's Urn A is a known known: You can be sure it has a 50/50 mix of red and black balls. Urn B, on the other hand, is a known unknown: You can be sure it contains both red and black balls, but you have no idea how many of each. Urn B is brimming with what Ellsberg called "ambiguity," and that feels scary. After all, what if 99 of the balls in Urn B somehow turn out to be red? Then you will stand a very high chance of winning nothing on the draw for black balls. The less sure we can be about the probabilities, the more we worry about the consequences. So we avoid Urn B, regardless of basic logic.

Ellsberg found that people persisted in choosing Urn A even after they realized it made no sense, and even if he asked them to bet money on whether they had picked the right urn. When Ellsberg tried his experiment on the leading economists and decision theorists of his time, many of them made the same mistake as the man in the street.

That's no surprise, since Ellsberg's Paradox is rooted in the same tension between thinking and feeling that drives so many of our investing decisions. A team of researchers recently scanned the brains of people who were asked to pick from a deck of 20 cards. Sometimes the players knew that the deck contained 10 red and 10 blue cards; at other times, all they knew was that the deck contained both red and blue cards. (They would miss out on a $3 gain if they picked the wrong card.) The first deck, like Ellsberg's Urn A, was a known known; the second, like Urn B, was a known unknown. When people considered picking from the ambiguous deck, the fear center in the amygdala went into overdrive. What's more, thinking about an ambiguous bet dampened activity in the caudate, one of the brain's reward centers that, as we saw in

Chapter Five, helps us trust someone and feel the pleasure of being in control of a situation. Not knowing the odds not only inflames our fears, but also strips us of the feeling that we are in charge.[23]

Ellsberg's Paradox often shows up in the stock market. Even though the growth rate of every company is uncertain, some rates seem more predictable than others. When a company's growth seems reliable, Wall Street says it has "high visibility." Ellsberg might say it has "low ambiguity." Whatever you call it, investors pay a premium for this illusion of predictability:

- Stocks that are followed by more security analysts on Wall Street have higher trading volume, suggesting that investors prefer betting on companies that are eyeballed by more "experts."

- The more closely analysts agree about how much a company will earn over the coming year, the more investors will pay for the stock. (As we saw in Chapter Four, analysts are lousy at predicting corporate earnings; yet investors prefer a precise but wrong forecast over a vague but accurate one.)

- Among security analysts, 78 percent agree that ambiguity about future earnings "tends to make me less confident" investing in small stocks than large stocks.

- On average, the earnings of so-called "value" companies are more than twice as volatile as those of "growth" companies.[24]

---

[23] Aldo Rustichini, "Neuroscience: Emotion and Reason in Making Decisions," *Science*, vol. 310, no. 5754 (9 December 2005):1624–1625; Ming Hsu et al., "Neural Systems Responding to Degrees of Uncertainty in Human Decision-Making," *Science*, vol. 310 (9 December 2005):1680–1683. (The frontal lobe is also involved: Scott A. Huettel et al., "Neural Signatures of Economic Preferences for Risk and Ambiguity," *Nature*, vol. 49, no. 5 [2 March 2006]:765–775.) Not knowing what the odds are is very different from knowing that the odds are low; as we saw in Chapter Three, nothing is quite as thrilling as a long-shot gamble on a big jackpot. When the probabilities of winning are remote, many people prefer an ambiguous over a certain gamble; see Hillel J. Einhorn and Robin M. Hogarth, "Decision Making Under Ambiguity," *Journal of Business*, vol. 59, no. 4, pt. 2 (October 1986):S225–S250.

[24] Michael J. Brennan, "The Individual Investor," *Journal of Financial Research*, vol. 18, no. 1 (1995):59–74; Robert A. Olsen and George H. Troughton, "Are Risk Premium Anomalies Caused by Ambiguity?," *Financial Analysts Journal*, vol. 56, no. 2 (March/April 2000):24–31; Thomas K. Philips, "The Source of Value," *Journal of Portfolio Management*, vol. 28, no. 4 (Summer 2002):36–44; Brad Barber et al., "Reassessing the Returns to Analysts' Stock Recommendations," *Financial Analysts Journal*, vol. 59, no. 2 (March/April 2003):88–96; John A. Doukas, Chansog (Francis) Kim, and Christos Pantzalis, "Divergent Opinions and the Performance of Value Stocks," *Financial Analysts Journal*, vol. 60, no. 6 (Nov/Dec 2004):55–64; Eugene F. Fama and Kenneth R. French, "The Anatomy of Value and Growth Stock Returns," CRSP Working Papers (September 2005): http://ssrn.com/abstract=806664.

All this makes investing in value stocks or small stocks the equivalent of trying to pick a black ball from Urn B: The higher ambiguity makes your odds of success feel less certain. Picking from the "predictable" growth stocks in Urn A simply feels safer. So most investors steer clear of value companies and small stocks, driving their share prices down, and pile into big growth companies, sending their stocks soaring—at least in the short run. Over longer periods, however, growth stocks and the stocks most popular with analysts tend to earn lower returns than value stocks and underanalyzed companies. By avoiding stocks that are high in ambiguity, the investing public makes them underperform in the short run—creating bargains that go on to outperform over the long run.

Fighting Your Fears

When you confront risk, your reflexive brain, led by the amygdala, functions much like a gas pedal, revving up your emotions. Fortunately, your reflective brain, with the prefrontal cortex in charge, can act like a brake pedal, slowing you down until you are calm enough to make a more objective decision. The best investors make a habit of putting procedures in place, in advance, that help inhibit the hot reactions of the emotional brain. Here are some techniques that can help you keep your investing cool in the face of fear:

Get It Off Your Mind. You'll never find the presence of mind to figure out what to do about a risk gone bad unless you step back and relax. Joe Montana, the great quarterback for the San Francisco 49ers, understood this perfectly. In the 1989 Super Bowl, the 49ers trailed the Cincinnati Bengals by three points with only three minutes left and 92 yards—almost the whole length of the field—to go. Offensive tackle Harris Barton felt "wild" with worry. But then Montana said to Barton, "Hey, check it out—there in the stands, standing near the exit ramp, there's John Candy." The players all turned to look at the comedian, a distraction that allowed their minds to tune out the stress and win the game in the nick of time. When you feel overwhelmed by a risk, create a John Candy moment. To break your anxiety, go for a walk, hit the gym, call a friend, play with your kids.[25]

Use Your Words. While vivid sights and sounds fire up the emotions in your reflexive brain, the more complex cues of language activate the prefrontal cortex and other areas of your reflective brain. By using words to counteract the stream of images the markets throw at you, you can put the hottest risks in cooler perspective.[26]

---

[25]Paul Zimmerman, "The Ultimate Winner," *Sports Illustrated* (13 August 1990):72–83; Larry Schwartz, "No Ordinary Joe" (www.espn.go.com/classic/biography/s/Montana_Joe.html).

[26]James J. Gross, "Antecedent- and Response-Focused Emotion Regulation: Divergent Consequences for Experience, Expression, and Physiology," *Journal of Personality and Social Psychology*, vol. 74, no. 1 (January 1998):224–237.

In the 1960s, Berkeley psychologist Richard Lazarus found that showing a film of a ritual circumcision triggered instant revulsion in most viewers, but that this disgust could be "short-circuited" by introducing the footage with an announcement that the procedure was not as painful as it looked. Viewers exposed to the verbal commentary had lower heart rates, sweated less, and reported less anxiety than those who watched the film without a soundtrack. (The commentary wasn't true, by the way—but it worked.)

More recent, disgusting film clips—featuring burn victims being treated and closeups of an arm being amputated—have been shown to viewers by the aptly named psychologist James Gross. (Although I do not recommend watching it on a full stomach, you can view the amputation clip at http://psych.stanford.edu/~psyphy/movs/surgery.mov.) He has found that viewers feel much less disgusted if they are given written instructions, in advance, to adopt a "detached and unemotional" attitude.

As we've learned, if you view a photograph of a scary face your amygdala will flare up, setting your heart racing, your breath quickening, your palms sweating. But if you view the same photo of a scary face accompanied by words like *angry* or *afraid*, activation in the amygdala is stifled and your body's alarm responses are reined in. As the prefrontal cortex goes to work trying to decide how accurately the word describes the situation, it overrides your original reflex of fear.[27]

Taken together, these discoveries show that verbal information can act as a wet blanket flung over the amygdala's fiery reactions to sensory input. That's why using words to think about an investing decision becomes so important whenever bad news hits. To be sure, formerly great investments can go to zero in no time; once Enron and WorldCom started to drop, it didn't pay to think analytically about them. But for every stock that goes into a total meltdown, there are thousands of other investments that suffer only temporary setbacks— and selling too soon is often the worst thing you can do. To prevent your feelings from overwhelming the facts, use your words and ask questions like these:

Other than the price, what else has changed?

Are my original reasons to invest still valid?

---

[27] Ahmad Hariri, interview by JZ via e-mail (14 April 2005); Ahmad R. Hariri, S.Y. Bookheimer, and J.C. Mazziotta, "Modulating Emotional Responses: Effects of a Neocortical Network on the Limbic System," *NeuroReport*, vol. 11, no. 1 (17 January 2000):43–48; Ahmad R. Hariri et al., "Neocortical Modulation of the Amygdala Response to Fearful Stimuli," *Biological Psychiatry*, vol. 53, no. 6 (15 March 2003):494–501; Kezia Lange et al., "Task Instructions Modulate Neural Responses to Fearful Facial Expressions," *Biological Psychiatry*, vol. 53, no. 3 (2003):226–232; Florin Dolcos and Gregory McCarthy, "Brain Systems Mediating Cognitive Interference by Emotional Distraction," *Journal of Neuroscience*, vol. 26, no. 7 (15 February 2006):2072–2079.

If I liked this investment enough to buy it at a much higher price, shouldn't I like it even more now that the price is lower?

What other evidence do I need to evaluate in order to tell whether this is really bad news?

Has this investment ever gone down this much before? If so, would I have done better if I had sold out—or if I had bought more?

Track Your Feelings. In Chapter Five, we learned the importance of keeping an investing diary. You should include what neuroscientist Antoine Bechara calls an "emotional registry," tracking the ups and downs of your moods alongside the ups and downs of your money. During the market's biggest peaks and valleys, go back and read your old entries from similar periods in the past. Chances are, your own emotional record will show you that you tend to become overenthusiastic when prices (and risk) are rising, and to sink into despair when prices (and risk) go down. So you need to train yourself to turn your investing emotions upside down. Many of the world's best investors have mastered the art of treating their own feelings as reverse indicators: Excitement becomes a cue that it's time to consider selling, while fear tells them that it may be time to buy. I once asked Brian Posner, a renowned fund manager at Fidelity and Legg Mason, how he sensed whether a stock would be a moneymaker. "If it makes me feel like I want to throw up," he answered, "I can be pretty sure it's a great investment." Likewise, Christopher Davis of the Davis Funds has learned to invest when he feels "scared to death." He explains, "A higher perception of risk can lower the actual risk by driving prices down. We like the prices that pessimism produces."[28]

Get Away from the Herd. In the 1960s, psychologist Stanley Milgram carried out a series of astounding experiments. Let's imagine you are in his lab. You are offered $4 (about $27 in today's money) per hour to act as a "teacher" who will help guide a "learner" by penalizing him for wrong answers on a simple memory test. You sit in front of a machine with 30 toggle switches that are marked with escalating labels from "slight shock" at 15 volts, up to "DANGER: SEVERE SHOCK" at 375 volts, and beyond to 450 volts (marked ominously with "XXX"). The learner sits where you can hear but not see him. Each time the learner gets an answer wrong, the lab supervisor instructs you to flip the next switch, giving a higher shock. If you hesitate to increase the voltage, the lab supervisor politely but firmly instructs you to continue. The first few shocks are

---

[28] Antoine Bechara, interview by JZ (2 April 2002); Jason Zweig, "What's Eating You," *Money Magazine*, vol. 30, no. 13 (December 2001):63–64; Beverly Goodman, "Family Tradition," *SmartMoney*, vol. 15, no. 3 (March 2006):64–67; Davis, interview by JZ via e-mail (27 June 2006).

harmless. But at 75 volts, the learner grunts. "At 120 volts," Milgram wrote, "he complains verbally; at 150 he demands to be released from the experiment. His protests continue as the shocks escalate, growing increasingly vehement and emotional. . . . At 180 volts the victim cries out, 'I can't stand the pain'. . . . At 285 volts his response can only be described as an agonized scream."29

What would you do if you were one of Milgram's "teachers"? He surveyed more than 100 people outside his lab, describing the experiment and asking them at what point they thought they would stop administering the shocks. On average, they said they would quit between 120 and 135 volts. Not one predicted continuing beyond 300 volts.

However, inside Milgram's lab, 100 percent of the "teachers" willingly delivered shocks of up to 135 volts, regardless of the grunts of the learner; 80 percent administered shocks as high as 285 volts, despite the learner's agonized screams; and 62 percent went all the way up to the maximum ("XXX") shock of 450 volts. With money at stake, fearful of bucking the authority figure in the room, people did as they were told "with numbing regularity," wrote Milgram sadly. (By the way, the "learner" was a trained actor who was only pretending to be shocked by electric current; Milgram's machine was a harmless fake.)

Milgram found two ways to shatter the chains of conformity. One is "peer rebellion." Milgram paid two people to join the experiment as extra "teachers"— and to refuse to give any shocks beyond 210 volts. Seeing these peers stop, most people were emboldened to quit, too. Milgram's other solution was "disagreement between authorities." When he added a second supervisor who told the first that escalating the voltage was no longer necessary, nearly everyone stopped administering the shocks immediately.

Milgram's discoveries suggest how you can resist the pull of the herd:

- Before entering an internet chat room or a meeting with your colleagues, write down your views about the investment you are considering: why it is good or bad, what it is worth, and your reasons for those views. Be as specific as possible—and share your conclusions with someone you respect who is not part of the group. (That way, you know someone else will keep track of whether you change your opinions to conform with the crowd.)

- Run the consensus of the herd past the person you respect the most who is not part of the group. Ask at least three questions: Do these people sound reasonable? Do their arguments seem sensible? If you were in my shoes, what else would you want to know before making this kind of decision?

---

29 Stanley Milgram, *Obedience to Authority* (New York: Harper & Row, 1974):4, 23, 107, 117–119, 123.

- If you are part of an investment organization, appoint an internal sniper. Base your analysts' bonus pay partly on how many times they can shoot down an idea that everyone else likes. (Rotate this role from meeting to meeting to prevent any single sniper from becoming universally disliked.)

- Alfred P. Sloan, Jr., the legendary chairman of General Motors, once abruptly adjourned a meeting this way: "Gentlemen, I take it we are all in complete agreement on the decision here. . . . Then I propose we postpone further discussion of this matter until our next meeting to give ourselves time to develop disagreement and perhaps gain some understanding of what the decision is all about." Peer pressure can leave you with what psychologist Irving Janis called "vague forebodings" that you are afraid to express. Meeting with the same group over drinks in everyone's favorite bar may loosen some of your inhibitions and enable you to dissent more confidently. Appoint one person as the "designated thinker," whose role is to track the flow of opinions set free as other people drink. According to the Roman historian Tacitus, the ancient Germans believed that drinking wine helped them "to disclose the most secret motions and purposes of their hearts," so they evaluated their important decisions twice: first when they were drunk and again when they were sober.[30]

Jason Zweig is a personal finance columnist at the Wall Street Journal.

---

[30]Irving L. Janis, *Groupthink*, 2nd edition (Boston: Houghton Mifflin, 1982):271; Tacitus, *Germania*.

Irrational Exuberance Revisited
Robert J. Shiller

Big market moves are historic events. And to understand historic events, a broad perspective is needed. We would not think of trying to understand the causes of World War II just in terms of changes in interest rates or inflation rates, and neither should we think of trying to understand events in the stock market in just such terms. As market observers, we need to understand more than just finance *per se*.

Understanding human psychology, culture, and institutions matters. Alan Greenspan's now famous phrase "irrational exuberance" is a good name for the variety of factors that has produced market excesses. I thought it was such a good term that in 2000 I wrote a book entitled *Irrational Exuberance*. I wish to talk about just what this term means. In particular, this presentation is about the psychology of the markets applied to the booms in the stock market in the 1990s and in the housing market just recently—essentially, a theory of bubbles based on all the perspectives I can muster from the social sciences. Finally, I will discuss new hedging vehicles for residential real estate.

The Psychology of Confidence

During a dinner speech on 5 December 1996, Alan Greenspan asked, "How do we know when irrational exuberance has unduly escalated asset prices?" As far as I can tell, that was the only time he ever uttered the words "irrational exuberance." He did not say there was irrational exuberance; he simply asked a question. Even though his words made no assertive statement, they spooked the markets. The Nikkei Index in Japan was open at the time and dropped 3.2 percent immediately on those words. Then, those words, and the reaction to them, spread around the world. I think the market response to his words more than the words themselves made "irrational exuberance" his most famous quote.

In the U.S. Federal Reserve's Economic Outlook of 20 October 2005, Chairman Ben Bernanke made the following statement about inflated home prices: "Although speculative activity has increased in some areas, at a national level, these price increases largely reflect strong economic fundamentals, including robust growth in jobs and incomes, low mortgage rates, steady rates of household formation, and factors that limit the expansion of housing supply in some areas." Bernanke is a very smart man, but based on this statement, he just

This presentation comes from Defining, Measuring, and Managing Uncertainty: The CFA Institute Risk Symposium held in New York City on 22–23 February 2006.

Reprinted with permission from CFA Institute Conference Proceedings Quarterly, *vol. 23, no. 3 (September 2006):16–25.*

does not get what is going on with home prices. In recent testimony, Bernanke did say that the clouds on the horizon are oil prices and home prices and that if home prices slow enough, it could weaken the economy. Note, however, no words about "bubble."

A bubble is a market situation in which news of price increases spurs investor enthusiasm. Thus, it is based on psychology and emotion. The bubble expands by psychological contagion from person to person, and this contagion is important. It brings in more and more investors who, despite doubts about fundamental value, find themselves drawn to the investment partly through envy and a gambler's excitement. Gambling behavior is part of human behavior, and anthropologists say it exists in every society and is an aspect of a human entrepreneurial spirit. My use of the word "gambler" could be provocative, but I am not criticizing gambling.

Bubbles are not purely psychological phenomena. They are an epidemic, and an epidemic requires contagion. An epidemic (bubble) can exist only if conditions favor contagion. For example, influenza, another contagious agent, tends to occur in the winter because people are inside more often than outside. Influenza is spread by droplets in the air, so when people are enclosed in a space, the contagion rate goes up. The contagion rate has to exceed the removal rate (the rate at which people recover from their illness), however, if an epidemic is to grow. One reason financial bubbles are mysterious is that their time pattern depends on the contagion rate of the enthusiasm, the spread of optimism and excitement for the market, and this contagion is hard to observe objectively.

The contagion rate is not just psychological. It depends on other things, such as monetary policy. The Fed can burst the bubble. It may not want to because of the collateral effects, but it has the opportunity to do so. Regulators in the past have stopped bubbles. After the Dutch tulip mania in 1637, authorities were aghast at what was happening and shut down the tulip markets.

I went on an expedition to find out who first defined the term "bubble." The earliest clear statement I could find was in an extraordinary book by Charles MacKay written in 1841 called *Extraordinary Popular Delusions and the Madness of Crowds*, which was a best-seller. I recommend it still today. In it, he talks about tulip mania, an event that occurred 200 years earlier. In describing the event, he uses vivid phrases: "Individuals suddenly grew rich," "A golden bait hung temptingly out before the people," and "They rushed to the tulip marts like flies around a honey-pot." As the bubble expanded, people who were not initially interested in the markets became interested, so it had elements of contagion. Then, MacKay writes about the inevitable bursting of the speculative bubble when the prices got too high. If prices get high, they are supported only by people's expectations that they will go up further, which cannot go on forever. A bubble has an inherent internal contradiction that brings it to an end. A bubble does not need any event to end it. It will end itself.

So, 1841 sounds like a long time ago, but for my scholarly perspective, I was not satisfied. I researched back to the tulip mania to find reference to a bubble. Old Dutch manuscripts of the time, however, do not include a definition of a bubble. But I did find evidence that hinted at one. A pamphlet from the year 1637, when the tulip mania bubble burst, contains a fictitious dialog between two men, Gaergoedt and Waermondt. Gaergoedt has just made a lot of money in the tulip market, and he is very proud of himself. He is talking to Waermondt, who is not in the tulip market. Gaergoedt talks expansively about the returns—10 percent, 100 percent, even 1,000 percent—trading tulips, and Waermondt is skeptical. He is worried that he is getting in too late. (Note that this was the very first big speculative bubble, and already it was obvious investors had to worry about getting in too late.) Gaergoedt just says some nonsense: "It's never too late to make a profit. You make money while sleeping."

One can picture the emotional response that Waermondt—a poor weaver who has been working all this time on his trade and never making much money—has to this kind of bragging behavior. Waermondt is uncomfortable because he knows logically that the boom might be coming to the end. He does not know what to do. Then, finally, he asks the question, "Do you know anyone who has become rich with your trade?" Gaergoedt gleefully gives him some examples. These stories seemed to convince Waermondt, and he seems ready to go into the tulip market, but he is saved by luck because Gaergoedt's wife comes in with news that the tulip market has just crashed.

That is the end of that pamphlet, but it is interesting that this writer from 1637 chose to explain the tulip mania in the form of a dialog because it illustrates the contagion as it works. It is word of mouth, person-to-person contagion. The human species is very empathetic; we feel others' feelings. The human species is also interconnected, and when we hear talk like this, it gets us emotionally involved, which is what happens in a bubble. I believe, but I cannot prove, that the writer of this pamphlet heard conversations like this in 1637 and made them the basis of the story. It is revealing of human nature. This same thing happens today.

Bubbles remain mysterious because they cannot be judged based simply on psychology. If it is just human psychology, then why don't we have a bubble all the time? That is always a difficult question. The theory of bubbles connected to the stock market has four elements:

1. precipitating factors, or what gets the bubble started;
2. amplification mechanism, the epidemic that gets the bubble to propagate;
3. cultural factors; and
4. psychological factors.

Precipitating Factors. Precipitating factors are the truly exogenous factors that begin to change the demand for stocks and start the epidemic on its path. A critical precipitating factor for the stock market boom of the late 1990s was the internet revolution. In the late 1990s, the internet was such a spectacular technological advance that it made people believe they were entering a "new era" and allowed them to think that stock prices could really soar.

Amplification Mechanism. The amplification mechanism propels the precipitating factors into irrational exuberance. The simplest amplification mechanism, as seen with Gaergoedt and Waermondt, is price to price. Prices start going up. It attracts attention. It spurs conversation and brings people into the market; they then buy and bid the price up more. The amplification mechanism can also be a price-to-GDP-to-price feedback. When the stock market is up, people feel optimistic and they spend more money, so the economy starts to boom. People see the booming economy, which encourages them to bid prices of stocks up even more. Finally, there is a price-to-earnings-to-price mechanism. When the stock market goes up, consumers spend more and corporate sales and earnings go up as long as costs are largely fixed. So, people can say that price was predicting the earnings growth. They believe that the reason the market is going up is because companies are doing so well when, in fact, it is all part of a cycle, albeit one that is self-limiting.

Cultural Factors. Cultural factors are the stories that surround the bubble. Stories are essential because humans are story-oriented animals. Listen to people on the way to and from a casino. Rarely are they talking about probability distributions or kurtosis or anything related to the science of gambling—probability and statistics. They are telling stories. They will say, "You know my friend? He went in. His wife told him not to go. But he did, and he won $10,000." That sort of story can justify a market boom. Many of these stories are stories about why the world is different this time. I call them "new era" stories.

Psychological Factors. To understand the vulnerability of markets to psychological errors, one has to understand the principles of psychology. One psychological factor is overconfidence. Most people (both men and women) think they are above average, and people have a tendency to believe in themselves, which is part of self-esteem. Another factor is the representativeness heuristic, which is a tendency to see patterns in data and expect them to repeat. Another factor is framing, which occurs when an individual lets his or her judgments be affected by the way a choice is presented, so people do not always judge things in a purely rational way. Finally, attention anomalies are mistakes that people make because of inattention. People get focused on one thing and miss the obvious.

Trends in the Stock Market

The stock market can be viewed from the perspective of bubble theory. The top line in **Figure 1** is the stock price from 1871 to 2005 corrected for inflation. It clearly has lots of ups and downs, with some ups that are quite sharp, such as the peaks in 1929 and 2000. These two peaks are cusp-shaped; they are classic bubbles. The market was increasing at an increasing rate, and then when nothing in particular happened, it suddenly turned. The bubble had its own end in sight.

Figure 1. S&P Composite Real Price and Earnings, January 1871–October 2005

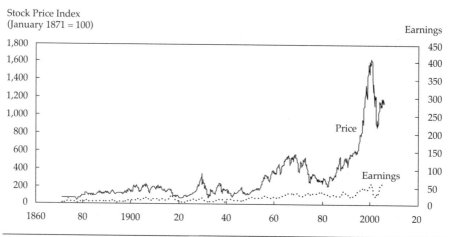

Source: Shiller (2005).

The top line in **Figure 2** is the P/E for January 1871 to October 2005, and the bottom line is long-term interest rates. The P/E is computed using Graham and Dodd's 1934 definition, which is price divided by 10-year rolling-average earnings. In this period, one can see a few historic peaks, most notably in 2000. Also note that since roughly 1970, an inverse relationship seems to have existed between interest rates and P/E. That relationship was talked about a lot around 2000; the so-called Fed model said that the frothy market was justified by the lower interest rates. Since 2000, that correlation has broken down, and also before 1970, there really was not a correlation. Thus, people seem to have been exaggerating the impact of interest rates on the stock market.

Figure 2. Real S&P P/E and Interest Rates, January 1881–October 2005

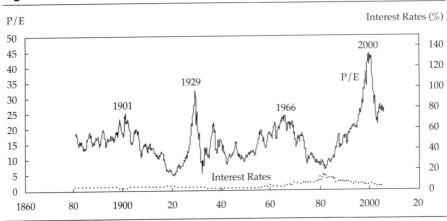

Source: Shiller (2005).

The stock market boom of the 1990s was a worldwide phenomenon. Brazil, China, France, Germany, the United States—all went up and down around the same time. Meanwhile, India, Japan, and South Korea did not share that same pattern, but even between 1998 and 2000, those countries all had dramatic booms. It seems as if the contagion reached these countries last, perhaps because the attention of people in these countries was on something else (e.g., the Asian financial crisis) and it took longer for the excitement to start there. Whatever the differences across countries, eventually the contagion spreads worldwide because the market culture is becoming worldwide more and more.

Figure 3 is a scatter diagram showing how P/E predicts future returns. Note that my colleague John Campbell and I showed an earlier version of this diagram to Alan Greenspan two days before he gave his irrational exuberance speech. A regression would not indicate a terribly good fit, but it is a good enough fit to suggest that there is something to this model. I see a negative slope to that scatter, and what it shows is that when the P/E has been high, subsequent returns have been low, and when the P/E has been low, subsequent returns have been high. For the years 1919, 1920, and 1921, the P/E was about 7—quite low—and the subsequent real returns were more than 15 percent a year. When the P/E has been high, say, 20–25 times, the subsequent 10-year returns have been just a little above zero. So, this relationship indicates that investors should expect low returns over the next 10 years because the P/E is about 25 times. Obviously, this is not a solid forecasting tool, but I still think that we are in exuberant times and that the market is still highly priced.

Figure 3.   Subsequent Annualized 10-Year Return vs. P/E, 1881–1995

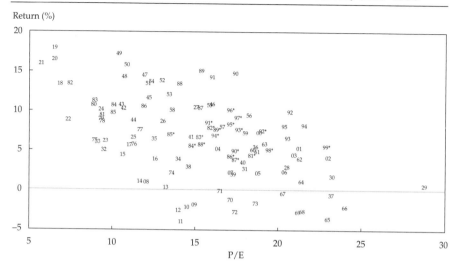

Notes: The numbers in the figure represent a year, and an asterisk next to a number indicates the 19th century. For example, 90* refers to the year 1890. P/E is for January of the indicated year.

Figure 4 shows the One-Year Confidence Index, which I started calculating in 1989 based on a survey both of individual and institutional investors and which is now maintained by the Yale School of Management.[1] The index equals the percentage of people who think the stock market will go up over the next year. It rose rapidly through the 1990s both for individual and institutional investors, but after 2000, it either flattened out or began sagging slightly. Nevertheless, confidence is still high.

Figure 5 shows the Valuation Confidence Index, which is the percentage of investors who think the market is *not* overvalued. Interestingly, the percentage for both individual and institutional investors declined through the 1990s and bottomed out right before the peak of the market. After the market crashed, it shot back up again, which is maybe one of the best pieces of evidence that the stock market boom was a bubble.

Since 1996, I have asked the following question to individual investors: "Do you agree with the following statement: 'The stock market is the best investment for long-term holders who can just buy and hold through the ups and downs of the market.'" Surprisingly, the percentage of individual investors

---

[1] For more information on the confidence indices, see http://icf.som.yale.edu/confidence.index/index.shtml.

Figure 4. One-Year Confidence Index: U.S. Six-Month Averages, 1989–2005

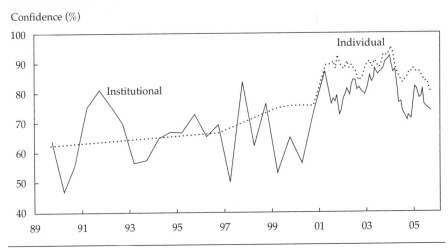

Confidence (%)

Note: Data for 2005 are through September.

Figure 5. Valuation Confidence Index: U.S. Six-Month Averages, 1989–2005

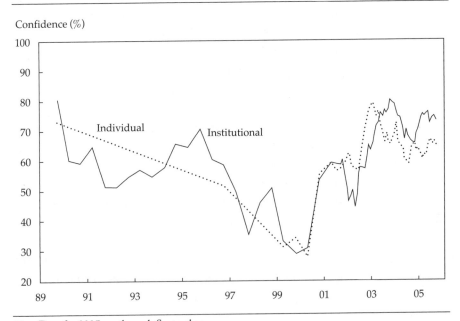

Confidence (%)

Note: Data for 2005 are through September.

responding that they strongly agree did not grow through the 1990s, but it certainly declined afterwards. So, the experience of the declining market has weakened people's enthusiasm for the stock market.

Another question I have been asking is, "Do you agree with this statement: 'If there is another crash like October 19, 1987, the market will surely be back up to its former levels in a couple years or so.'" The percentage of investors saying they strongly agree has never been as high as 50 percent, but it grew through the 1990s and has fallen sharply since then. These opinions should not be changing so fast; people should know that the stock market has a history of more than 100 years, and the last few years do not add much evidence about the behavior of the stock market. People are focusing on the latest events, and they are changing their confidence in the market rather sharply.

Trends in Real Estate

Although the stock market bubble has burst, we are currently in what appears likely to be a housing bubble. This is significant. It is, in an important sense, a new phenomenon. Since 1980, I have been counting (using electronic searches) the times the phrase "housing bubble" appears in newspapers. The phrase was not used at all before 1987. Then, it began to appear right after the stock market crash in 1987 but died out again. It suddenly reappeared in 2002.

We have entered a speculative phase, and now, a lot of people think we are in a housing bubble. Many people are buying real estate today because they think real estate prices will go up for a while. This mentality, of course, propels the bubble, for a while.

Regulators should pay attention. Nontraditional mortgages have helped fuel the housing boom. We have seen a deterioration in lending standards and a proliferation of adjustable-rate mortgages (ARMs) and option ARMs. People with very small down payments are buying houses, and too many of them are considered lower income or have poor credit histories. Unfortunately, the regulators do not move fast.

Because no long historical time series for home prices exists, I had to create one, shown in **Figure 6**. I looked at every price index for homes to try to get a quality control price index—pricing a standard home, which is not constant over time because homes have gradually gotten bigger over the past century. I found a number of series, but I had to fill in gaps to create this index. Notice that starting in 1890, home prices in real terms did not grow much until 1997, when they started shooting up—apparently a bubble period.

Back in the 1950s, economists reasoned that home prices are driven by building costs. They found that the change in real home prices very roughly mirrored the change in building costs. But that relationship seems to have broken

Figure 6.   Long-Term Trends in Single-Family Homes, 1890–2005

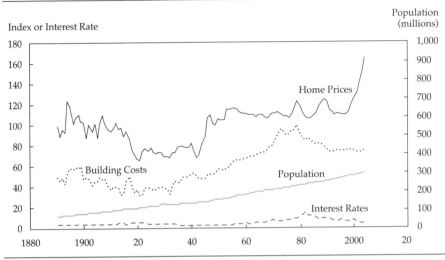

Notes: For home prices, 1890 = 100. For building costs, 1890 = 50.

down; recently, no correlation exists between the two. Furthermore, the jump in home prices cannot be explained by population increases because the population has been growing steadily—with no sudden jump after 1997. Finally, interest rates cannot explain the sudden increase in home prices after 1997 because interest rates have been on a rather steady decline since the early 1980s, with no sudden move down after 1997. Therefore, I think the increase is psychological.

Home prices have not gone up in real terms over long periods of time. Thus, a house has not been a great investment, unless, of course, one has a sufficiently high valuation of the "dividends" the house pays in terms of housing services.

Why haven't home prices gone up? The price of a house relates mostly to its structure. And houses are getting cheaper to build, not more expensive, because of technical progress. In 1890, homes were handmade by skilled artisans. Now, people can purchase modular, prefabricated homes, circumventing the skilled artisans. Land has been getting more expensive, but if a person wants a house and does not care where it is, land can cost almost nothing. The population spreads out into formerly rural areas, taking the pressure off of prices in city centers.

Why do people believe home prices will do well in the long term? I think it is partly because of inflation confusion: Homes cannot be split like shares when they become highly priced, and so the rise in nominal home prices caused by inflation is much more apparent than the rise in stock prices. Another possible explanation is popular perceptions of the decline in real interest rates.

I constructed a long-term real interest rate series back to 1890, shown in **Figure 7**, and compared it with the same home price series shown in Figure 6. But popular perceptions notwithstanding, declining real interest rates actually cannot justify the home price boom today. Real interest rates have been declining since the early 1980s (note the inverted scale), but they do not match up well with home prices. I separately tested the relationship between government expenditure and home prices and found no meaningful relationship. And remarkably, the unemployment rate shows no correlation with real home prices. The United States had two high periods of unemployment (the 1890s and the 1930s), and neither of those periods experienced a decline in real home prices. Finally, people are now saying that the boom in housing prices cannot deflate because no recession looms on the horizon.

Figure 7. Home Prices and Real Interest, 1890–2005

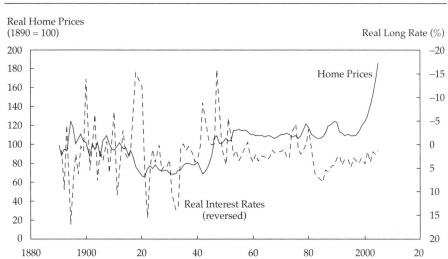

Another factor to examine is rental prices. Since 1913, real rents of primary residences, as reported by the U.S. Bureau of Labor Statistics (BLS), have gradually declined. Thus, home prices have gone up recently without any concomitant increase in real rents. But rents are different from home prices. A renter does not have any speculative interest in the property, but the buyer does. **Figure 8** shows the ratio of my home price index to the BLS rent index, which can be thought of as the P/E for housing. Since 1913, this ratio has exhibited a strong uptrend. Some have criticized the BLS rent index for not accounting properly for quality change, but at the very least, the available data do not show that recent home price increases are justified by rent increases.

Figure 8. Ratio of Shiller Home Price Index to Rent of Primary Residence Index, 1913–2004

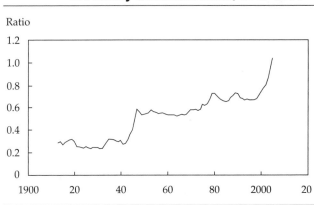

Eichholtz (1997) computed a housing price index that went back to 1628, which includes the tulip mania, for the upscale Herengracht neighborhood of Amsterdam. Although it has shown boom and bust cycles, it has not shown an uptrend. If I were to ask people what they thought the return on housing should be in a glamorous metropolitan area, a lot of people would answer even better than the stock market—say, 10 percent a year. Think about it. Amsterdam has been a booming metropolis since 1628. It was the financial center of the world in the 1600s. It ought to have done well. Could it have done 10 percent a year since 1628? No. Compounding 10 percent a year for 370 years would produce a total return of 443,031,891,418,593,000 percent, which would bring us beyond the galaxy—not possible. Real prices have actually doubled in 350 years, and that is only a 0.2 percent increase a year. Thus, this beautiful downtown section in Amsterdam has not changed in price adjusted for inflation.

Why can someone buy an apartment there today and pay the same price as in 1628, adjusted for inflation? Because people do not have to live there. Other locations are competing with the Herengracht neighborhood. Amsterdam is now spread out over a huge area and is continuing to spread. Prices are not going to go up in the center because people can go somewhere else. It is elementary supply and demand, and that is why home prices will not go up strongly in real terms over long periods of time.

Expectations of future price appreciation, however, are quite different. I asked homeowners in Los Angeles and Milwaukee the following: "On average over the next 10 years, how much do you expect the value of your home to change each year?" The results are shown in **Table 1**. These are extraordinary expectations, especially because home prices are already high. Milwaukee had lower expectations until recently, so what I think is happening now is the bubble has gotten so much publicity that even in Milwaukee people are getting optimistic.

Table 1. Long-Term Expectations for Housing Appreciation, Los Angeles and Milwaukee

City/Measure	1988	2003	2004	2005
Los Angeles				
Mean	14.3%	13.0%	22.5%	22.7%
Median	10	8	10	9
Milwaukee				
Mean	7.3%	11.7%	13.4%	13.6%
Median	5	5	5	7.5

I then asked people whether they agreed that real estate is the best investment for long-term holders, who can just buy and hold through the ups and downs of the market. In Los Angeles, more than 50 percent said they strongly agree. But as I have just demonstrated for real home prices in Amsterdam over a 350-year history, real estate has about a 0 percent real return in the long run. These survey respondents do not know that. In Milwaukee, however, respondents seemed more rational; only about one-third thought that real estate is the best long-term investment.

Hedging Vehicles for Real Estate

According to the Federal Reserve Board, real estate owned by households is the second largest asset class in the United States, valued at $21.6 trillion in the fourth quarter of 2005. But until recently, unlike for stocks and bonds, investors could not hedge real estate risk efficiently. Many investors are exposed to real estate risk because it is concentrated in one geographical area, and especially for ordinary retail investors, real estate may be the biggest part of their portfolios. Many are hoping to use this "asset" when they retire, but it may be in one of these volatile sections.

Various attempts have been made to develop hedging vehicles for real estate. The first such attempt was in London in 1991. The London Futures and Options Exchange (London Fox) started trading property futures in 1991 on U.K. home price indices. It was a cash-settled futures market, but it lasted only a few months because the volume of trade was disappointing, eventually leading to London Fox officers making fraudulent trades to inflate the volume of trade.

Around 2002, a futures market in U.K. housing began: City Index and IG Index. These are spread-betting firms in London, and they have some trading of home price indices in the United Kingdom, but they are not very successful. In 2004, Hedgestreet.com set up an online trading site aimed at retail investors with price indices for single-family homes. As far as I can tell, it is not a big success, although it just announced that it is teaming up with the Chicago Board Options Exchange to develop new products.

In May 2006, the Chicago Mercantile Exchange (CME) opened a futures market based on the S&P/Case–Shiller Metro Area Home Price Indices, which were originally developed in the 1980s.[2] Cash-settled futures are available in 10 U.S. cities, as is a national composite index, with the highest weightings given to New York (27 percent), San Francisco (12 percent), and Chicago (9 percent). The futures are traded on CME Globex. The value for each contract is 250 times the value of any index. With the opening composite index at $231, the value of one futures contract is $57,750. So, a homeowner wishing to hedge a $570,000 house could sell 10 contracts for a complete hedge. The CME has also created an options market, based on the same home price index.

These new markets may start slowly and grow, but as people get used to liquid markets for home prices, they should garner more and more interest. Perhaps within a few years, investors will be hearing on the news that New York closed up 2 points and Los Angeles closed down 2 points, just like the stock market. The cash market for homes is inefficient right now. It has very strong momentum compared with the stock market, not at all the random walk that financial theory describes. I hope that the housing market will become more like the stock market and that investment professionals will have the opportunity to participate in these markets on behalf of their clients on a global scale.

Robert J. Shiller is the Arthur M. Okun Professor of Economics at Yale University, New Haven, Connecticut.

REFERENCES

Eichholtz, Piet M.A. 1997. "A Long Run House Price Index: The Herengracht Index, 1628-1973." *Real Estate Economics*, vol. 25, no. 2 (Summer):175–192.

Shiller, Robert J. 2005. *Irrational Exuberance*. 2nd ed. Princeton, NJ: Princeton University Press.

[2]*Editor's Note*: Professor Shiller is a co-founder of, and stockholder in, MacroMarkets LLC, the producer of a series of home price indices that are licensed to the CME and that form the basis for the futures contracts referenced in this article.

Question and Answer Session
Robert J. Shiller

Question: Who would naturally be on the long side of a futures trade given that so many individual investors, in particular, are already long real estate?

Shiller: Yes, indeed, a lot of people are saying everyone wants to be short the market these days because we are all worried that the prices are going to go down. But all that means is that the futures market is likely to go into backwardation (futures prices lower than spot prices).

I believe the futures market for housing will be one of those markets (like the oil futures market) that is frequently seen in backwardation. With backwardation in place, the longs will see that they are buying cheaply and will have an incentive to come in. Even when the futures market is not actually in backwardation, it will be attractive to longs if the price increase "predicted" in the futures market is less than the actual expected price increase.

It is important to note that even though I have said home prices have not gone up much in the long run, taking long positions in the futures market is likely to be a good investment for longs. Note also that because of a low correlation between home prices and other investments, long futures is a good diversifying investment too.

Question: Could the tax deductibility of mortgage interest be a material factor in explaining trends in housing prices?

Shiller: The federal income tax came into force in 1913, which is exactly the beginning of our series. Then, it was a millionaire's tax, but it became important after World War II. I don't think that explains the phenomenon well because the boom in the housing market really occurred in many countries. I think it started first in London. It wasn't first in the United States. I haven't heard a good tax explanation for all of these events around the world.

Question: Do you expect Fannie Mae and other government-sponsored enterprises to be active participants in the futures markets?

Shiller: We would love to have Fannie and Freddie hedge their portfolios in our markets. We've been trying to tell them that. I'm hoping that they will because they have an exposure to real estate risk, and I think they are in a somewhat risky situation because home prices may start falling. If they do fall, it could cause mortgage defaults, so they should be hedged against this.

Question: What are the macroeconomic implications of a housing price boom followed by a crash?

Shiller: The real estate boom that we've been in is quite a dramatic event, and it has been driving the economy substantially. The personal savings rate is negative now, at least in part because people view themselves as "saving" through increased home prices. But if home prices start to fall, their "saving" could suddenly evaporate, which could affect confidence and then consumption expenditure, which, in turn, could cause a recession.

If history is a guide, we might have a recession as part of the unraveling of a housing boom, but recessions tend to be rather short lived, 6–18 months typically, and we would see declining prices in real estate for five years or more. Keep in mind that this home price boom is essentially unprecedented. The only one that's similar is the post–World War II boom, but the World War II boom was different because during the war, 25 percent of the men were in uniform, which shut down the construction industry. The government also didn't want people building houses and diverting materials from the war effort. When the soldiers came back, that was a fundamental shock that drove the housing market. Recently, we haven't had a fundamental shock. There has been no world war. We're in a really different set of circumstances. This is more of a speculative shock this time.

Question: Does your caution about residential housing apply equally to the commercial realty market?

Shiller: Yes, I think that the correlation between home prices over the recent sample period and especially commercial apartment buildings has been fairly substantial; they are substitutes for each other. So, if we see a drop in home prices, we might see a drop in commercial real estate prices as well.

Eight Lessons from Neuroeconomics for Money Managers

Steven G. Sapra, CFA
Paul J. Zak

The 1970s ushered in the ascendance of the rational school of thought in economics. In particular, the development of the theory of rational expectations (Lucas 1972) led to substantially improved predictive models in economics and finance. By the 1980s, dynamic general equilibrium expectation models were being used to understand macroeconomic phenomena, such as business cycles and consumption patterns, as well as to characterize variations in financial markets and guide economic policies. The Nobel Prizes awarded to economists Robert Lucas, Jr., Edward Prescott, Finn Kydland, Harry Markowitz, Myron Scholes, Robert Merton, and William Sharpe reflect the importance of this research.

By the late 1980s, the dominance of rational expectations models had led many economists to categorically accept the assumption that human decisions are made with full foresight and rational deduction. In finance, the logical conclusion was that traded assets are always (or nearly always) fairly priced because investors consider all relevant outcomes and their related probabilities of occurrence. In other words, the theory of rational expectations led to the conclusion that markets are *efficient* because investors use all relevant information in forming their investment decisions. The development of index funds has been largely a result of the conclusions drawn from rational expectations models.

Recently, however, a revolutionary change has occurred in financial economics. The field of cognitive psychology—and, more recently, behavioral neuroscience—has allowed economists to observe the limits of human cognitive abilities and to appreciate the extent to which human biases often result in decisions starkly at odds with those predicted by models of rational choice. Even casual observation shows that human beings often behave, particularly in the financial markets, in ways vastly different from what is predicted by economic theory.

More than 200 years ago, in "The Theory of Moral Sentiments," Adam Smith characterized human beings as struggling between an "impartial spectator" and the "passions" (Smith 1759). This characterization will sound familiar to any modern-day student of psychology or cognitive neuroscience. Now we can measure these psychological constructs physiologically. In many respects, we have come full circle back to Smith: Modern neuroscience has shown us that our brains are indeed characterized by a struggle between our need for novelty and instant gratification (i.e., the passions) and our uniquely human ability to "know better" (i.e., the impartial spectator). Smith's ideas have been proven correct by modern neuroscience.

The new transdisciplinary field of neuroeconomics (Zak 2004; Zak forthcoming) identifies the brain regions that are most active when people are making economic decisions. This advance allows neuroeconomists to explain a number of prominent behavioral anomalies, or deviations from rational choice. The rapid development of the techniques used to measure brain activity, in conjunction with the decline in their costs, has produced a plethora of new findings in neuroeconomics since 2000. Neuroeconomics is providing an understanding of why real people, rather than "economic agents," behave the way they do. Furthermore, this emerging field has caused a growing body of economists to openly question the appropriateness of putting *homo economicus* into every economic model.

Modern neuroscience has shown that the vast majority of human information processing and decision making occurs on autopilot. The brain's autonomic mechanisms often execute decisions with little deliberate thought. The reasons the brain processes much information without conscious deliberation are discussed in Lesson 7, but in short, the brain is resource constrained. As a result, the brain does not invest its scarce resources to fully optimize every decision. In economic terms, the costs associated with fully evaluating every option often exceed the benefits of doing so. Hence, our brains have evolved to work largely without the need for conscious "intervention" into their operations.

Depending on the situation, the brain's automatic responses can be adaptive or maladaptive. Automatic processes in the brain react strongly when environmental conditions suddenly change; change may provoke such emotional responses as fear or hostility, for example. When these automatic processes occur, the brain increases the body's heart rate, blood pressure, and respiration, which sets off a cascade of "fight or flight" responses. When people are emotionally aroused, decisions narrow to the immediate; the primary objective in such a situation is to seek safety. When trading in financial markets, these evolved responses may be maladaptive. That is, as we discuss in Lesson 2, our brains treat volatility in markets as equivalent to spotting a lion on the savannah. Our automatic reaction is fear when the market falls precipitously or when returns are highly volatile.

This article not only identifies how the brain reacts to market conditions but also provides solutions for maladaptive responses. Importantly, how the brain responds to stimuli can change with training and experience. Our intention is to make financial professionals conscious of the brain's automatic processes so that they can train themselves to override those processes that negatively affect portfolio performance and focus on the brain processes that can enhance performance.

The human brain shares autonomic functions with other animals but differs primarily in the large and evolutionarily new prefrontal cortex. This is the area of the brain in the foremost part of the frontal cortex that lies directly behind the forehead. (The general organization of the brain is shown in **Figure 1.**[1]) Our deliberate thought and "executive functions," such as planning actions and evaluating outcomes, take place in the prefrontal cortex. This brain region engages cognitive resources to make decisions and recruits older brain regions

Figure 1. General Organization of the Human Brain

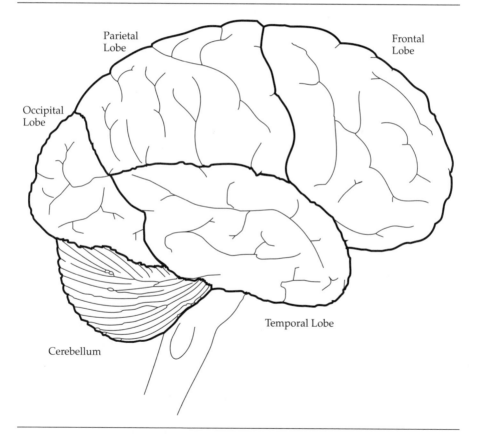

---

[1]Zak (2004) provides a primer on brain structure and function.

to provide access to memories (what have I done previously? what have others done?), affective states (how do I feel about each option?), and calculations of expected risk and return (what do I expect to get? how much risk am I willing to bear?). Experience, then, is a two-edged sword. To conserve brain resources, memories allow the brain to automate responses to similar tasks. At the same time, memories provide a store of related decisions and outcomes from which to draw comparisons and potentially change strategies. The key issue is when to engage our cognitive resources to undertake new analyses that may change decisions and when, instead, to use memories and experiences of past similar events when making choices.

Eight Lessons from Neuroeconomics

We present eight lessons from the recent literature in neuroeconomics that we hope will improve the practice of money management. As part of each lesson, we present practical applications for investment professionals. The sources of these lessons are cited, but additional information on the brain and investing can be found in Peterson (2007) and Shermer (2007).

Lesson 1: Anticipating Rewards. As any gambler knows, and modern neuroscience has now shown, what keeps the gambler coming back to the tables is the anticipation of reward.

Receiving a reward is pleasurable in the brain—and even more so if the reward is unexpected. Because the human brain evolved in an environment of scarcity, acquiring such primary rewards as food or sex is highly reinforcing: It makes us feel good, so our brain reminds us to keep doing it. Recent research by Knutson and Bossaerts (2007) has shown that acquiring money is similarly rewarding in the brain.

Acquiring resources is essential for the survival of all animals, and the evolutionarily old brain region that encodes rewards is found even in reptiles. This midbrain region, found near the brainstem at the base of the brain in Figure 1, is known as the "wanting" system because it motivates us to expend effort and accept risk to acquire things we need. To do this, the wanting system makes the pursuit of rewards highly pleasurable; it engages our emotions. Indeed, many drugs of abuse, such as methamphetamine and cocaine, hijack this area of the brain. The emotion investors feel when they anticipate a gain from investing is similar to the rush associated with drug use.

Yet, the activity of the brain's wanting system occurs largely outside of our conscious awareness. This brain system adapts to the environment in which we find ourselves, so the "drug" no longer provides the same high; we thus seek to acquire more. As a result, making the same or similar choices is no longer pleasurable. In other words, after an investor makes dozens of million-dollar trades, doing so becomes routine and the brain begins to process this type of decision automatically. When the brain becomes accustomed to making large trades, there is little novelty associated with this activity, and therefore, the emotional valence to large trades is diminished.

When an investor faces a new choice—a new market, a new asset class, or a larger than normal trade—the wanting system kicks back in and refocuses the investor's attention on acquiring reward. In a literal sense, then, we are biologically driven to seek novelty.

The brain's reward system is also hungry; it is constantly on the lookout for possible reward targets. As we mature, we learn how to say "no" to some of these rewards. The prefrontal executive regions of the brain modulate how strongly rewards are felt and how the anticipation of rewards affects behavior. Unfortunately, the prefrontal regions are the last to mature in humans; full maturity is not reached until people are 30 years of age. Furthermore, the prefrontal region "wires up" more slowly in men than in women. This lag is one reason that young men take more risks than young women. Communication between the prefrontal cortex and reward system requires experience to work effectively.

Even in those who are over 30, the prefrontal modulation of reward anticipation can be clouded by circumstances. Recent research has revealed that when the wanting system is in high gear, the reward signal swamps the prefrontal weighing of costs and benefits (Knutson, Wimmer, Kuhnen, and Winkielman 2008). In this experiment, a group of heterosexual men were shown pornographic photographs of women, stimulating the viewers' reward systems. Then, the men were asked to choose portfolios of risky stocks and safe bonds that would earn them money. Compared with men who saw nonpornographic pictures, those who viewed pornographic pictures had overactive wanting systems and chose riskier portfolios.

Investors who skydive, use illegal drugs, or drive too fast may also be overstimulating their reward systems. Periods of excessive risk taking, often accompanied by high leverage, can result from reward system overactivation and may negatively affect the performance of their investments.

■ *Application*: The pleasure of investing must be modulated so that excessive risk taking does not occur. Excessive risk taking is more likely when an investor has had several recent successes that push the wanting system to seek greater and greater rewards. For this reason, managers should monitor indicators of daily trading volume to prevent excessive trading. Assiduous use of risk budgeting and risk limits is essential to identify traders who are taking excessive risks.

Knowing that they are susceptible to trading for the thrill, the high, means that investment professionals themselves should learn to recognize when trading becomes sport. This is the time to throttle back on risk or manage a different portfolio. This self-analysis is critically important in highly volatile markets with high, often speculation-induced, share volumes. High volumes are likely to stimulate the reward system, as we discuss in Lesson 4.

Lesson 2: Balancing Risk. Modern portfolio theory (MPT) describes the yin and yang of risk and reward, the distinct and theoretically independent components of active money management. Return is defined as the realized outcome of a random variable (the market outcome), and risk is defined as the expected statistical deviation from expected return (volatility). Consistent with MPT, Knutson, Fong, Bennett, Adams, and Hommer (2003) showed that risk is processed in an evolutionarily new brain region that monitors body states and activates when a person experiences painful or aversive stimuli.

We literally *feel* risk in the same way that we feel fear when riding a roller coaster, disgust when we smell rotten food, or pain when we slice a finger while cooking. Our brain system says "stay away" from these things. Like all parts of the brain, the risk system also adapts to experience: The prefrontal cortex tells us that the roller coaster is safe, and we choose to go on it even though we know it will frighten us. Experience is essential for modulating emotional responses to visceral signals. Lo and Repin (2002) discovered that all traders have heightened fear responses when the markets are volatile by measuring physiological responses in professional foreign currency traders while they worked. Importantly, fear responses were reduced with trading experience. Experience reduces the weight put on fear signals by providing memories that we can use to relate the present state of arousal to similar signals and their associated outcomes. When fear is so high that we have little experience with which to compare it, the desire for safety can lead to excessive risk aversion.

The prefrontal cortex integrates information on reward and risk to generate a physiological utility calculation. That is, three primary brain regions are involved in a trading decision: the wanting system, the risk-aversion system, and the integration of these systems into a utility function. (Yes, the foundational notion in economics, utility, is a real physiological entity in the human brain.) The three regions that inform decisions are in broadly different areas of the brain: The wanting system is in the evolutionarily ancient midbrain; the risk system is in the newer temporal lobe of the brain; and utility calculations occur in the last area to evolve in humans, the prefrontal cortex.

■ *Application*: Because distinct brain regions process risk and reward, a disconnect can occur between them and the brain's utility function in the prefrontal cortex. This disconnect could result from a lesion (scar) on the connecting fibers or simply from fewer connections for communication existing between regions, as could be the case in chronic risk takers. Cross-talk between other brain regions can also dull the communication between risk and reward regions when choices are being weighed. Furthermore, the brain may encode the risk associated with investing other people's money differently from the way it treats risk when one's own money is at stake. This may reduce risk aversion for professional money managers.

Recall rogue trader Nick Leeson, who caused the collapse of Barings Bank after losing $1.4 billion on futures contracts. Leeson took excessive risk to offset losses from highly leveraged investments gone sour, doubling-down just like a gambler playing a losing strategy. The Bank of England's report stated:

> Barings' collapse was the result of the unauthorized and ultimately cata-strophic activities of, it appears, one individual that went undetected because of a failure of management and other internal controls of the most basic kind. (U.K. Parliament 1995)

Leeson may have become so accustomed to substantial risk that his visceral avoidance signal was muted.

In highly trending markets, the brain's risk monitor may also be underac-tive. Traders may undertake too little risk. Risk taking is appropriate for investment professionals, and managers should be alerted if traders have the bulk of their portfolios in cash for an extended period of time. This behavior is the equivalent of a deer freezing when headlights illuminate it on a country road; freezing may be adaptive in some circumstances, but it is often maladap-tive for investors.

To combat the possibilities of traders' taking too much risk or not enough risk, firms should have systems in place to monitor risk levels by sending alerts if risk is too high or too low. A simple way to do this is to have a manager who gets a risk report on each trader daily.

Lesson 3: Wait for It. Human beings are the only animals known that can delay gratification for more than a few minutes. Recent studies in neuroeco-nomics have shown that forgoing a current payoff to get a larger, later return requires intense activity in the prefrontal cortex (McClure, Laibson, Loewen-stein, and Cohen 2004).

Even with our large prefrontal cortices, we find waiting hard to do. With immediate rewards available, the midbrain wanting system is in high gear. Worse yet, Shiv and Fedorikhin (1999) showed that individuals' ability to exercise self-control fails in the presence of other demands on the prefrontal cortex. When markets are volatile, investors' deliberative prefrontal cortices are heavily taxed. This is precisely the situation in which an investor is more likely to make decisions based on immediate gratification and little deliberation, rather than on the basis of the bigger, later payoff.

■ *Application*: Volatility absorbs our cognitive resources as we cope with a multitude of information—much of it noise. Trading effectively in volatile markets often requires that we slow down decisions and look for opportunities deliberately. Going with our "gut instincts" has some merit—it draws on our visceral memories of related events—but it assesses our memories imperfectly and with hindsight bias (we may just have been lucky last time, so repeating our actions has no guarantee of success). In a volatile-market situation, making no decision is preferable to making a poor decision. When cognitive load is high, a good decision often entails stepping away from the situation and coming back later. This behavioral truth is precisely the reason behind the three-day waiting period for the purchase of a handgun. Recognizing the danger of cognitive overload when monitoring multiple streams of information requires that we train ourselves to step back and reflect before pulling the investment trigger.

Lesson 4: Following the Herd. Human beings are hypersocial creatures. Most of us like to be around other humans (at least some of them!). One of the values of being hypersocial is that we learn from each other easily and naturally. Studies have shown that social attachment occurs when the brain chemical oxytocin is released (Zak, Stanton, and Ahmadi 2007). Oxytocin is evolutionarily old and activates both emotion and reward pathways in the brain (Zak forthcoming). Like it or not, we are a herd species, and our brain makes us feel good when we follow the herd.

What was beneficial for our ancestors on the African savannah does not always serve us well in financial markets (Shermer 2007). Social learning is great when mastering calculus or riding a bicycle, but herd behavior in markets is typically detrimental. Herd behavior violates the "all else being equal" rule in economics in that investor decisions are not independent, and mispricing is thus likely to occur. Trading does not occur in a vacuum; often traders buy an asset because they see it going up in value. As more investors jump on the bandwagon, herd mentality results in a price bubble.

Our brains have evolved to make us desperately want to follow the crowd. Riots, overly popular restaurants, and asset market bubbles are the results. Herd behavior can occur even when individuals do not coordinate with each other but trade only on the basis of private information and prices (Bikhchandani, Hirshleifer, and Welch 1992).

■ *Application*: We know mathematically that all asset bubbles must burst, ultimately restoring equilibrium. The key issue, of course, is the timing of the rupture. Except for those who get into and out of a market quickly, profits often are found in going against the herd (just ask Warren Buffett). But evaluating alternatives while others follow trends goes against our nature because our brains bias us to follow the crowd. Desperate buying and panic selling are the inevitable consequences of herd mentality. Instead, investment professionals should discount their evolved bias toward following others and be contrarian. This approach will make them feel alone and exposed—two things our ancestors feared the most. The primitive fear response can be suppressed, however, by the deliberative prefrontal cortex—and through practice.

Investment professionals should be aware of their natural instinct to follow the crowd and consider whether their purchase of an asset is based on its fundamental value or the fact that it is in vogue at the moment. Conscious awareness of the herding bias will help to suppress the instinct to follow the crowd. Join the herd in dining out—but not in investing.

Lesson 5: The New New Thing. As discussed in Lesson 1, anticipation of gains activates the reward regions of the brain. Unfortunately, this reward system is multipurpose. *Any* new information we stumble upon will cause it to activate. Focusing on "the new new thing" (the motto of James H. Clark, the man who founded, among other companies, Silicon Graphics International and Netscape Communications) will continually "juice" this system.

Our brains are designed to seek out novelty and make finding it rewarding; this drive is what makes us want to acquire new information. Acquiring new information is obviously useful, and it evolved to be rewarding for important reasons, but how much of the "new new" is needed by investment professionals? As discussed in Lesson 3, the brain is subject to information overload that can impair decision making. Furthermore, discriminating between signal and noise in information flows is not easy, especially in these Bloombergian days of continual news feeds. Yet, our brains bias us to search for the new new thing—constantly.

Application: Novelty and reward are confounded in the brain, so it is important—but can be difficult—to keep them from being confused with each other when making investment decisions. Constant information flows rev up the wanting system, leading to increased risk taking, as discussed in Lesson 1. In addition, information flows demand cognitive resources in the prefrontal cortex as we seek to categorize and sort. This demand reduces such executive functions as evaluating and executing decisions. The (perhaps surprising) conclusion is that it is best to turn off Bloomberg and CNBC when making investment decisions. Listening to classical music will probably result in better decision making than trying to concentrate over the incessant banter of television commentators. Financial news has its place, but much of today's financial news is noise rather than signal and can impair financial decision making.

Of course, receiving new information is important in making up-to-date decisions. Eliminating Bloomberg entirely may not be the answer, but for most traders, viewing can be limited to once or twice a day. Adding some noise to your decision making via news feeds can actually improve decisions because it moves the deliberations away from the brain's automatic responses. At the same time, following established trading rules is essential, and one should not be distracted by rumor and innuendo—two things that stimulate the brain's wanting system.

Lesson 6: Checking References. Psychologist Daniel Kahneman was awarded the Nobel Prize in Economics in 2002 for his many clever experiments that called into question traditional rational expectations utility theory. For instance, Kahneman showed that the subjective value of an outcome is determined relative to a reference point (see, for example, Kahneman and Tversky 1979). The brain works similarly, making comparisons of relative value rather than absolutes as it seeks to sustain balance, or *homeostasis*.

Studies in monkeys (Platt and Glimcher 1999) and humans (Knutson and Peterson 2005) show that rewards are evaluated relative to a baseline of what one already has. As a result, people are *reference dependent* decision makers. For example, several studies have shown that after a gain, people take on more risk: The brain's reward system is cranked up and wants more. Similarly, after losses, many people increase their risk exposure to get back to their break-even reference point, just what Nick Leeson did at Barings Bank. Taking additional risk because of a focus on a reference point may lead to decisions that are not warranted.

Application: Clear the slate. Avoid radically changing positions in the presence of recent losses or gains except as guided by previously chosen stop-loss or limit orders. Understand that the reference point bias can work against the effective application of trading rules. In addition to avoiding herd behavior as described in Lesson 4, investment professionals should not use a colleague's profits or positions as reference points for their own trades. Other investment professionals may have different risk profiles, liquidity, or time horizons. Comparing performance with that of a colleague only clouds a manager's ability to objectively assess a situation. Investment professionals should analyze investments on their merits alone and ignore the path they took to get where they are today.

Lesson 7: Rational Rationality. All biological systems are economical: They have limited resources to accomplish necessary goals and, therefore, have evolved ways to use resources efficiently.

Our brains economize on scarce metabolic resources in two primary ways. The first is the cellular basis for learning: Brain circuits that are repeatedly used develop a bias to activate when they encounter the same or similar stimuli (Haier, Siegel, MacLachlan, Soderling, Lottenberg, and Buchsbaum 1992). This process in the brain leads, of course, to biases in behavior. Once something is learned, extra effort is needed to unlearn it. The phrase "think outside the box" is used precisely to encourage people to unlearn behavior that has become routine.

The second energy-saving technique the brain uses is to perform tasks we do repeatedly without conscious direction. In fact, nearly all of our brain processes occur outside our conscious awareness. Because of this ability, we can drive a car and talk or listen to the radio at the same time: We do not need to be consciously aware of driving—until the driver in the car in front of us slams on the brakes. Both learning and unconscious processing cause us to perform tasks on autopilot without burning the extra energy needed to consciously deliberate on best options.

This means that the human brain is a lazy Bayesian updater. Although large deviations from expectations (for example, the market crash of 1987) do lead to an updating of beliefs, small deviations do not cause us to integrate new information into our decision scaffolding. The human brain is "rationally rational" (Zak 2007, 2008a) rather than perfectly rational or irrational. The model of rational rationality predicts that for a range of decisions, "good enough" will prevail. Rational rationality is the brain basis for what Herbert Simon, Nobel laureate in economics, called "satisficing." Unless the expected benefits or costs are high, rational rationality uses memories of similar situations to serve as beliefs to guide decisions. Belief-based decisions do not use the full complement of cognitive resources to analyze available options.

Application: Investment professionals are paid to go beyond what nonprofessionals do in markets. Unfortunately, the longer these professionals do their job, the less effort their brains will put into it—rational rationality. Therefore, when new circumstances arise, investment professionals may continue to treat them as the "same old, same old."

The brain can be fooled by occasionally changing things around. Move to a new office or turn the desk a different way. Open or close the blinds, take a walk, put on music, read a different kind of book, or simply take a vacation. These changes can be enough to knock the brain out of its inertia and get an investment professional to start thinking differently. Just eat a good breakfast for energy; the brain runs on glucose, so a hungry brain is learning impaired.

Lesson 8: Portfolio Love. Zak's lab has shown that the human oxytocin-mediated empathy (HOME) circuit is extraordinarily powerful (Zak 2008b; Zak forthcoming). HOME leads us to "attach" and care about not only our families (the classic purpose of oxytocin and the physiological basis for love) but also complete strangers—and even cars, pets, and houses. The key is exposure. If we are around anyone or anything long enough, we develop either an aversion or an attachment to him/her/it. This attachment behavior is part of the evolution of humans as hypersocial creatures.

Although HOME allows us to live and work with those unrelated to us by motivating us to cooperate with others, HOME is constantly looking for targets and releasing rewarding neurochemicals when we find one. Unfortunately, companies and their stocks can also activate the HOME brain circuit. What is important for survival is rewarded in the brain, but it is not necessarily rewarded in markets. This brain bias manifests as the endowment effect: We value what we own more than what we do not own.

■ *Application*: Because HOME is so powerful, concentration using the prefrontal cortex is needed to override its attachment effects. Your portfolio does not love you, and you should not be too attached to it. Recognizing this bias is the first step.

It is hard to detach from a portfolio that was painstakingly chosen and nurtured. One way to deal with this bias is to have an investment professional who did not choose the portfolio be the one to manage it. This action protects us from our natural tendency to defend our creations, often beyond the bounds of stated risk–return metrics. Managing someone else's portfolio makes it easier to apply the trading rules he or she has developed. Investment firms can, and have, instituted swapped portfolio management.

Quantitative asset management, whereby trading decisions are driven by computer models, is another way of taking the emotional attachment out of holding particular stocks. Because buy and sell decisions are driven by computer algorithms, human emotion is entirely removed from the investment process. The goal is to apply strict trading rules without the financially maladaptive influence of portfolio love.

Conclusion

Unfortunately, we human beings are characterized by numerous biases that can cloud our ability to make good investment decisions. These traits were selected through evolution for their ability to propagate the species, but they sometimes work against profitable performance in financial markets. Neuroeconomics research is now uncovering the brain basis for behavioral biases. Awareness of these biases can help investment professionals learn to use the important signals the brain receives from markets (for example, a response to increased risk) while minimizing or ignoring signals that detract from performance (for example, portfolio love).

Investment professionals need to use all the brain resources at their disposal to think clearly and deliberately when making investment decisions. One of the characteristics that distinguishes humans from other animals is our large prefrontal cortex. Most of our analytical power resides in the prefrontal cortex, but it is also metabolically expensive to use. When we are mindful of the brain's evolved biases, our prefrontal cortex can be fully engaged to integrate information from *all* the brain regions. Acknowledging and integrating all information regularly will improve financial analysis and portfolio performance.

Steven G. Sapra, CFA, is a professor of finance at the Marshall School of Business, University of Southern California, Los Angeles.

Paul J. Zak is a professor of economics in the Department of Economics and director of the Center for Neuroeconomics Studies at Claremont Graduate University, Claremont, California.

REFERENCES

Bikhchandani, S., D. Hirshleifer, and I. Welch. 1992. "A Theory of Fads, Fashion, Custom, and Cultural Change as Information Cascades." *Journal of Political Economy*, vol. 100, no. 5 (October):992–1026.

Haier, R.J., B.V. Siegel, A. MacLachlan, E. Soderling, S. Lottenberg, and M.S. Buchsbaum. 1992. "Regional Glucose Metabolic Changes after Learning a Complex Visuospatial/Motor Task: A Positron Emission Tomographic Study." *Brain Research*, vol. 570, no. 1–2 (January):134–143.

Kahneman, D., and A. Tversky. 1979. "Prospect Theory: An Analysis of Decision under Risk." *Econometrica*, vol. 47, no. 2 (March):263–291.

Knutson, B., and P. Bossaerts. 2007. "Neural Antecedents of Financial Decisions." *Journal of Neuroscience*, vol. 27, no. 31 (August):8174–8177.

Knutson, B., and R. Peterson. 2005. "Neurally Reconstructing Expected Utility." *Games and Economic Behavior*, vol. 52, no. 2 (August):305–315.

Knutson, B., G.E. Wimmer, C.M. Kuhnen, and P. Winkielman. 2008. "Nucleus Accumbens Activation Mediates the Influence of Reward Cues on Financial Risk Taking." *Neuroreport*, vol. 19, no. 5 (March):509–513.

Knutson, B., G.W. Fong, S.M. Bennett, C.M. Adams, and D. Hommer. 2003. "A Region of Mesial Prefrontal Cortex Tracks Monetarily Rewarding Outcomes: Characterization with Rapid Event-Related fMRI." *NeuroImage*, vol. 18, no. 2 (February):263–272.

Lo, A.W., and D.V. Repin. 2002. "The Psychophysiology of Real-Time Financial Risk Processing." *Journal of Cognitive Neuroscience*, vol. 14, no. 3 (April):323–339.

Lucas, R.E., Jr. 1972. "Expectations and the Neutrality of Money." *Journal of Economic Theory*, vol. 4, no. 2 (April):103–124.

McClure, S.M., D.I. Laibson, G. Loewenstein, and J.D. Cohen. 2004. "Separate Neural Systems Value Immediate and Delayed Monetary Rewards." *Science*, vol. 306, no. 5695 (October):503–507.

Peterson, R.L. 2007. *Inside the Investor's Brain: The Power of Mind over Money*. Hoboken, NJ: Wiley.

Platt, M.L., and P.W. Glimcher. 1999. "Neural Correlates of Decision Variables in Parietal Cortex." *Nature*, vol. 400, no. 6741 (July):233–238.

Shermer, M. 2007. *The Mind of the Market: Compassionate Apes, Competitive Humans, and Other Tales from Evolutionary Economics*. New York: Times Books.

Shiv, B., and A. Fedorikhin. 1999. "Heart and Mind in Conflict: The Interplay of Affect and Cognition in Consumer Decision Making." *Journal of Consumer Research*, vol. 26, no. 3 (December):278–292.

Smith, A. 1759. "The Theory of Moral Sentiments." Reprinted in *Glasgow Edition of the Works and Correspondence of Adam Smith*, vol. 1. Edited by D.D. Raphael and A.L. Macfie. Indianapolis: Liberty Fund, 1982.

U.K. Parliament. 1995. "Banking Supervision." *Daily Hansard* (21 July): www.parliament.the-stationery-office.co.uk/pa/ld199495/ldhansrd/vo950721/text/50721-14.htm.

Zak, P.J. 2004. "Neuroeconomics." *Philosophical Transactions of the Royal Society B (Biology)*, vol. 359, no. 1451:1737–1748.

———, ed. 2007. *Moral Markets: The Critical Role of Values in the Economy*. Princeton, NJ: Princeton University Press.

———. 2008a. "Rational Rationality." *The Moral Molecule, Psychology Today Blog* (10 October 2008): www.psychologytoday.com/blog/the-moral-molecule/200810/rational-rationality.

———. 2008b. "The Neurobiology of Trust." *Scientific American* (June):88–95.

———. Forthcoming. "The Physiology of Moral Sentiments." *Journal of Economic Behavior & Organization*.

Zak, P.J., A.A. Stanton, and S. Ahmadi. 2007. "Oxytocin Increases Generosity in Humans." *PLoS ONE*, vol. 2, no. 11:e1128.

Investing in the Unknown and Unknowable

Richard Zeckhauser

David Ricardo made a fortune buying bonds from the British government four days in advance of the Battle of Waterloo. He was not a military analyst, and even if he were, he had no basis to compute the odds of Napoleon's defeat or victory, or hard-to-identify ambiguous outcomes. Thus, he was investing in the unknown and the unknowable. Still, he knew that competition was thin, that the seller was eager, and that his windfall pounds should Napoleon lose would be worth much more than the pounds he'd lose should Napoleon win. Ricardo knew a good bet when he saw it.

This essay discusses how to identify good investments when the level of uncertainty is well beyond that considered in traditional models of finance. Many of the investments considered here are one-time only, implying that past data will be a poor guide. In addition, the essay will highlight investments, such as real estate development, that require complementary skills. Most readers will not have such skills, but many will know others who do. When possible, it is often wise to make investments alongside them.

Though investments are the ultimate interest, the focus of the analysis is how to deal with the unknown and unknowable, hereafter abbreviated *uU*. Hence, I will sometimes discuss salient problems outside of finance, such as terrorist attacks, which are also unknown and unknowable.

Putting It in Context

What triggered you to write this piece? And how do you think it should be helpful to professional investment practitioners?

I have had twin careers in academia and in real-world finance. The role of uncertainty has played a central part in my academic work, which lies at the juncture of economics and decision theory. My research, and that of others, shows that the more profound the uncertainties, the worse individuals' decision processes. This insight pointed the way to profitable investment opportunity: Knowing well where others feared to tread, the potential profits were correspondingly great. My article extends these lessons to profound uncertainties, the unknown and the unknowable. I seek to distill profitable lessons for such a world. The financial events surrounding 2008 showed the extreme relevance of this area of inquiry.

Professionals should read my article to see if they can identify situations in their own experience where the world was not merely uncertain but tended to the unknown and the unknowable. If the answer, as I expect, is yes, they should then take the lessons imparted here seriously and extend them with their own experience and insights. The lessons of my article are identified as such.

Editor's Note: An earlier version of this paper appeared as "Investing in the Unknown and Unknowable," *Capitalism and Society*, vol. 1, issue 2 (2006): www.bepress.com/cas/vol1/iss2/art5.

This essay takes no derivatives, and runs no regressions.[1] In short, it eschews the normal tools of my profession. It represents a blend of insights derived from reading academic works and from trying to teach their insights to others, and from lessons learned from direct and at-a-distance experiences with a number of successful investors in the *uU* world. To reassure my academic audience, I use footnotes where possible, though many refer to accessible internet articles in preference to journals and books. Throughout this essay, you will find speculations and maxims, as seems called for by the topic. They will be labeled in sequence.

This informal approach seems appropriate given our present understanding of the topic. Initial beliefs about this topic are highly uncertain, or as statisticians would phrase it: "Prior distributions are diffuse." Given that, the judicious use of illustrations, and prudent attempts to provide taxonomies and sort tea leaves, can substantially hone our beliefs, that is, tighten our future predictions.

Part I of this essay talks about risk, uncertainty, and ignorance, the last carrying us beyond traditional discussions. Part II looks at behavioral economics, the tendency for humans to deviate in systematic ways from rational decision, particularly when probabilities are involved, as they always are with investments. Behavioral economics pervades the *uU* world. Part III addresses the role of skilled mathematical types now so prevalent in finance. It imparts a general lesson: If super-talented people will be your competitors in an investment arena, perhaps it is best not to invest. Its second half discusses a dispute between math types on money management, namely how much of your money to invest when you do have an edge. Part IV details when to invest when you can make more out of an investment but there is a better informed person on the other side of the transaction. Part V tells a Buffett tale, and draws appropriate inferences. Part VI concludes the discussion.

I. Risk, Uncertainty and Ignorance

Escalating Challenges to Effective Investing. The essence of effective investment is to select assets that will fare well when future states of the world become known. When the probabilities of future states of assets are known, as the efficient markets hypothesis posits, wise investing involves solving a sophisticated optimization problem. Of course, such probabilities are often unknown, banishing us from the world of the capital asset pricing model (CAPM) and thrusting us into the world of uncertainty.[2]

---

[1] Ralph Gomory's (1995) literary essay on the unknown and unknowable provided inspiration. Miriam Avins provided helpful comments. Nils Wernerfelt provided effective research assistance.
[2] The classic description of uncertainty, a situation where probabilities could not be known, is due to Frank Knight (1921).

Were the financial world predominantly one of mere uncertainty, the greatest financial successes would come to those individuals best able to assess probabilities. That skill, often claimed as the domain of Bayesian decision theory, would swamp sophisticated optimization as the promoter of substantial returns.

The real world of investing often ratchets the level of nonknowledge into still another dimension, where even the identity and nature of possible future states are not known. This is the world of ignorance. In it, there is no way that one can sensibly assign probabilities to the unknown states of the world. Just as traditional finance theory hits the wall when it encounters uncertainty, modern decision theory hits the wall when addressing the world of ignorance. I shall employ the acronym *uU* to refer to situations where both the identity of possible future states of the world as well as their probabilities are unknown and unknowable. **Table 1** outlines the three escalating categories; entries are explained throughout the paper.

Table 1. Escalating Challenges to Effective Investing

	Knowledge of States of the World	Investment Environment	Skills Needed
Risk	Probabilities known	Distributions of returns known	Portfolio optimization
Uncertainty *U*	Probabilities unknown	Distributions of returns conjectured	Portfolio optimization Decision theory
Ignorance *uU*	States of the world unknown	Distributions of returns conjectured, often from deductions about other's behavior. Complementary skills often rewarded alongside investment	Portfolio optimization Decision theory Complementary skills (ideal) Strategic inference

This essay has both dreary and positive conclusions about investing in a *uU* world. The first dreary conclusion is that unknowable situations are widespread and inevitable. Consider the consequences for financial markets of global warming, future terrorist activities, or the most promising future technologies. These outcomes are as unknowable today as were the 1997 Asian meltdown, the 9/11 attacks, or the NASDAQ soar and swoon at the end of the century shortly before they were experienced.

These were all aggregate unknowables, affecting a broad swath of investors. But many unknowables are idiosyncratic or personal, affecting only individuals or handfuls of people, such as: If I build a 300-home community ten miles to the west of the city, will they come? Will the Vietnamese government let me sell my insurance product on a widespread basis? Will my friend's new software program capture the public fancy, or if not might it succeed in a completely different application? Such idiosyncratic *uU* situations, I argue below, present the greatest potential for significant excess investment returns.

The second dreary conclusion is that most investors—whose training, if any, fits a world where states and probabilities are assumed known—have little idea of how to deal with the unknowable. When they recognize its presence, they tend to steer clear, often to protect themselves from sniping by others. But for all but the simplest investments, entanglement is inevitable—and when investors do get entangled they tend to make significant errors.

The first positive conclusion is that unknowable situations have been and will be associated with remarkably powerful investment returns. The second positive conclusion is that there are systematic ways to think about unknowable situations. If these ways are followed, they can provide a path to extraordinary expected investment returns. To be sure, some substantial losses are inevitable, and some will be blameworthy after the fact. But the net expected results, even after allowing for risk aversion, will be strongly positive.

Do not read on, however, if blame aversion is a prime concern: The world of *uU* is not for you. Consider this analogy. If in an unknowable world none of your bridges falls down, you are building them too strong. Similarly, if in an unknowable world none of your investments looks foolish after the fact, you are staying too far away from the unknowable.

Warren Buffett, a master at investing in the unknowable, and therefore a featured player in this essay, is fond of saying that playing contract bridge is the best training for business. Bridge requires a continual effort to assess probabilities in at best marginally knowable situations, and players need to make hundreds of decisions in a single session, often balancing expected gains and losses. But players must also continually make peace with good decisions that lead to bad outcomes, both one's own decisions and those of a partner. Just this peacemaking skill is required if one is to invest wisely in an unknowable world.

The Nature of Unknowable Events. Many of the events that we classify as unknowable arrive in an unanticipated thunderclap, giving us little or no time to anticipate or prepare. But once they happen, they do not appear that strange. The human mind has an incredible ability to find a rationalization for why it should have been able to conjecture the terror attack of 9/11 or the Asian tsunamis of 1997 and 2005, respectively, caused by currency collapse and underwater earthquake. This propensity to incorporate hindsight into our memories—and to do so particularly when Monday morning quarterbacks may attack us—hinders our ability to anticipate extreme events in the future. We learn insufficiently from our misestimates and mistaken decisions.

Other unknowable events occur over a period of time, as did the collapse of the Soviet Union. Consider most stock market swings. Starting in January 1996, the NASDAQ rose fivefold in four years. Then it reversed field and fell by two-thirds in three years. Similarly, the 50% collapse in the broad stock market from

May 2008 till March 2009 was a fairly steady progression, with only a brief period of truly steep decline in fall 2008. Such developments are hardly thunderclaps. They are more like blowing up a balloon and then dribbling out the air. In retrospect, these remarkable swings have lost the flavor of an unknowable event, even though financial markets are not supposed to work that way. If securities prices at any moment incorporate all relevant information, a property that is usually posited, long-term movements in one direction are hardly possible, since strong runs of unanticipated good news or bad news will be exceedingly rare. Similarly, the AIDS scourge now seems familiar territory, though 25 years ago— when there had been only 31 cumulative deaths in the U.S. from AIDS—no one would have predicted a world-wide epidemic killing tens of millions and vastly disrupting the economies of many poor nations.

Are uU events to be feared? Warren Buffett once noted that virtually all surprises are unpleasant. Most salient uU events seem to fall into the left tail of unfortunate occurrences. This may be more a matter of perception than reality. Often an upside unknowable event, say the diminution of terror attacks or recovery from a dread disease, is difficult to recognize. An attack on any single day was not likely anyway, and the patient still feels lousy on the road to recovery. Thus, the news just dribbles in, as in a financial market upswing. B.F. Skinner, the great behavioral psychologist, taught us that behavior conditioned by variable interval reinforcement—engage in the behavior and from time-to-time the system will be primed to give you a payoff—was the most difficult to extinguish. Subjects could never be sure that another reward would not be forthcoming. Similarly, it is hard to discern when a string of inconsistently spaced episodic events has concluded. If the events are unpleasant, it is not clear when to celebrate their end.

Let us focus for the moment on thunderclap events. They would not get this title unless they involved something out of the ordinary, either good or bad. Casual empiricism—judged by looking at local, national and international headlines—suggests that thunderclap events are disproportionately adverse. Unlike in the old television show, *The Millionaire*, people do not knock on your door to give you a boatload of money, and in Iraq terror attacks outnumber terrorist arrests manifold.

The financial arena may be one place with an apparently reasonable ratio of upside to downside uU events, particularly if we include events that are drifts and not thunderclaps. By the end of 2004, there were 2.5 million millionaires in the United States, excluding housing wealth (http://money.cnn.com/2005/06/09/news/world_wealth/). Many of these individuals, no doubt, experienced upside uU events. Some events, such as the sustained boom in housing prices, were experienced by many, but many upside events probably only affected the individual and perhaps a few others. Such events include an unexpected lucrative job, or having a business concept take a surprisingly prosperous turn, or having a low-value real estate holding explode in value, and so on.

We hear about the lottery winner—the big pot, the thunderclap, and the gain for one individual makes it newsworthy. In contrast, the tens of thousands of *uU* events that created thousands of new real estate investment millionaires are mostly reported in dry aggregate statistics. Moreover, contrary to the ads in the back of magazines, there is usually not a good way to follow these "lucky folks," since some complementary skill or knowledge is likely to be required, not merely money and a wise choice of an investment. Thus, many favorable *uU* financial events are likely to go unchronicled. By contrast, bad news financial events, such as the foreclosure explosion of 2008–09, like other bad news events, such as murders and fires, tend to get media attention. In drawing inferences about the distribution of financial *uU* events, it is dangerous to rely on what you read in the papers.

To return to the Pollyannish side, it is worth noting the miracles of percentage symmetry given extreme events. Posit that financial prices move in some symmetric fashion. Given that negative prices are not possible, such changes must be in percentage rather than absolute terms.[3] We will not notice any difference between percentage and absolute if changes are small relative to the mean. Thus, if a price of 100 goes up or down by an average of 3 each year, or up by a ratio of 103/100 or down by 100/103 hardly matters. But change that 3 to a 50, and the percentage symmetry helps a great deal. The price becomes 100(150/100) or 100(100/150), which has an average of 117. If prices are anything close to percentage symmetric, as many believe they are, then big swings are both enemy and friend: enemy because they impose big risks, friend because they offer substantial positive expected value.

Many millionaires have made investments that multiplied their money 10-fold, and some 100-fold. The symmetric geometric model would expect events that cut one's stake to 1/10 or 1/100 of its initial value to be equally likely. The opportunity to get a 10 or 100 multiple on your investment as often as you lose virtually all of it is tremendously attractive.

There is, of course, no reason why investments must yield symmetric geometric returns. But it would be surprising not to see significant expected excess returns to investments that have three characteristics addressed in this

---

[3]This is sometimes expressed that things move geometrically rather than arithmetically, or that the logarithm of price has a traditional symmetric distribution. The most studied special case is the lognormal distribution. See "Life Is Log-Normal" by E. Limpert and W. Stahel, http://www.inf.ethz.ch/personal/gut/lognormal/brochure.html, for an argument on the widespread applicability of this distribution.

essay: (1) *uU* underlying features, (2) complementary capabilities are required to undertake them, so the investments are not available to the general market, and (3) it is unlikely that a party on the other side of the transaction is better informed. That is, *uU* may well work for you, if you can identify general characteristics of when such investments are desirable, and when not.

These very attractive three-pronged investments will not come along everyday. And when they do, they are unlikely to scale up as much as the investor would like, unlike an investment in an underpriced New York Stock Exchange (NYSE) stock, which scales nicely, at least over the range for most individual investors. Thus, the *uU*-sensitive investor should be constantly on the lookout for new opportunities. That is why Warren Buffett trolls for new businesses to buy in each Berkshire Hathaway annual report, and why most wealthy private investors are constantly looking for new instruments or new deals.

Uniqueness. Many *uU* situations deserve a third *U*, for unique. If they do, arbitrageurs—who like to have considerable past experience to guide them—will steer clear. So too will anybody who would be severely penalized for a poor decision after the fact. An absence of competition from sophisticated and well-monied others spells the opportunity to buy underpriced securities.

Most great investors, from David Ricardo to Warren Buffett, have made most of their fortunes by betting on *uUU* situations. Ricardo allegedly made 1 million pounds (over $50 million today)—roughly half of his fortune at death—on his Waterloo bonds.[4] Buffett has made dozens of equivalent investments. Though he is best known for the Nebraska Furniture Mart and See's Candies, or for long-term investments in companies like the Washington Post and Coca-Cola, insurance has been Berkshire Hathaway's fire hose of wealth over the years. And insurance often requires *uUU* thinking, and careful analysis of when to proceed and when to steer clear. Buffett and Berkshire know when the unknowables in a situation make clear steering the wise course. No insurance of credit default swaps for them. However, a whole section below discusses Buffett's success with what many experts saw as a *uUU* insurance situation, so they steered clear; but he saw it as offering excess premium relative to risk, so he took it all.

Speculation 1: uUU investments—unknown, unknowable and unique—drive off speculators, which creates the potential for an attractive low price.

---

[4] Ricardo's major competitors were the Baring brothers and the Rothschilds. Do not feel sorry for the Rothschilds. In the 14 years from 1814 to 1828 they multiplied their money 8-fold, often betting on *uU* situations, while the Baring brothers lost capital (http://www.businessweek.com/1998/49/b3607071.htm). Analysis based on Niall Ferguson's *House of Rothschild*.

Some *uU* situations that appear to be unique are not, and thus fall into categories that lend themselves to traditional speculation. Corporate takeover bids are such situations. When one company makes a bid for another, it is often impossible to determine what is going on or what will happen, suggesting uniqueness. But since dozens of such situations have been seen over the years, speculators are willing to take positions in them. From the standpoint of investment, uniqueness is lost, just as the uniqueness of each child matters not to those who manufacture sneakers.

Weird Causes and Fat Tails. The returns to *uUU* investments can be extreme. We are all familiar with the bell curve (or normal distribution), which nicely describes the number of flips of a fair coin that will come up heads in a large number of trials. But such a mechanical and controlled problem is extremely rare. Heights are frequently described as falling on a bell curve. But in fact there are many too many people who are extremely tall or extremely short, due say to glandular disturbances or genetic abnormalities. The standard model often does not apply to observations in the tails. So too with most disturbances to investments. Whatever the explanation for the October 1987 crash, it was not due to the usual factors that are used to explain market movements.[5]

More generally, movements in financial markets and of investments in general appear to have much thicker tails than would be predicted by Brownian motion, the instantaneous source of bell curve outcomes. That may be because the fundamental underlying factors produce thicker tails, or because there are rarely occurring anomalous or weird causes that produce extreme results, or both. The *uU* and *uUU* models would give great credence to the latter explanation, though both could apply.[6]

Complementary Skills and *uU* Investments. A great percentage of *uU* investments, and a greater percentage of those that are *uUU*, provide great returns to a complementary skill. For example, many of America's great

---

[5]Hart and Tauman (2004) show that market crashes are possible purely due to information processing among market participants, with no new information. They observe that the 1987 crash—20% in a day—happened despite no new important information becoming available, nor negative economic performance after the crash. Market plunges due to ordinary information processing defies any conventional explanation, and is surely a *uU* event.

[6]Nassim Taleb and Benoit Mandelbrot posit that many financial phenomena are distributed according to a power law, implying that the relative likelihood of movements of different sizes depends only on their ratio. Thus, a 20% market drop relative to a 10% drop is the same as a 10% drop relative to a 5% drop (http://www.fooledbyrandomness.com/fortune.pdf). Power distributions have fat tails. In their empirical studies, economists frequently assume that deviations from predicted values have normal distributions. That makes computations tractable, but evidence suggests that tails are often much thicker than with the normal (Zeckhauser and Thompson 1970).

fortunes in recent years have come from real estate. These returns came to people who knew where to build, and what and how. Real estate developers earn vast amounts on their capital because they have complementary skills. Venture capitalists can secure extraordinary returns on their own monies, and charge impressive fees to their investors, because early stage companies need their skills and their connections. In short, the return to these investments comes from the combination of scarce skills and wise selection of companies for investment. High tech pioneers—Bill Gates is an extreme example—get even better multiples on their investment dollars as a complement to their vision and scientific insight.[7]

Alas, few of us possess the skills to be a real estate developer, venture capitalist or high tech pioneer. But how about becoming a star of ordinary stock investment? For such efforts an ideal complementary skill is unusual judgment. Those who can sensibly determine when to plunge into and when to refrain from *uUU* investments gain a substantial edge, since mispricing is likely to be severe.

Warren Buffett's unusual judgment operates with more prosaic companies, such as oil producers and soft drink firms. He is simply a genius at everyday tasks, such as judging management capability or forecasting company progress. He drains much of the unknowable in judging a company's future. But he has other advantages. A number of Buffett's investments have come to him because companies sought him out, asking him to make an investment and also to serve on their board, valuing his discretion, his savvy, and his reputation for rectitude— that is, his complementary skills, not merely his money. And when he is called on for such reasons, he often gets a discounted price. Even though Buffett flubbed it when he invested heavily in companies like Goldman Sachs and General Electric in fall 2008, his pain was surely diminished because he had a 10% preferred coupon in both companies, quite apart from the now well-out-of-the-money options he received. Those like Buffett who can leverage complementary skills in stock market investment will be in a privileged position of limited competition. But that will accomplish little if they do not show courage and make big purchases where they expect high payoffs. But the lesson for regular mortals is not to imitate Warren Buffett; that makes no more sense than trying to play tennis like Roger Federer. Each of them has an inimitable skill. If you lack Buffett capabilities, you will get chewed up as a bold stock picker.

---

[7]Complementary skills can also help the less affluent invest. Miriam Avins, a good friend, moved into an edgy neighborhood in Baltimore because the abandoned house next door looked like a potential community garden, she knew she had the skills to move the project forward, and she valued the learning experience the house would bring to her family. Her house value doubled in 3 years, and her family learned as well.

Note, by the way, the generosity with which great investors with complementary skills explain their successes—Buffett in his annual reports, any number of venture capitalists who come to lecture MBAs, and the highly successful investors who lecture my executive students about behavioral finance.[8] These master investors need not worry about the competition, since few others possess the complementary skills for their types of investments. Few *uU* investment successes come from catching a secret, such as the whispered hint of "plastics" in the movie *The Graduate*. Mayer Amschel Rothschild had five sons who were bright, disciplined, loyal and willing to disperse. These were the complementary skills. The terrific investments in a *uU* world—and the Rothschild fortune—followed.

Before presenting a maxim about complementary skills, I present you with a decision problem. You have been asked to join the Business Advisory Board of a company named Tengion. Tengion was founded in 2003 to develop and commercialize a medical breakthrough: "developing new human tissues and organs (*neo-tissues* and *neo-organs*) that are derived from a patient's own cells . . . [this technology] harnesses the body's ability to regenerate, and it has the potential to allow adults and children with organ failure to have functioning organs built from their own (*autologous*) tissues." (http://www.tengion.com/)

This is assuredly a *uU* situation, doubly so for you, since until now you had never heard the term neo-organ. A principal advantage of joining is that you would be able to invest a reasonable sum on the same basis as the firm's insiders and venture capitalists. Would you choose to do so?

I faced this decision problem because I had worked successfully with Tengion's president on another company many years earlier. He was an individual of high capability and integrity. I was delighted with the *uU* flavor of the situation, and chose to join and invest because I would be doing so on the same terms as sophisticated venture capital (VC) firms with track records and expertise in relevant biotech areas. They would undertake the due diligence that was beyond my capability. This was an investment from which virtually everyone else would be excluded. In addition, it would benefit from the complementary skills of the VCs.

Sidecar Investments. Such undertakings are "sidecar investments"; the investor rides along in a sidecar pulled by a powerful motorcycle. Perhaps the premier sidecar investment ever available to the ordinary investor was

---

[8] They speak to my Investment Decisions and Behavioral Finance executive program at Harvard. The first was Charlie Munger, Buffett's partner, in the 1980s. The two most recent were Jeremy Grantham of GMO and Seth Klarman of the Baupost Group. Some investment wizards do have a "magic sauce" that they will not reveal. Thus, the unbelievably successful Renaissance Technologies hedge fund, which relies on mathematical and computer models, reveals nothing.

Berkshire Hathaway, many decades back. One could have invested alongside Warren Buffett, and had him take a ridiculously low compensation for his services. (In recent years, he has been paid $100,000, with no bonus or options.) But in 1960 who had heard of Warren Buffett, or knew that he would be such a spectacular and poorly compensated investor? Someone who knew Buffett and recognized his remarkable capabilities back then was in a privileged *uU* situation.

> *Maxim A:* **Individuals with complementary skills enjoy great positive excess returns from** *uU* **investments. Make a sidecar investment alongside them when given the opportunity.**

Do you have the courage to apply this maxim? It is January 2006 and you, a Western investor, are deciding whether to invest in Gazprom, the predominantly government-owned Russian natural gas giant in January 2006. Russia is attempting to attract institutional investment from the West; the stock is sold as an ADR, and is soon to be listed on the OTC exchange; the company is fiercely profitable, and it is selling gas at a small fraction of the world price. On the upside, it is generally known that large numbers of the Russian elite are investors, and here and there it is raising its price dramatically. On the downside, Gazprom is being employed as an instrument of Russian government policy; for example, gas is sold at a highly subsidized price to Belarus, because of its sympathetic government, yet the Ukraine is being threatened with more than a four-fold increase in price, in part because its government is hostile to Moscow. And the company is bloated and terribly managed. Finally, experiences, such as those with Yukos Oil, make it clear that the government is powerful, erratic, and ruthless.

This is clearly a situation of ignorance, or *uU*. The future states of the world are simply not known. Will the current government stay in power? Will it make Gazprom its flagship for garnering Western investment? If so, will it streamline its operations? Is it using foreign policy concerns as a device mainly to raise prices, a strong positive, and is it on a path to raise prices across the board? Will it complete its proposed pipelines to Europe? What questions haven't you thought of whose answers could dramatically affect your payout? Of course, you should also determine whether Western investors have distinct disadvantages as Gazprom shareholders, such as unique taxes and secondary voting status. Finally, if you determine the investment is favorable given present circumstances, you should ask how quickly Russia could change conditions against outsiders, and whether you will be alert and get out if change begins.

You could never learn about the unknowables sufficiently well to do traditional due diligence on a Gazprom investment. The principal arguments for going ahead would be that speculation 1 and maxim A apply. If you could comfortably determine that the Russian elite was investing on its own volition, and that foreigners would not be discriminated against, or at least not quickly, this would make a sensible sidecar investment.[9]

II. Behavioral Economics and Decision Traps

Behavioral decision has shaken the fields of economics and finance in recent decades. Basically, this work shows in area after area that individuals systematically deviate from making decisions in a manner that would be admired by Jimmie Savage (1954) and Howard Raiffa (1968), pioneers of the rational decision paradigm. As one illustration, such deviators could be turned into money pumps: They would pay to pick gamble B over gamble A. Then with A reframed as A', but not changed in its fundamentals, they would pay to pick A over B.

That is hardly the path to prudent investment, but alas behavioral decision has strong descriptive validity. Behavioral decision has important implications for investing in *uU* situations. When considering our own behavior, we must be extremely careful not to fall prey to the biases and decision traps it chronicles. Almost by definition, *uU* situations are those where our experience is likely to be limited, where we will not encounter situations similar to other situations that have helped us hone our intuition.

Virtually all of us fall into important decision traps when dealing with the unknowable. This section discusses two, overconfidence and recollection bias, and then gives major attention to a third, misweighting differences in probabilities and payoffs. But there are dozens of decision traps, and some will appear later in this essay. The Nobel Prize-winning work of Daniel Kahneman and Amos Tversky (the latter was warmly cited, but died too soon to win)[10] and the delightful and insightful *Poor Charlie's Almanack*, written by Charles Munger (Warren Buffett's partner), respectively, provide academic and finance-oriented discussions of such traps.

There are at least three major objections to behavioral economics: First, in competitive markets, the anomalies it describes will be arbitraged away. Second, the anomalies only appear in carefully crafted situations; they are much like optical illusions, intriguing but rarely affecting everyday vision. Third, they describe the way people do behave, but not the way they should behave. The first objection is tangential to this discussion; competitive markets and arbitrage are not present in many *uU* situations, and in particular not the ones that interest us. The second objection is relatively unimportant because, in essence, *uU*

---

[9]This investment was proposed when this paper was presented at a conference sponsored by the Wharton School on January 6, 2006. The price was then 33.60. The stock peaked above 60 in spring 2008, but then collapsed with oil prices and the Russian stock market.

[10]See http://nobelprize.org/nobel_prizes/economics/laureates/2002/public.html.

situations are those where optical illusions rule the world. A *uU* world is not unlike a fun house. Objection three I take up seriously below; this essay is designed to help people behave more rationally when they invest.

Let us first look at the biases.

Overconfidence. When individuals are assessing quantities about which they know very little, they are much too confident of their knowledge (Alpert and Raiffa 1982). Appendix A offers you a chance to test your capabilities in this regard. For each of eight unknown quantities, such as the area of Finland, you are asked to provide your median estimate, then your 25th and 75th percentile estimates (i.e., it is one-quarter likely the true value will be more extreme than either of the two), and then your 1st and 99th percentiles, what are referred to as surprise points. In theory, an individual should have estimates outside her surprise points about 2% of the time. In fact, even if warned about overconfidence, individuals are surprised about 35% of the time.[11] Quite simply, individuals think they know much more about unknowable quantities than they do.

> *Speculation 2:* Individuals who are overconfident of their knowledge will fall prey to poor investments in the *uU* world. Indeed, they are the green plants in the elaborate ecosystem of finance where there are few lions, like Warren Buffett; many gazelles, like you and me; and vast acres of grass ultimately nourishing us all.

Recollection Bias. A first lesson in dealing with *uU* situations is to know thyself. One good way to do this is to review successes and failures in past decisions. However, since people do not have a long track record, they naturally turn to hypotheticals from the past: Would I have judged the event that actually occurred to be likely? Would I have made that good investment and steered clear of the other bad one? Would I have sold out of NASDAQ stocks near New Year 2001? Alas, human beings do not do well with such questions. They are subject to substantial recollection bias.[12]

Judging by articles in the *New York Times* leading up to September 11, 2001, there was virtually no anticipation of a major terrorist attack on the United States; it was a clear *uUU* event. But that is not what respondents told us one to three years later. They were asked to compare their present assessments of the likelihood of a massive terrorist attack with what they estimated that likelihood to be on September 1, 2001. Of more than 300 Harvard Law and

---

[11] Approximate average from Investment Decisions and Behavioral Finance, executive program, annually fall 2001–2006, and API-302, Analytic Frameworks for Policy course. The former is chaired, the latter taught by Richard Zeckhauser, Kennedy School, Harvard University.
[12] See Gilbert (2006) for insightful discussions of the problems of rationalization and corrigibility.

Kennedy School students surveyed, 31% rated the risk as now lower, and 26% rated the risk as the same as they had perceived the 9/11 risk before the event.[13] We can hardly be confident that investors will be capable of judging how they would have assessed uU risks that occurred in the past.

Misweighting Probabilities and Preferences. The two critical components of decision problems are payoffs and probabilities. Effective decision requires that both be carefully calibrated. Not surprisingly, prospect theory, the most important single contribution to behavioral decision theory to date, finds that individuals' responses to payoffs and probabilities are far from rational.[14] To my knowledge, there is no tally of which contributes more to the loss of expected utility from the rational norm. (Some strong supporters of behavioral decision theory, however, think it is our norms that are misguided, and that the way the brain naturally perceives outcomes, not the prescriptions of decision theorists and economists, should be the guideline.) Whether drawing from Prospect Theory or observation, it seems clear that individuals draw insufficient distinctions among small probabilities. Consider the experiment shown in **Table 2**, in which an individual is asked to pick A or B.

Table 2. Lottery Choice: Payoffs versus Probabilities

	Payoff	Probability
A	$2,000	0.01
B	$1,000	0.025

A rational, risk averse individual should opt for B, since it offers a higher expected value—$25 versus $20—and less risk. Yet past experiments have shown that many individuals choose A, since in accordance with Prospect Theory they do not distinguish sufficiently between two low probability events. We speculate further that if we used named contingencies—for example, the Astros or the Blue Jays win the World Series—alongside their probabilities, the frequency of preference for A would increase. The contingencies would be selected, of course, so that their likelihood of occurrence, as indicated by odds in Las Vegas, would match those in the example above.

This hypothetical experiment establishes a baseline for another one that involves uU events. This time the prizes are based on events that are as close to the spectrum of uU events as possible, subject to the limitation that they must

---

[13] See Viscusi and Zeckhauser (2005).
[14] Kahneman and Tversky (1979).

be named.[15] Thus, a contingency might be that a 10,000-ton asteroid passed within 50,000 miles of Earth within the past decade, or that more than a million mammals crossed the border from Tanzania to Kenya last year. To begin our experiment, we ask a random sample of people to guess the likelihood of these contingencies. We then alter the asteroid distance or the number of animals in the question until the median answer is 0.03. Thus, if 50,000 miles got a median answer of 0.05, we would adjust to 40,000 miles, etc.

We now ask a new group of individuals to choose between C and D, assuming that we have calibrated the asteroid and mammal question to get to 0.03 (see **Table 3**). Lotteries C and D should yield their prizes with estimated probabilities of 1% and 3% respectively. Still, we suspect that many more people would pick C over D than picked A over B, and that this would be true for the animal movement contingency as well.[16]

**Table 3. Lottery Choice: Payoffs versus Probability or
uU Event**

	Payoff	Required contingency
C	$2,000	Draw a 17 from an urn with balls numbered 1 to 100
D	$1,000	10,000-ton asteroid passed within 40,000 miles of Earth

A more elaborated version of this problem would offer prizes based on alternative *uU* contingencies coming to pass. For example, we might recalibrate the mammal-crossing problem to get a median response of 0.01. We would then have the choices shown in **Table 4**. Here the values have been scaled so the median response is three times higher for the asteroid event than the animal crossing. We would conjecture again that E would be chosen frequently.[17] People do not like to rely on the occurrence of *uU* events, and choices based on distinguishing among their probabilities would be an unnatural act.

---

[15]This illustration employs events that may have happened in the past, but subjects would not know. The purpose is to make payoffs immediate, since future payoffs suffer from a different form of bias.

[16]The experiment is at a disadvantage in getting this result, since people's assessments of the contingencies' probabilities would vary widely. Some would pick D because they attached an unusually high probability to it. In theory, one could ask people their probability estimate after they made their choice, and then look only at the answers of those for whom the probability was in a narrow range. However, individuals would no doubt adjust their retrospective probability estimates to help rationalize their choice.

[17]This experiment and the choice between lotteries C and D above only approximate those with numerical probabilities, since they are calibrated for median responses and individuals' estimates will differ.

Table 4. Lottery Choice: Payoffs versus *uU* Events

	Payoff	Required contingency
E	$2,000	Calibrated large number of animals crossed the Tanzania–Kenya border
F	$1,000	10,000-ton asteroid passed within 40,000 miles of Earth

Daniel Ellsberg (1961) alerted us to ambiguity aversion long before he created a *uU* event by publishing the Pentagon papers. In an actual experiment, he showed, in effect, that individuals preferred to win a prize if a standard coin flip came up heads, rather than to win that prize by choosing either heads or tails on the flip of a mangled coin whose outcome was difficult to predict.[18] Such ambiguity aversion may be a plausible heuristic response to general decisions under uncertainty, since so often there is a better-informed person on the other side—such as someone selling a difficult-to-assess asset.[19] Whatever the explanation, ambiguity aversion has the potential to exert a powerful effect. Extending Ellsberg one step further, it would seem that the more ambiguous the contingencies, the greater the aversion. If so, *uU* investments will drive away all but the most self-directed and rational thinking investors. Thus, speculation 1 is reinforced.

III. Math Whizzes in Finance and Cash Management

The major fortunes in finance, I would speculate, have been made by people who are effective in dealing with the unknown and unknowable. This will probably be truer still in the future. Given the influx of educated professionals into finance, those who make their living speculating and trading in traditional markets are increasingly up against others who are tremendously bright and tremendously well-informed.[20]

By contrast, those who undertake prudent speculations in the unknown will be amply rewarded. Such speculations may include ventures into uncharted areas, where the finance professionals have yet to run their regressions, or may

---

[18]In fact, Ellsberg's experiment involved drawing a marble of a particular color from an urn. Subjects preferred a situation where the percentage of winning marbles was known, even if they could bet on either side when it was unknown.

[19]Fox and Tversky (1995, p. 585) found that ambiguity aversion was "produced by a comparison with less ambiguous events or with more knowledgeable people. . . . [it] seems to disappear in a noncomparative context." Ambiguity aversion is still relevant for investments, if alternative investments are available and contemplated.

[20]Paul Samuelson, who attends closely to most aspects of the finance field, attests to this challenge. He observed that Renaissance Technologies, run by former Stony Brook math professor James Simons, is "perhaps the only long-time phenomenal performer [in traditional financial markets] on a risk-corrected basis." Private communication, June 15, 2006.

take completely new paths into already well-traveled regions.[21] It used to be said that if your shoeshine boy gave you stock tips it was time to get out of the market. With shoeshine boys virtually gone and finance Ph.D.'s plentiful, the new wisdom might be:

> When your math whiz finance Ph.D. tells you that he and his peers have been hired to work in the XYZ field, the spectacular returns in XYZ field have probably vanished forever.

Similarly, the more difficult a field is to investigate, the greater will be the unknowns and unknowables associated with it, and the greater the expected profits to those who deal sensibly with them. Unknowables can't be transmuted into sensible guesses—but one can take one's positions and array one's claims so that unknowns and unknowables are mostly allies, not nemeses. And one can train to avoid one's own behavioral decision tendencies, and to capitalize on those of others.

Assume that an investor is willing to invest where he has an edge in uU situations. How much capital should then be placed into each opportunity? This problem is far from the usual portfolio problem. It is afflicted with ignorance, and decisions must be made in sequential fashion. Math whizzes have discussed this problem in a literature little known to economists, but frequently discussed among gamblers and mathematicians. The most famous contribution is an article published 50 years ago by J.L. Kelly, an AT&T scientist. His basic formula, which is closely related to Claude Shannon's information theory, tells you how much to bet on each gamble as a function of your bankroll, with the probability of winning and the odds as the two parameters. Perhaps surprisingly, the array of future investment opportunities does not matter.

Kelly's Criterion, as it is called, is to invest an amount equal to $W - (1 - W)/R$, where W is your probability of winning, and R is the ratio of the amount you win when you win to the amount you lose when you lose.[22]

---

[21] I saw such path blazing by my former business partner Victor Niederhoffer in the 1970s, when he ventured into commodity investing. His associates hand recorded commodity prices at 15-minute intervals. He lined up a flotilla of TRS-80 Radio Shack computers to parallel process this information. His innovative data mining, spurred by accompanying theories of how markets behave, gave him a giant advantage over major investment houses. Niederhoffer continues along unusual paths, now making a second fortune after losing his first in the collapse of the Thai baht in 1997. http://www.greenwichtime.com/business/scn-sa-black1jun18,0,3887361.story?page=5&coll=green-business-headlines.

[22] http://www.investopedia.com/articles/trading/04/091504.asp. In an interesting coincidence, Elwyn Berlekamp, a distinguished Berkeley math professor who was Kelly's research assistant, was an extremely successful investor in a brief stint managing a fund for James Simons. See footnote 20.

Thus, if you were 60% likely to win an even money bet, you would invest $0.6 - (1 - 0.6)/1 = 0.2$ or 20% of your capital.

It can be shown that given sufficient time, the value given by any other investment strategy will eventually be overtaken by value following the Kelly Criterion, which maximizes the geometric growth rate of the portfolio. That might seem to be definitive. But even in the mathematical realm of optimal dynamic investment strategies, assuming that all odds and probabilities are known, we encounter a uU situation.

Paul Samuelson, writing in a playful mood, produced an article attacking the Kelly Criterion as a guide for practice. His article uses solely one-syllable words. His abstract observes: "He who acts in N plays to make his mean log of wealth as big as it can be made will, with odds that go to one as N soars, beat me who acts to meet my own tastes for risk."[23] In short, Samuelson shows that the Kelly Criterion, though mathematically correct, does not tell us how much to invest when one has an edge, since it ignores the structure of preferences.

I lack both the space and capability to straighten out the sequential investment problem. But a few observations may be worthwhile: (1) Most uU investments are illiquid for a significant period, often of unknown length. Monies invested today will not be available for reinvestment until they become liquid. (2) Markets charge enormous premiums to cash out illiquid assets.[24] (3) Models of optimal sequential investment strategies tend to assume away the most important real-world challenges to such strategies, such as uncertain lock-in periods. (4) There are substantial disagreements in the literature even about "toy problems," such as those with immediate resolution of known-probability investments. The overall conclusion is that: (5) Money management is a challenging task in uU problems. It afflicts even those with a substantial edge when making such investments. And when the unknowable happens, as it did with the air-pocket plunge in the 1987 stock market or the 1997 Asian crisis, unforeseen short-term money-management problems—e.g., transferring monies across markets in time to beat margin calls—tend to emerge. These five points

---

[23] Paul A. Samuelson, "Why We Should Not Make Mean Log of Wealth Big Though Years to Act Are Long," *Journal of Banking & Finance*, vol. 3, no. 4 (December 1979):305–307.

[24] For example, in real estate, a limited partnership interest that will come due in a few years is likely to sell about 30% below discounted expected future value. The significant discount reflects the complementary skills of acquirers, who must be able to assess and unlock the value of idiosyncratic partnerships. Personal communication, Eggert Dagbjartsson, Equity Resource Investments, December 2005. That firm earns substantial excess returns through its combination of effective evaluation of uU situations, the ability to structure complex financial transactions, and the unusual complementary skill of being able to deal effectively with a great range of general partners. Experience with Dagbjartsson's firm—at which the author is a principal—helped inspire this paper.

imply that even if it were clear how one should invest in a string of favorable gambles each of which is resolved instantaneously, that would help us little in the real world of *uU* investing, which presents a much more difficult task.

IV. Investing with Someone on the Other Side

One of the more puzzling aspects of the financial world is the volume of transactions in international currency markets. Average daily volume is $1.9 trillion, which is slightly more than all U.S. imports in a year. There are hedgers in these markets, to be sure, but their volume is many times dwarfed by transactions that cross with sophisticated or at least highly paid traders on both sides. Something no less magical than levitation is enabling all players to make money, or think that they are making money.

But let us turn to the micro situation, where you are trading against a single individual in what may or may not be a *uU* situation. If we find that people make severe mistakes in this arena even when there is merely risk or uncertainty, we should be much more concerned, at least for them, when *uU* may abound.

Bazerman–Samuelson Example and Lessons. Let us posit that you are 100% sure that an asset is worth more to you than to the person who holds it, indeed 50% more. But assume that she knows the true value to her, and that it is uniformly distributed on [0, 100], that is, her value is equally likely to be 0, 1, 2, . . . 100. In a famous game due to Bazerman and Samuelson (1983), hereafter BS, you are to make a single bid. She will accept if she gets more than her own value. What should you bid?

When asked in the classroom, typical bids will be 50 or 60, and few will bid as low as 20. Students reason that the item will be worth 50 on average to her, hence 75 to them. They bid to get a tidy profit. The flaw in the reasoning is that the seller will only accept if she will make a profit. Let's make you the bidder. If you offer 60, she will not sell if her value exceeds 60. This implies that her average value conditional on selling will be 30, which is the value of the average number from 0 to 60. Your expected value will be 1.5 times this amount, or 45. You will lose 15 on average, namely 60 – 45, when your bid is accepted. It is easy to show that any positive bid loses money in expectation. The moral of this story is that people, even people in decision analysis and finance classrooms, where these experiments have been run many times, are very poor at taking account of the decisions of people on the other side of the table.

There is also a strong tendency to draw the wrong inference from this example, once its details are explained. Many people conclude that you should never deal with someone else who knows the true value when you know only the distribution. In fact, BS offer an extreme example, almost the equivalent of an optical illusion. You might conclude that when your information is very diffuse and the other side knows for sure, you should not trade even if you have a strong absolute advantage.

That conclusion is wrong. For example, if the seller's true value is uniform on [1, 2] and you offer 2, you will buy the object for sure, and its expected value will be 1.5 times 1.5 = 2.25. The difference between this example and the one with the prior on [0, 1] is that here the effective information discrepancy is much smaller. To see this, think of a uniform distribution from [100, 101]; there is virtually no discrepancy. (In fact, bidding 2 is the optimal bid for the [1, 2] example, but that the extreme bid is optimal also should not be generalized.)

Drawing Inferences from Others. The general lesson is that people are naturally very poor at drawing inferences from the fact that there is a willing seller on the other side of the market. Our instincts and early training lead us not to trust the other guy, because his interests so frequently diverge from ours. If someone is trying to convince you that his second-hand car is wondrous, skepticism and valuing your own information highly helps. However, in their study of the heuristics that individuals employ to help them make decisions, Tversky and Kahneman (1974) discovered that individuals tend to extrapolate heuristics from situations where they make sense to those where they do not.

For example, we tend to distrust the other guy's information even when he is on our side. This tendency has serious drawbacks if you consider sidecar investing—free riding on the superior capability of others—as we do below. Consider two symmetrically-situated partners with identical interests who start with an identical prior distribution about some value that is described by a two-parameter distribution. They each get some information on the value. They also have identical prior distributions on the information that each will receive. Thus, after his draw, each has a posterior mean and variance. Their goal is to make a decision whose payoff will depend on the true value. The individuals begin by submitting their best estimate, namely their means. After observing each other's means, they then simultaneously submit their new best estimate. Obviously, if one had a tight (loose) posterior his estimate would shift more (less) toward that of his partner. In theory, two things should happen: (a) The two partners should jump over each other between the first and second submission half of the time. (b) The two partners should give precisely the same estimate for the third submission.

In practice, unless the players are students of Robert Aumann[25]—his article "Agreeing to Disagree" (1976) inspired this example—rarely will they jump over each other. Moreover, on the third submission, they will not come close to convergence.

The moral of this story is that we are deeply inclined to trust our own information more than that of a counterpart, and are not well trained to know when this makes good sense, and when it inclines us to be a sucker. One should also be on the lookout for information disparities. Rarely are they revealed through carnival-barker behavior. For example, when a seller merely offers you an object at a price, or gets to accept or reject when you make a bid (as with BS), he will utilize information that you do not possess. You had better be alert and give full weight to its likely value, e.g., how much the object is worth on average were he to accept your bid.

In the financial world one is always playing in situations where the other fellow may have more information and you must be on your guard. But unless you have a strictly dominant action—one that is superior no matter what the other guy's information—a maximin strategy will almost always push you never to invest. After all, his information could be just such to lead you to lose large amounts of money.

Two rays of light creep into this gloomy situation: First, only rarely will his information put you at severe disadvantage. Second, it is extremely unlikely that your counterpart is playing anything close to an optimal strategy. After all, if it is so hard for you to analyze, it can hardly be easy for him.[26]

Absolute Advantage and Information Asymmetry. It is helpful to break down these situations into two components. A potential buyer's absolute advantage benefits both players. It represents the usual gains from trade. In many financial situations, as we observed above, a buyer's absolute advantage stems from her complementary skills. An empty lot in A's hands may be worth much less than it would be in B's. Both gain if A trades to B, due to absolute advantage. But such an argument would not apply if A was speculating that the British pound would fall against the dollar when B was speculating that it would rise. There is no absolute advantage in such a situation, only information asymmetries.

---

[25] Robert Aumann and Thomas Schelling won the 2005 Nobel Memorial Prize in Economics for their contributions to game theory.

[26] Given the potential for imperfect play, it is sometimes dangerous to draw inferences from the play of others, particularly when their preferences are hard to read. The Iraqi weapons of mass destruction provide a salient example. Many people were confident that such weapons were present not because of intelligence, but because they believed Saddam Hussein could have saved himself and his regime simply by letting in inspectors, who in the instance would find nothing.

If both parties recognize a pure asymmetric information situation, only the better informed player should participate. The appropriate drawing of inferences of "what-you-know-since-you-are-willing-to-trade" should lead to the well known no-trade equilibrium. Understanding this often leads even ordinary citizens to a shrewd stratagem:

> *Maxim B:* **When information asymmetries may lead your counterpart to be concerned about trading with you, identify for her important areas where you have an absolute advantage from trading. You can also identify her absolute advantages, but she is more likely to know those already.**

When you are the buyer, beware; seller-identified absolute advantages can be chimerical. For example, the seller in the bazaar is good at explaining why your special characteristics deserve a money-losing price—say it is the end of the day and he needs money to take home to his wife. The house seller who does not like the traffic noise in the morning may palter that he is moving closer to his job, suggesting absolute advantage since that is not important to you. Stores in tourist locales are always having "Going Out of Business Sales." Most swindles operate because the swindled one thinks he is in the process of getting a steal deal from someone else.

If a game theorist had written a musical comedy, it would have been *Guys and Dolls*, filled as it is with the ploys and plots of small-time gamblers. The overseer of the roving craps game is Nathan Detroit. He is seeking action, and asks Sky Masterson—whose good looks and gambling success befit his name—to bet on yesterday's cake sales at Lindy's, a famed local deli. Sky declines and recounts a story to Nathan:

> On the day when I left home to make my way in the world, my daddy took me to one side. "Son," my daddy says to me, "I am sorry I am not able to bankroll you to a large start, but not having the necessary lettuce to get you rolling, instead I'm going to stake you to some very valuable advice. One of these days in your travels, a guy is going to show you a brand-new deck of cards on which the seal is not yet broken. Then this guy is going to offer to bet you that he can make the jack of spades jump out of this brand-new deck of cards and squirt cider in your ear. But, son, do not accept this bet, because as sure as you stand there, you're going to wind up with an ear full of cider."

In the financial world at least, a key consideration in dealing with *uU* situations is assessing what others are likely to know or not know. You are unlikely to have mystical powers to foresee the unforeseeable, but you may be able to estimate your understanding relative to that of others. Sky's dad drew an inference from someone else's willingness to bet. Presumably Ricardo was not a military expert, but just understood that bidders would be few and that the market would over discount the *uU* risk.

Competitive Knowledge, Uncertainty, and Ignorance.

Let us assume that you are neither the unusually skilled Warren Buffett nor the unusually clear-thinking David Ricardo. You are just an ordinary investor who gets opportunities and information from time to time. Your first task is to decide into which box an investment decision would fall. We start with unknown probabilities shown in **Table 5**.

Table 5. Investing with Uncertainty and Potential Asymmetric Information

	Easy for Others to Estimate	Hard for Others to Estimate
Easy for You to Estimate	A. Tough markets	B. They're the sucker
Hard for You to Estimate	C. Sky Masterson's dad, you're the sucker	D. Buffett's reinsurance sale California Earthquake Authority

The first row is welcome and relatively easy, for two reasons: (1) You probably have a reasonable judgment of your knowledge relative to others, as would a major real estate developer considering deals in his home market. Thus you would have a good assessment of how likely you are to be in box B or box A. (2) If you are in box B, you have the edge. Box A is the home of the typical thick financial market, where we tend to think prices are fair on average.

The second row is more interesting, and brings us to the subject matter of this paper. In Part V below, we will see Buffett sell a big hunk of reinsurance because he knew he was in box D. His premium was extremely favorable, and he knew that it was exceedingly unlikely that the other side possessed private information that would significantly shift the odds. Box C consists of situations where you know little, and others may know a fair amount. The key to successfully dealing with situations where you find probabilities hard to estimate is to be able to assess whether others might be finding it easy.

Be sensitive to telling signs that the other side knows more, such as a smart person offering too favorable odds. Indeed, if another sophisticated party is willing to bet, and he can't know that you find probabilities hard to estimate, you should be suspicious. For he should have reasonable private knowledge so as to protect himself. The regress in such reasoning is infinite.

Maxim C: In a situation where probabilities may be hard for either side to assess, it may be sufficient to assess your knowledge relative to the party on the other side (perhaps the market).

Let us now turn to the more extreme case, situations where even the states of the world are unknown, as they would be for an angel investment in a completely new technology, or for insuring infrastructure against terrorism over a long period (see **Table 6**).

Table 6. Investing with Ignorance and Potential Asymmetric Information

	Known to Others	Unknown to Others
Unknown to You	Dangerous waters Monday morning quarterback risk	Low competition Monday morning quarterback risk

In some ignorance situations, you may be confident that others know no better. That would place you in box F, a box where most investors get deterred, and where the Buffetts of this world, and the Rothschilds of yesteryear have made lots of money. Investors are deterred because they employ a heuristic to stay away from *uU* situations, because they might be in E, even though a careful assessment would tell them that outcome was highly unlikely. In addition, both boxes carry the Monday morning quarterback (MMQ) risk; one might be blamed for a poor outcome if one invests in ignorance, when it was a good decision that got a bad outcome; might not have allowed for the fact that others might have had better knowledge when in fact they didn't; or might not have allowed for the fact that others might have had better knowledge, when in fact they did, but that negative was outweighed by the positive of your absolute advantage. The criticisms are unmerited. But since significant losses were incurred, and knowledge was scant, the investment looks foolish in retrospect to all but the most sophisticated. An investor who could suffer significantly from any of these critiques might well be deterred from investing.

Let us revisit the Gazprom lesson with this thought in mind. Suppose you are a Russia expert. It is still almost inevitable that real Russians know much more than you. What then should you do? The prudent course, it would seem, would be first to determine your MMQ risk. It may actually be reduced due to your largely irrelevant expertise. But if MMQ is considerable, steer clear. If not, and Russian insiders are really investing, capitalize on box E, and make that sidecar investment. You have the additional advantage that few Westerners will be doing the same, and they are your prime competition for ADRs.[27]

Speculation 3: uU situations offer great investment potential given the combination of information asymmetries and lack of competition.

Boxes E and F are also the situations where other players will be attempting to take advantage of us and, if it is our inclination, we might take advantage of them. This is the area where big money changes hands.

A key problem is to determine when you might be played for a sucker. Sometimes this is easy. Anyone who has small oil interests will have received many letters offering to buy, no doubt coming from people offering far less than

---

[27]In January 2006, Gazprom traded in the West as an ADR, but soon became an over-the-counter stock.

fair value. They are monopsonists after all, and appropriately make offers well below the market. They may not even have any inside knowledge. But they are surely taking advantage of the impulsive or impatient among us, or those who do not understand the concepts in this paper.

Being a possible sucker may be an advantage if you can gauge the probability. People are strongly averse to being betrayed. They demand much stronger odds when a betraying human rather than an indifferent nature would be the cause of a loss (Bohnet and Zeckhauser 2004). Given that, where betrayal is a risk, potential payoffs will be too high relative to what rational decision analysis would prescribe.

Investing in *uU* with Potentially Informed Players on the Other Side. Though you may confront a *uU* situation, the party or parties on the other side may be well informed. Usually you will not know whether they are. Gamblers opine that if you do not know who the sucker is in a game that you are the sucker. That does not automatically apply with *uU* investments. First, the other side may also be uninformed. For example, if you buy a partially completed shopping center, it may be that the developer really did run out of money (the proffered explanation for its status) as opposed to his discovery of deep tenant reluctance. Second, you may have a complementary skill, such as strong relations with Walmart, that may give you a significant absolute advantage multiple.

The Advantage Multiple versus Selection Formula. Let us simplify and leave risk aversion and money management matters aside. Further posit, following BS, that you are able to make a credible take-it-or-leave-it offer of 1. The value of the asset to him is v, an unknown quantity. The value to you is av, where a is your absolute advantage. Your subjective prior probability distribution on v is $f(v)$. The mean value of your prior is $m < 1$.[28] In a stripped-down model, three parameters describe this situation: your advantage multiple, a; the probability that the other side is informed, p; and the selection factor against you, s, if the other side is informed.[29] Thus s is the fraction of expected value that will apply, on average, if the other side is informed, and therefore only sells when the asset has low value to her. Of course, given the *uU* situation, you do not know s, but you should rely on your mean value of your subjective distribution for that parameter.

---

[28] It is important that $m < 1$. Otherwise the seller would refuse your offer if he were uninformed.
[29] In health care, this process is called adverse selection, with sicker people tending to enroll in more generous health plans.

If you knew $p = 0$, that the other side knew no more than you, you would simply make the offer if $am > 1$. If you knew there were selection, that is, $p = 1$, you would invest if your multiple more than compensated for selection, namely if $ams > 1$. The general formula is that your return will be:

$$am\left[ps + (1-p)1\right]. \tag{1}$$

Maxim D: **A significant absolute advantage offers some protection against potential selection. You should invest in a uU world if your advantage multiple is great, unless the probability is high the other side is informed and if, in addition, the expected selection factor is severe.**

Following maxim D, you should make your offer when the expression in (1) exceeds 1.

In practice, you will have a choice of offer, t. Thus, s will vary with t, that is, $s(t)$.[30] The payoff for any t will be

$$am\left[ps(t) + (1-p)1\right] - t. \tag{2}$$

If at the optimal offer t^*, this quantity is positive, you should offer t^*.

Playing the Advantage Multiple versus Selection Game.

Our formulation posited a take-it-or-leave-it offer with no communication. In fact, most important financial exchanges have rounds of subtle back-and-forth discussion. This is not simply cheap talk. Sometimes real information is provided, such as accounting statements, geological reports, antique authentications. And offers by each side reveal information as well. Players on both sides know that information asymmetry is an enemy to both, as in any agency problem.

It is well known that if revealed information can be verified, and if the buyer knows on what dimensions information will be helpful, then by an unraveling argument all information gets revealed.[31] Consider a one-dimension case where a value can be between 1 and 100. A seller with a 100 would surely reveal, implying the best unrevealed information would be 99. But then the 99 would reveal, and so on down through 2.

When the buyer is in a uU situation, unraveling does not occur, since he does not know the relevant dimensions. The seller will keep private unfavorable

---

[30] Let $\underline{v}$ be the conditional mean of $x < v$. The value of s will be constant if $\underline{v}/v$ = positive k for all v. This will be the case if $f(v)$ is homogeneous, i.e., $f(kv) = k_n f(v)$, as with the uniform or triangular distribution starting at 0.

[31] See Grossman (1981) on unraveling. If information is costly to reveal, then less favorable information is held back and signposting applies (Zeckhauser and Marks 1996).

information on dimensions unknown to the buyer. She will engage in signposting: announcing favorable information, suppressing unfavorable.[32]

The advantage multiple versus selection game will usually proceed with the seller explaining why she does not have private information, or revealing private information indicating that m and a are large. Still, many favorable deals will not get done, because the less informed party can not assess what it does not know. Both sides lose *ex ante* when there will be asymmetry on common value information, or when, as in virtually all *uU* situations, asymmetry is suspected.

Auctions as *uU* Games. Auctions have exploded as mechanisms to sell everything from the communications spectrum to corporate securities, and, in 2009, toxic assets. Economic analyses of auctions—how to conduct them and how to bid—have exploded alongside. The usual format is that an informed seller faces a group of less-knowing buyers. The usual prescription is that the seller should reveal his information about elements that will affect all buyers' valuations, such as geologic information on an oil lease or evidence of an antique's pedigree, to remove buyers' concerns about the winner's curse. The winner's curse applies when an object, such as an oil lease, is worth roughly the same to all. The high bidder should be aware that every other bidder thought it was worth less than he did. Hence, his estimate is too high, and he is cursed for winning.

Real-world auctions are often much more complex. Even the rules of the game may not be known. Consider the common contemporary auction phenomenon, witnessed often with house sales in hot markets, and at times with the sale of corporations.[33] The winner, who expected the final outcome to have been determined after one round of bidding, may be told there will be a best and final offer round, or that now she can negotiate a deal for the item.

Usually the owner of the object establishes the rules of the game. In theory, potential buyers would insist that they know the rules. In practice, they often have not. When Recovery Engineering, makers of PUR water purifiers, was sold in 1999, a "no one knows the rules" process ensued, with Morgan Stanley representing the seller. A preliminary auction was held on an August Monday. Procter and Gamble (P&G) and Gillette bid, and a third company expressed

---

[32]To be sure, the shrewd buyer can deduce: "Given the number of unknown dimensions I suspected, the seller has revealed relatively few. Hence, I assume that there are a number of unfavorable dimensions," etc. When seller revelation is brief, only high m buyers will make exchanges. The doubly shrewd buyer may be informed or get informed on some dimension without the seller knowing which. He can then say: "I have unfavorable information on a dimension. Unless you reveal on all dimensions, this information will stay private, and I will know that you are suppressing information." The triply shrewd buyer, knowing nothing, will make the same statement. The shrewd seller has countermeasures, such as insisting on proof that the buyer is informed, e.g., by third party attestation, and if evidence is received then revealing some but not all, hoping to hit the lucky dimension.

[33]See Subramanian and Zeckhauser (2005), who apply the term "negotiauctions" to such processes.

interest but said it had difficulties putting its bid together. Gillette's bid was $27 per share; P&G's was $22. P&G was told by the investment banker that it would have to improve its bid substantially. Presumably, Gillette was told little, but drew appropriate inferences, namely that it was by far high. The final auction was scheduled for that Friday at noon. Merrill Lynch, Gillette's investment banker, called early on Friday requesting a number of additional pieces of due diligence information, and requesting a delay till Monday. Part of the information was released—Gillette had had months to request it—and the auction was delayed till 5 p.m. Friday. P&G bid $34. At 5 p.m., Merrill Lynch called, desperate, saying it could not get in touch with Gillette. Brief extensions were granted, but contact could not be established. P&G was told that it was the high bidder. Over the weekend a final deal was negotiated at a slightly higher price; the $300 million deal concluded. But would there have been a third round of auction if Gillette had bid $33.50 that Friday? No one knows.

The Recovery board puzzled over the unknowable question: What happened to Gillette? One possibility was that Gillette inferred from the fact that it was not told its Monday bid was low that it was in fact way above other bidders. It was simply waiting for a deal to be announced, and then would propose a price perhaps $2 higher, rather than bid and end up $5 higher.[34] Gillette never came back. A while later, Recovery learned that Gillette was having—to that time unreported—financial difficulties. Presumably, at the moment of truth Gillette concluded that it was not the time to purchase a new business. In short, this was a game of unknowable rules, and unknowable strategies.[35] Not unusual.

At the close of 2005, Citigroup made the winning bid of about $3 billion for 85% of the Guangdong Development Bank, a financially troubled state-owned Chinese bank. As the *New York Times* reported the deal, Citigroup "won the right to negotiate with the bank to buy the stake." If successful there, its "control might allow Citigroup to install some new management and have some control over the bank's future. . .one of the most destitute of China's big banks. . .overrun by bad loans."[36] Citigroup is investing in a uU situation, and knows that both the rules of the game and what it will win are somewhat undefined. But it is probably confident that other bidders were no better informed, and that both the bank and the Chinese government (which must

---

[34] Recovery created a countermeasure to raise any post-deal bid by inserting a breakup fee in its deal with P&G that declined (ultimately to 0) with the price premium paid by a new buyer.

[35] Details confirmed by Brian Sullivan, then CEO of Recovery Engineering, in personal communication, January 2006. Zeckhauser was on the Recovery board due to a sidecar privilege. He had been Sullivan's teacher, and had gotten him the job.

[36] *New York Times* (31 December 2005):B1 and B4. Citigroup had several Chinese state-owned companies as partners, but they probably gave more political cover than knowledge of the value of the bank.

approve the deal) may also not know the value of the bank, and were eager to secure foreign control. Great value may come from buying a pig in a poke, if others also can not open the bag.

Ideal Investments with High and Low Payoffs. In many *uU* situations, even the events associated with future payoff levels—for example, whether a technology supplier produces a breakthrough or a new product emerges—are hard to foresee. The common solution in investment deals is to provide for distributions of the pie that depend not on what actually happens, but solely on money received. This would seem to simplify matters, but even in such situations sophisticated investors frequently get confused.

With venture capital in high tech, for example, it is not uncommon for those providing the capital to have a contractual claim to all the assets should the venture go belly up. Similarly, "cram down" financings, which frequently follow when startups underperform, often give VCs a big boost in ownership share. In theory, such practices could provide strong incentives to the firm's managers. In reality, the managers' incentives are already enormous. Typical VC arrangements given bad outcomes cause serious ill will, and distort incentives—for example, they reward gambling behavior by managers after a bleak streak. Worse still for the VCs, they are increasing their share of the company substantially when the company is not worth much. They might do far better if arrangements specified that they sacrifice ownership share if matters turn out poorly, but gain share if the firm does particularly well.

Maxim E: In *uU* situations, even sophisticated investors tend to underweight how strongly the value of assets varies. The goal should be to get good payoffs when the value of assets is high.

No doubt Ricardo also took maxim E into account when he purchased the "Waterloo bonds." He knew that English money would be far more valuable if Wellington was victorious and his bonds soared in value than if he lost and the bonds plummeted.

A *uU* Investment Problem. Now for a harder decision. Look at the letter in **Exhibit A**, which offers you the chance to make a modest investment in an oil well. You have never heard of Davis Oil, and the letter came out of the blue, and without letterhead. You inquire, and find out that it is the company previously owned by the famous, recently deceased oilman Marvin Davis. Your interest is offered because the Davis Company bought the managing partner's interest in the prospect from a good friend and oilman who invited you into his prospect.[37] Davis is legally required to make this offer to you. Decide whether to invest or merely wait for your costless override before you read on.

---

[37] That man was Malcolm Brachman, president of Northwest Oil, a bridge teammate and close friend. Sadly, Malcolm had died in the interim. One consequence was that he could not advise you.

EXHIBIT A

September 19, 2005

WORKING INTEREST OWNER: Richard Zeckhauser

Re: Well Proposal

David Petroleum Corp.

Devlin #1-12

Section 12-T8N-R19W

Washita County, Oklahoma

Gentlemen:

Davis Petroleum Corp. ("Davis") proposes the drilling of a 17,000' Sub-Thrusted Springer test at a surface location of 660' FNL and 1980' FWL and a bottom hole location of 1,650' FNL and 990' FWL of Section 12-T8N-R19W, Washita County, Oklahoma. Enclosed for your review is our AFE reflecting estimated dry hole costs of $6,869,100.00 and estimated completion costs of $2,745,400.00. As a working interest owner within the referenced unit and per the terms and conditions of that certain Order 450325, Cause CD 200100725-T, dated March 29, 2001, Davis respectfully requests that you elect one of the afforded options as follows:

1.   Participate in the drilling and completing of said well by paying your proportionate share of well costs as stipulated by Order 450325;

2.   Elect not to participate in the proposed test well, electing to farm out your unit interest delivering to Davis your interest at a proportionate 75% net revenue interest.

Per the terms of Order 450325 you have **15 days** upon receipt of this proposal to make your election as outlined above. Failure to respond within the 15 day period will evidence your election not to participate thus relinquishing your interest under paragraph 2, above.

Please indicate the option of your choice by signing below and returning one copy of this letter to my attention. This proposal may be terminated without further notice. Should you have any questions, please contact me at (713) 439-6750 or Bill Jaqua at (405) 329-0779.

Sincerely,

Davis Petroleum Corp.

Alan Martinkewiz
Landman

THE UNDERSIGNED HEREBY ACCEPTS OPTION NO._____, THIS _____
DAY OF _____, 2005

By: _____

Title: _____

Company: _____

Here is what your author did. He started by assessing the situation. Davis could not exclude him, and clearly did not need his modest investment. The letter provided virtually no information, and was not even put on letterhead, presumably the favored Davis approach if it were trying to discourage investment. Davis had obviously spent a fair amount of effort determining whether to drill the well, and decided to go ahead. It must think its prospects were good, and you would be investing as a near partner.

Bearing this in mind, he called Bill Jaqua—a contact Davis identified in the letter—and asked about the well. He was informed it was a pure wildcat, and that it was impossible to guess the probability of success. Some geologic technical discussion followed, which he tried to pretend he understood. He then asked what percent of Davis wildcat wells had been successful in recent years, and got a number of 20–25%. He then asked what the payoff was on average if the wells were successful. The answer was 10 to 1. Beyond that, if this well was successful, there would be a number of other wells drilled in the field. Only participation now would give one the right to be a future partner, when presumably the odds would be much more favorable. This appeared to be a reasonably favorable investment, with a healthy upside option of future wells attached. The clinching argument was that Jaqua courteously explained that Davis would be happy to take his interest and give him the free override, thus reinforcing the message of the uninformative letter not placed on letterhead. (It turned out that the override would have only been 1% of revenue—an amount not mentioned in the letter—as opposed to 76% if he invested.)[38] In short, the structure of the situation and the nature of Davis's play made a sidecar investment imperative. The well has not yet been started.

Davis was in a tough situation. It had to invite in undesired partners on favorable terms when it had done all the work. It reversed the usual ploy where someone with a significant informational advantage tries to play innocent or worse, invoke some absolute advantage story. Davis tried to play up the uU aspect of the situation to discourage participation.

Review of the Bidding. You have been asked to address some decision problems. Go back now and grade yourself first on the overconfidence questionnaire. The answers are in the footnote.[39]

You were asked about three investments: Tengion, Gazprom and Davis Oil. Go back and reconsider your choices, and decide whether you employed the appropriate principles when making them, and then assess the more general

---

[38]Not mentioned in the letter was that 24% went off the top to priority claims, and that Davis charges 75% if you take the free override.

[39]1) 173,710, 2) 2,716, 3) 2,007,901, 4) 130,119, 5) 13, 6) 12,212,000, 7) $259B, 8) 13.45%, 9) 853,000.

implications for investment in *uU* situations. Though this essay pointed out pitfalls with *uU* investing, it was generally upbeat about the potential profits that reside in *uU* arenas. Hopefully you have been influenced, at least a bit.

V. Some Cautions: Herding, Cascades and Meltdowns

Understanding the *uU* world presents great opportunity, but it also suggests some cautions. We shall focus on just the three: herding, cascades, and meltdowns.

Herding. Animals gather together because there is safety in numbers. Investors cluster as well. That may help them fend off criticism, but it will not protect them from meltdowns in value, be they for individual assets or for the market as a whole. There are two main ingredients in such meltdowns, information cascades and fat-tailed distributions. A cascade is experienced when the information from one individual spills over to inform another individual, and then a whole group gets informed. Fat tails, as we mentioned above, refers to the fact that financial assets have more big movements in price than experience with small movements would suggest, including some movements so large they would seem nearly impossible.

Information Cascades. Information cascades occur when individuals draw inferences about the information that others possess from the actions they take. Thus one individual's information cascades to affect the action of another. The danger with an information cascade is that it is very difficult for the players to know how much information is possessed in total. When the total possessed is much less than the total assessed, prices can be well out of line. Just such a situation may be responsible for the meltdown in housing prices in the United States in 2008. Each family purchasing a house looks to comparable sales for guidance. Using that basis, it seems sensible to pay say $300,000 for this home, since other equivalent homes nearby sold for as much as $320,000. The trouble is that all the other home buyers were also relying on the market price. In effect, there was herding on the information. Everyone would be happy to know that they bought close to the correct price, namely what others would buy for in the future. But unfortunately, there was no hard basis to determine that correct price. One possibility would be to rely on the prices in equivalent nearby towns, but this just raises the herding on information issue one level. A whole region or nation can find its housing prices inflated.

Economists would say that there are multiple equilibria in such markets, at least one high priced and one low priced. The high-priced equilibrium of late 2007 proved to be unstable. A moderate shock knocked it away from that equilibrium, and prices spiraled downward to what will ultimately be a lower-priced equilibrium. People who bought houses in 2007 were unlikely to have thought about either information cascades or fat tails. That is, they did not contemplate that current house prices were based on little reliable information, and that big price movements, down as well as up, were quite possible.

In some circumstances, although there is abundant information in the system, and individuals closely monitor and behave in response to the actions of others, little of the information gets shared. Take a situation where each of 100 people gets a signal on whether housing prices are going down or up. The signal is not fully reliable. If prices are going down, it is 70% likely someone will get a down signal and 30% an up signal, and vice versa when the market is going up. Individuals choose whether to buy a house in numerical order, and will buy a house if on the basis of what they know, they think prices are going up, though a small group buys because they desperately need a house. They draw inferences from the actions of others. Person 1 gets an up signal and buys a house. Person 2 can't be sure that 1 did not buy because he was desperate for a house, so his information would outweigh 1's action as a signal. 2 would not buy if he got a down signal, but he got an up signal. He too buys a house. Person 3 gets a down signal, but reasons that 1 and 2 probably got up signals, so his signal is outvoted; prices are likely to go up. Beyond that, everyone, whatever his signal, will buy. That is what we call an information cascade. Almost certainly, the aggregate information from all 100 people would indicate a down market, but the cascade of information from the first two individuals is what dominates the market.

Meltdowns. We are most likely to get prices far from equilibrium in those markets where prices rose rapidly. Individuals within might reason as follows: "Prices went up by roughly 8% each of the last three years. Thus, the price I should pay should depend not only on some multiple of rent—a normal metric—but must incorporate how much prices will go up next year. Others think that $300,000 is an appropriate price for such a house. That price builds in consensus expectations." This reasoning may be correct, but it represents a fragile situation. If prices do not go up by 8%, the price will not merely soften; it will collapse, since rapid appreciation was the basis for its high price.

Matters would be far different in unglamorous cities, say Indianapolis or Buffalo. House prices hardly budged in them for a long time. They were set in relation to rental rates, and did not rely on future expectations. In short, there was much more information in the system. People could make decisions on whether it was cheaper to rent or buy.

Experience with the NASDAQ and California home prices is instructive. From 1995 to 2000 the NASDAQ had multiplied more than six times in value before peaking in March 2000. It then fell by 60% in a year.[40] The median price of an existing detached home in California had tripled in eight years before mid 2007, and then fell in half in one year.[41]

In each case there was a dramatic run up before the big run down. Investors in the first case and home buyers in the second were trying to guess how prices would move in the future. All participants were watching and taking comfort from the decisions of others. They moved with the herd as prices moved up. Once prices stopped their rapid ascent, they could not be sustained, since current values anticipated rapid appreciation. The participants were victims of the fat-tail phenomenon. Meltdowns were experienced.

> *Maxim F:* **When there may be herding on information, beware. Be doubly beware if the information comes from extrapolating a successful past to a successful future.**

Some very major financial players ignored maxim F, to their peril. Many of our most prestigious investment houses lost many billions of dollars because they went with the herd to get a little extra kick by buying mortgage-backed securities. Perhaps more surprising, Fannie Mae and Freddie Mac effectively collapsed because they failed to examine their own markets.

The implication of maxim F is that effective decision makers must—as a recent insightful book for business and financial executives puts it in its first lesson—"Go to the Source," namely engage in the "relentless pursuit of information from the field." It tells the story of Bill George, the newly appointed president of medical equipment giant Medtronic, who went into the operating room where he witnessed the dreadful performance of the company's catheter during an angioplasty. By starting at the source, he discovered that the company's information system systematically covered up information about low quality: "People do not want to pass on bad news, and engineers [or any other group] can be in denial about a problem."[42] That last sentence distills our findings about much in the recent collapse of mortgage markets and financial institutions.

---

[40] Yahoo! Finance.

[41] California Association of Realtors (2008).

[42] See Zeckhauser and Sandoski (2008), pp. 7–43. The book's second lesson (pp. 44–72) is also instructive if one wishes to elicit information from all and to avoid herding. It is "Fill a Room with Barbarians." The central finding is that: "Seeking and fostering dissent provides two advantages. . . .[participants must] expose their opinions to a wide range of counterarguments. . .[and] diverse, well-founded arguments can reframe a problem so that everyone sees it in a new way."

Maxim G: Be triply beware of herding when there is evidence that there have been significant changes in the basic structure of markets, however stable they have been in the past.

The mortgage market, a stable and successful market for decades, had undergone dramatic changes in the decade or so before it collapsed. Mortgages, originally the obligations of the banks that wrote them, had evolved into derivative products, with large numbers of mortgages packaged together and sold as a unit. That dramatically reduced the incentives for the banks that wrote them to scrutinize their safety. It also meant that no one really understood the risk characteristics of any package. A second major development, no doubt pushed along by the derivative developments, was that mortgages had come to be written with extraordinarily low down payments. Indeed, looking back four years from 2007, 25% of mortgages on new houses were written with down payments of 2% or less.[43]

Investment houses often warn us that past performance is not necessarily indicative of future results. Maxim G would tell us that past performance is particularly unreliable if basic assumptions from the past have been overturned. Our big losers among investment houses ignored their own warning when it came to mortgage-backed securities, and maxims F and G as well.

While issuing cautions, consider a final word about statistical inference. In the classroom, we are used to drawing inferences from multiple trials. Thus, to determine whether a new drug offers benefits, we might give it to 100 people, and an existing drug to another 100, and see which performs better, say in lowering cholesterol. This mental model of independent trials may not carry over to financial markets. The excess performance of 100 firms investing in mortgage-backed securities in a particular year is far from 100 independent trials. They will all do well if housing markets rise, but if such markets plummet, they will all be in trouble. A single year with 100 firms is closer to 1 observation than 100 independent observations. Hedge funds announced their ability to do well in up or down financial markets, and from 1987 to 2007 they averaged almost a 14% return. But they were not really tested till 2008, when they were down on average 19.83% for the year.[44]

---

[43] *American Housing Survey for the United States: 2007.*
[44] Data from the Hennessee Group's Hedge Fund Index (see http://www.hennesseegroup.com/indices/index.html).

VI. A Buffett Tale

Let us conclude with a happier tale. The following story encapsulates the fear of uU situations, even by sophisticated investors, and the potential for shrewd investors to take great advantage of such situations. In 1996, I was attending a National Bureau of Economic Research (NBER) conference on insurance. One participant was the prime consultant to the California Earthquake Authority. He had been trying to buy a $1 billion slice of reinsurance—to take effect after $5 billion in aggregate insured losses—from the New York financial community. The Authority was offering five times estimated actuarial value, but had no takers. It seemed exceedingly unlikely that the parties requesting coverage had inside information that a disastrous earthquake was likely. Hence, there was a big advantage, in effect $a = 5$, and p was close to 0. Maxim D—weigh absolute advantage against informational disadvantage—surely applied.

My dinner table syndicate swung into action, but ended up $999.9 million short. A couple days later, we learned that Buffett had flown to California to take the entire slice. Here is his explanation.

> . . .we wrote a policy for the California Earthquake Authority that goes into effect on April 1, 1997, and that exposes us to a loss more than twice that possible under the Florida contract. Again we retained all the risk for our own account. Large as these coverages are, Berkshire's after-tax "worst-case" loss from a true mega-catastrophe is probably no more than $600 million, which is less than 3% of our book value and 1.5% of our market value. To gain some perspective on this exposure, look at the table on page 2 and note the much greater volatility that security markets have delivered us.
>
> —Chairman's letter to the shareholders of Berkshire Hathaway, 1996, http://www.ifa.com/Library/Buffet.html

Reinsurance for earthquakes is certainly a venture into the unknown, but had many attractive features beyond its dramatic overpricing. Unlike most insurance, it was exceedingly unlikely that the parties taking insurance had inside knowledge on their risk. Thus, Buffett—despite attention to money management—was willing to take 100% of a risk of which Wall Street firms rejected taking even part. Those fancy financial entities were not well equipped to take a risk on something that was hard for them to estimate. Perhaps they did not recognize that others had no inside information, that everyone was operating with the same probability. And perhaps they were just concerned about Monday Morning Quarterbacking.

It is also instructive to consider Buffett's approach to assessing the probabilities in this *uU* situation, as revealed in the same annual report:

> So what are the true odds of our having to make a payout during the policy's term? We don't know—nor do we think computer models will help us, since we believe the precision they project is a chimera. In fact, such models can lull decision-makers into a false sense of security and thereby increase their chances of making a really huge mistake. We've already seen such debacles in both insurance and investments. Witness "portfolio insurance," whose destructive effects in the 1987 market crash led one wag to observe that it was the computers that should have been jumping out of windows.

Buffett was basically saying to Wall Street firms: "Even if you hire 100 brilliant Ph.D.s to run your models, no sensible estimate will emerge." These are precisely the types of *uU* situations where the competition will be thin, the odds likely favorable, and the Buffetts of this world can thrive.

As Buffett has shown on repeated occasions, a multibillionaire will rush in where mathematical wizards fear to tread. Indeed, that explains much of his success. In 2006 hurricane insurance met two Buffett desiderata, high prices and reluctant competitors. So he plunged into the market:

> Buffett's prices are as much as 20 times higher than the rates prevalent a year ago, said Kevin Madden, an insurance broker at Aon Corp. in New York. On some policies, premiums equal half of its maximum potential payout, he said. [In a May 7, 2006, interview Buffett said:] "We will do more than anybody else if the price is right. . .We are certainly willing to lose $6 billion on a single event. I hope we don't." (http://seekingalpha.com/article/11697)

At least two important lessons emerge from thinking about the "advantage-versus-selection" problem, and observing Warren Buffett:

Maxim H: Discounting for ambiguity is a natural tendency that should be overcome, just as should be overeating.

Maxim I: Do not engage in the heuristic reasoning that just because you do not know the risk, others do. Think carefully, and assess whether they are likely to know more than you. When the odds are extremely favorable, sometimes it pays to gamble on the unknown, even though there is some chance that people on the other side may know more than you.

Buffett took another bold financial move in 2006, in a quite different field, namely philanthropy. He announced that he would give away 85% of his fortune or $37.4 billion, with $31 billion going to the Bill and Melinda Gates Foundation. Putting money with the Gates Foundation represents sidecar philanthropy. The Foundation is an extremely effective organization that focuses on health care and learning. It is soon to be led by Bill Gates, a fellow with creativity, vision and hardheadedness as strong complementary skills, skills which are as valuable in philanthropy as they are in business.

VII. Conclusion

This essay offers more speculations than conclusions, and provides anecdotal accounts rather than definitive data. Its theory is often tentative and implicit. But the question it seeks to answer is clear: How can one invest rationally in *uU* situations? The question sounds almost like an oxymoron. Yet clear thinking about *uU* situations, which includes prior diagnosis of their elements, and relevant practice with simulated situations, may vastly improve investment decisions where *uU* events are involved. If they do improve, such clear thinking will yield substantial benefits. For financial decisions at least, the benefits may be far greater than are available in run-of-the-mill contexts, since competition may be limited and prices well out of line.

How important are *uU* events in the great scheme of financial affairs? That itself is a *uU* question. But if we include only those that primarily affect individuals, the magnitude is far greater than what our news accounts would suggest. Learning to invest more wisely in a *uU* world may be the most promising way both to protect yourself from major investment errors, and to significantly bolster your prosperity.

Richard Zeckhauser is the Frank P. Ramsey Professor of Political Economy at the Kennedy School, Harvard University, Cambridge, Massachusetts.

Appendix A

Assessing Quantities[45]

1. Democratic votes in Montana, 2004 Presidential election

2. Length of Congo River (in miles)

3. Number of subscribers to *Field and Stream*

4. Area of Finland (in square miles)

5. Birth rate in France per 1,000 population

6. Population of Cambodia

7. Revenues of Wal-Mart Stores (largest in U.S.), 2003

8. Annual percent yields on 30-year Treasury bonds in 1981? (This year had the highest rate over the 1980–1998 period.)

9. Number of physicians in the United States, 2002

10. Number of electoral votes going to the Republican presidential candidate in 2008 (out of 538)

11. Value of Dow Jones Average on December 31, 2006 (on 6/30/06 closed at 11,150)

12. Value of the NASDAQ on December 31, 2006 (on 6/30/06 closed at 2,172)

---

[45]Question 1, http://www.uselectionatlas.org/RESULTS/state.php?f=0&year=2004&fips=30. Questions 2–6, *1995 Information Please Almanac*. Question 8, *1999 Wall Street Journal Almanac*. Questions 7 and 9, *World Almanac 2005*.

Table 7.

	1st percentile	25th percentile	50th percentile	75th percentile	99th percentile
Democratic votes MT 2004 presidential election					
Congo River (length in miles)					
Field & Stream (number of subscribers)					
Finland (area in square miles)					
Birth rate of France (per thousand)					
Population of Cambodia					
Revenues of Wal-Mart Stores, 2003					
% Yields on 30-year bonds, 1981					
Number of physicians in U.S., 2002					
Number of electoral college votes, Republican presidential candidate in 2008					
Dow Jones Average 12/31/06 (on 6/30/06 closed at 11,150)					
Value of NASDAQ 12/31/06 (on 6/30/06 closed at 2,172)					

REFERENCES

Alpert, M., and H. Raiffa. 1982. "A Progress Report on the Training of Probability Assessors." In *Judgment under Uncertainty: Heuristics and Biases*. Edited by D. Kahneman, P. Slovic, and A. Tversky. New York: Cambridge University Press (294–305).

Aumann, R.J. 1976. "Agreeing to Disagree." *Annals of Statistics*, vol. 4, no. 4 (November): 1236–1239.

Bazerman, M.H., and W.F. Samuelson. 1983. "I Won the Auction But Don't Want the Prize." *Journal of Conflict Resolution*, vol. 27, no. 4 (December):618–634.

Bohnet, I., and R. Zeckhauser. 2004. "Trust, Risk and Betrayal." *Journal of Economic Behavior & Organization*, vol. 55, no. 4 (December):467–484.

Ellsberg, D. 1961. "Risk, Ambiguity, and the Savage Axioms." *Quarterly Journal of Economics*, vol. 75, no. 4 (November):643–669.

Fox, C.R., and A. Tversky. 1995. "Ambiguity Aversion and Comparative Ignorance." *Quarterly Journal of Economics*, vol. 110, no. 3 (August):585–603.

Gilbert, D. 2006. *Stumbling on Happiness*. New York: Alfred A. Knopf.

Gomory, R.E. 1995. "The Known, the Unknown and the Unknowable." *Scientific American*, vol. 272, no. 6 (June):120.

Grossman, S.J. 1981. "The Informational Role of Warranties and Private Disclosure about Product Quality." *Journal of Law & Economics*, vol. 24, no. 3 (December):461–483.

Hart, S., and Y. Tauman. 2004. "Market Crashes without External Shocks." *Journal of Business*, vol. 77, no. 1 (January):1–8.

Kahneman, D., and A. Tversky. 1979. "Prospect Theory: An Analysis of Decision under Risk." *Econometrica*, vol. 47, no. 2 (March):263–291.

Knight, F.H. 1921. *Risk, Uncertainty and Profit*. Boston: Houghton Mifflin.

Munger, C.T. 2005. *Poor Charlie's Almanack: The Wit and Wisdom of Charles Munger*. Virginia Beach, VA: Donning Company Publishers.

Raiffa, H. 1968. *Decision Analysis*. Reading, MA: Addison-Wesley.

Samuelson, P.A. 1979. "Why We Should Not Make Mean Log of Wealth Big Though Years to Act Are Long." *Journal of Banking & Finance*, vol. 3, no. 4 (December):305–307.

Savage, L.J. 1954. *The Foundations of Statistics*. New York: Wiley.

Subramanian, G., and R. Zeckhauser. 2005. "'Negotiauctions': Taking a Hybrid Approach to the Sale of High Value Assets." *Negotiation*, vol. 8, no. 2 (February):4–6.

Tversky, A., and D. Kahneman. 1974. "Judgment under Uncertainty: Heuristics and Biases." *Science*, vol. 185, no. 4157 (September):1124–1131.

U.S. Bureau of the Census. Current Housing Reports, Series H150/07. In *American Housing Survey for the United States: 2007*. Washington, DC: U.S. Government Printing Office.

Viscusi, W.K., and R.J. Zeckhauser. 2005. "Recollection Bias and the Combat of Terrorism." *Journal of Legal Studies*, vol. 34, no. 1 (January):27–55.

Zeckhauser, B., and A. Sandoski. 2008. *How the Wise Decide: The Lessons of 21 Extraordinary Leaders*. New York: Crown Business.

Zeckhauser, R. 2006. "Investing in the Unknown and Unknowable." *Capitalism and Society*, vol. 1, no. 2 (August): http://www.bepress.com/cas/vol1/iss2/art5.

Zeckhauser, R., and M. Thompson. 1970. "Linear Regression with Non-Normal Error Terms." *Review of Economics and Statistics*, vol. 52, no. 3 (August):280–286.

Zeckhauser, R.J., and D. Marks. 1996. "Signposting: The Selective Revelation of Product Information." In *Wise Choices: Games, Decisions, and Negotiations*. Edited by R.J. Zeckhauser, R.L. Keeney, and J.K. Sebenius, 22–41. Boston: Harvard Business School Press.

A Psychological Profile of the Portfolio Manager

Have recent upheavals made the portfolio manager manic-depressive, a game player, or too much the organization man?

Dean LeBaron, CFA

The Psychology of the New Portfolio Managers

The fundamental theorem is that when confronted with unstructured stimuli the person will impose structure on them in such a way as to reflect his own needs and impulses; the subject's responses therefore are expected to serve as guides to his private world of fantasy, his attitudes, fears, aspirations and the like.

—L.K. Frank, 1939

Many have examined the working milieu of the investment manager in an effort to explain increased market volatility. No attempt, to my knowledge, has been made to examine the mind of the portfolio manager, the investment decision-maker, to understand and deal with this new phenomenon. This article is such an effort.

If we understand the filters, hypotheses, and assumptions that the portfolio manager uses to make his decisions, we shall be better able to interpret his deviations from "rational." Furthermore, we should be able to improve job-related learning and establish environments in which the new managers can flourish.

Finally, the article hopes to stimulate serious research by competent psychology professionals in this field. The field is not overcrowded, deals with interesting people, has ample quantitative data, and, because such research should lead to more optimum allocation of investment resources, it should pay well. Investment organizations need help now in the selection, training, organization, and prediction of the behavior of their own professional staffs. An important social-science function is wide open.

Putting It in Context

What triggered you to write this piece? And how do you think it should be helpful to professional investment practitioners?

The article remains relevant today, although when it was written we did not have the terminology "behavioral finance." But as a quantitative-oriented investor, I knew that the psychological filter of the researcher found in physics and most sciences had to be evident in our field too. Hence, I wrote the article to test whether or not I could pull some new data together to illustrate the principles and to develop my own arguments with sufficient rigor to stand the critique of my peers.

A large number of friends, colleagues, competitors, and academics have contributed thoughts to this short piece. I have elected to preserve their anonymity so they can continue to be unfettered observers of the investment scene, a role I risk losing. An exception to this rule is my public gratitude to my associate, Alexis Belash, a frequent translator of my writings into English.

Environment

Markets have been harsh lately. No sooner had the Fisher and Lorie long-term equity return figure of 9.3 percent per year been published when a 25-year bull market ended in 1966. Total return of bonds and stocks has been near zero since then, depending slightly, but not much, on when you wish to take the measurement. No sooner had the brightest business school graduates flocked to the investment industry in the mid-sixties to make their fortunes on the frontier of change, but change it did, and for the worse. Not only were careers not advancing, but jobs were threatened in one economy drive after another. The final irony is that the academics' notion of efficient markets—the random walk for portfolios—became widely accepted. Attacked by markets, client, employer, and teacher, the investment manager has withdrawn into a catatonic state. When he recovers, he will exhibit new behavior patterns learned from his experience.

A portfolio manager has one overriding requirement: to invest for his employer/client to produce the highest expected return, without ever assuming so much risk that future investment might become impossible. This is pure game theory, which has been well tested on humans and pigeons.

A more recent variant of game theory holds that there is a "utility" or "moral value" of money. A player may assign weights to various outcomes that from an objective, impersonal standpoint seem irrational. These arbitrary weights can be detected by the statistician over long observation periods and reveal the motivations, needs, and desires of the player. In fact, after determining which weighting systems are player-related, not game-related, new effective rules and compensating systems may be employed. These can improve the outcome without changing the players or their own non-optimizing weight assignments.

It is not very difficult to see how these weightings have changed in actual practice. The old definition of a portfolio manager's job was centered on stock picking. If one picked profitable investments, the job requirements were met. Now, the determination of risk level has replaced stock picking. Furthermore, stock picking has fallen into such disrepute that stock selection is assumed to be nearly impossible. Consequently, the portfolio manager has had to orient himself in wholly new ways: toward risks, toward diversification, and, of course, to clients.

Disorientation and Change

Thus, the new portfolio manager has acquired some new assumptions about his world from the experiences he has had in the last decade.

He is willing to accept the efficient market hypothesis, at least in private with his peers if not yet openly with his clients. This two-tier difference between fantasy and reality is causing far more anxiety among portfolio managers than the other, more widely publicized "two-tier" condition.

The second assumption is that the client's needs are paramount in determining the level of investment success. In most relationships between a professional and his client, the professional is in the superior position because of his specialized knowledge and facility. Although that assumption was true of the investment profession in the sixties, the investment world is undergoing rapid change, and the professional relationship here is being revised as well. Job security is most important in considering the manager's assumptions. Through economy drives and reorganizations, skilled investment people have been thrust out into an unreceptive job market.

Those who remain have a message: you do not win by trying to be a hero; stay in the middle as an unnoticed team-player, and feed your family. It has long been recognized that short-term job considerations penalize creative work; hence the tenure system in academia. The investment manager had been threatened at his most critical level, his own survival, and he may have put his own immediate interests ahead of those of his clients. If so, he has lost the principal mark of a professional, his independence and his ability to completely represent interests other than his own even if they are in conflict with his own.

The portfolio manager has a number of lesser filters that may influence his thinking. He thinks that trends endure and can be identified early enough to be profitably exploited. He thinks his peers are smart and is willing to copy them almost without question. After all, most of them went to the same schools he did, he often eats lunch with them, and he even lives the same life-style they do. He thinks most of the world can be quantified—numbers count. But exhaustive study is not productive. He looks for the key reasons and is willing to forgo the luxury of more detailed and thorough analysis. Finally, he is motivated by the achievement of capital power. Few of the top portfolio managers are wealthy in their own right. Most are striving to achieve freedom of occupational choice by acquiring sufficient capital to meet a high living standard. Their personal options will be greater with capital than with merely a high employment salary.

Most investment organizations have undergone a tightening of structure in the last five years or so. It is assumed that this trend has emanated from senior management levels. I doubt it. Portfolio managers today manifest an interest in having well-defined limits to their decision-making, are happy with approved policy guides and in avoiding individual assignment of responsibility for investment acts that may go astray. Several former military men who came to the investment business say that change was far easier to bring about in their first career than in their second.

Much of the change in the investment world seems to repeat the Hawthorne experiment of 1927. Contrary to the hypothesis there being tested, changes in light level, first increasing then decreasing, *both* produced increases in assemblers' output. Changes in industry assignments, changes in portfolio industry mix, field trips to company managements have some similarity to change for the sake of job interest, not content.

The Protestant Ethic was accepted during the sixties; a lot of hard work and occasional flashes of brilliance would allow the portfolio manager to control his own destiny. Now that is not the case. His destiny is in the hands of a system that looks random or efficient, of an organization that is reducing its manpower, of a client who distrusts his mystical skills, and of a personal ego that requires he reject all of these notions. Is it any wonder that the portfolio manager has begun to embrace marketing?

Characteristics of a Portfolio Manager

The portfolio manager job requirements stated by investment firms have escalated to the point that one man cannot fulfill the task. No longer is a determination of future earnings above or below trend the principal ingredient. Now one is expected to deal with inflation, Washington, international affairs . . . all the things that were once taken for granted. Clearly a team is called for, and in a team individual responsibility is very difficult to assign. These long-term factors are also very difficult to connect to specific decisions, so that individual performance review is impossible. Decisiveness and frequency of investment decisions are not important now. The long-term issues change slowly and the decision points are fewer. Few decisions, few actions, long-term considerations, and a team effort.

One of the common psychotic states is manic depressive. This is a state in which the subject cyclically changes between excited and depressed. Although there are behavior manifestations of the manic depressive in all of us at one time or another, they seem to be more apparent in investment people recently. Perhaps the tight organization and even the willingness of investment people for structure is a voluntary recognition of the psychological damage and the need for repair. An application of game theory suggests a change in game rules to adapt the non-reality player-related weights to a profit system.

The exaggerated behavior of the game-player is not alone in revealing his characteristics and experience. His associations are also clues. Group behavior studies have much to tell us about groups that are threatened, even with very mild threats. Panic sets in when team effort is required and the group is not meeting its norm. There is a classic experimental game involving removing pegs from a bottle for a small reward or punishment. It frequently leads to violence on the part of the participants. Non-conformity is the worst threat to the group, according to most studies. Homans (1950) found in his study of gangs that the closer one came to the norms of the leader, the closer one became to him in rank.

Rumor plays a key role in the group. Information passed on serially gets abbreviated and altered until it is passed on by rote and has no information content about reality. The sharing of the same information, no matter how useless or incorrect, is important in preserving the group.

Punishment for non-conformity, sharing useless information, striving for the leader's norms are all ways of dealing with a hostile environment. They do not happen to be job-related in the sense of enhancing investment performance. Appleman (1973a, 1973b) gave a questionnaire to readers of the *Financial Analysts Journal*. He concluded that portfolio managers were demoralized, unable to be rational.

Learning

We have discussed some of the weaknesses of the present state of mind. The purpose is not to add to the excessive criticism of portfolio managers, but rather to illuminate some of their problems. Assistance could come in two forms: one, an increase in organizational structure to remove some of the threats and fears (this is occurring); and, two, a relearning of old experiences that may counter-balance the weight of the more recent negative ones. The latter exercise is promising.

One of the most widely publicized experiments in learning was the Pavlov (1927) demonstration of a conditioned response in a dog. By association with a pleasurable experience (satisfaction of hunger), a dog was made to salivate at the ringing of a bell. The traditional ringing of the morning bell on the floor of the New York Stock Exchange may be too much of a coincidence. It is not difficult to draw the analogy that when investment decisions produce less than expected results at the ringing of the bell, the subject will exhibit behavior demonstrating that he has "learned" something painful is about to occur. Since pleasure and pain are far more evenly balanced in the study of market history, I would remind the portfolio manager not to be unduly concerned with recent events.

In animals and, I suspect, in humans, the early learning experiences tend to dominate. Thus, a portfolio manager of the fifties and sixties would tend to exhibit behavior appropriate for a rising trend, and deviances from that environment will initially be rejected. Those of more recent responsibility will display skills useful in a trendless condition and are likely to be equally confused by change. A knowledge of market history will even out these biases. It would be especially useful if market games could be played, like computer-generated war games, to simulate earlier periods, thereby developing and reinforcing skills unused in the current market phase.

Rationalization is the most important defense mechanism in one's arsenal of protective devices. But rationalization hinders learning by blocking useful information. The more used in the short-run, the more it is likely to be required in the long-run, through encouragement of mistakes. There are a number of nonthreatening methods of criticism and learning that do not involve forcing someone to establish a pattern of rationalization and self-justification. Games are one example. They should be used.

The Future

This article is not intended to have foresight; the study of the psychology of the portfolio manager is too new for that. I have some views, however, and there are changes now taking place that need assessment.

My own preferred investment environment is one characterized by rigid discipline and a loose organizational structure. The investment community seems headed for the converse: a willingness to adopt a series of expedient philosophies and a tight organization. This trend may protect the psyche of the portfolio manager and keep him from doing great damage in his present wounded state. It does not get at the root problem, his mental state, but merely allows him to function in a limited way.

The view that marketing is the key ingredient of the investment process needs critical examination before its acceptance. This doctrine of marketing primacy is being taught in the leading investment courses and is a contributing factor to the disinterest of top students in investments today. Like many disguised norms, it has a way of bringing about its own fulfillment. As one identified with endorsing the efficient market notion, I would prefer to see effort devoted to production considerations, such as economies of scale, and to searching out those places and times in the market when inefficiencies are present. The practitioner has given up too soon—perhaps another manifestation of his present mental condition.

I recently read a prescription for group brainwashing: "Segregate leaders, deny information, create distrust by informers, withdraw group privileges because of one person, publicly praise collaboration, pace demands for conformity slowly so that resistance seems illogical, maintain deprivation, and give small rewards for conforming." Most of these conditions seem to be at work in the investment world in 1974, and like the results of most brainwashing exercises, they seem unlikely to be of benefit to a constructive enterprise.

Having stated, and perhaps overstated, my fears, let me close by expressing my hope. The forces I seem to see at work are not invincible. They can be resisted, and such damage as they may have caused can be repaired. A prerequisite for doing so is that they and their impact be clearly identified and understood. This article is intended as a modest contribution to that end. From its very inception, one of the fundamental tenets of the psychoanalytical movement has been that unconscious tendencies rendered conscious could be corrected where there was the will to do so.

Of all the major factors that affect the behavior of the stock market, the psychology of the portfolio manager is probably the most neglected. Whether or not I have managed to shed any light on this area, it is my hope to stimulate greater interest in it.

Dean LeBaron, CFA, is the founder of Batterymarch Financial Management, Boston.

REFERENCES

Appleman, Mark J. 1973a. "How Professional Is the Professional Portfolio Manager?" *Financial Analysts Journal*, vol. 29, no. 2 (March/April):32–33.

———. 1973b. "The Three Minds of the Professional Investor." *Financial Analysts Journal*, vol. 29, no. 5 (September/October):49–52.

Homans, George Caspar. 1950. *The Human Group.* New York: Harcourt, Brace and Company.

Pavlov, Ivan P. 1927. *Conditioned Reflexes: An Investigation of the Physiological Activity of the Cerebral Cortex.* London: Routledge and Kegan Paul.

Using Behavioral Finance to Improve the Adviser–Client Relationship

Bryan Olson, CFA
Mark W. Riepe, CFA

Those persons who accept a fee for making investment recommendations to individuals are generally thought of as acting in a fiduciary capacity. One obligation of a fiduciary is to act solely in the best interests of the client. This obligation often applies whether or not the adviser has discretion over the assets of the client. Operating in such a world is challenging for the investment adviser, whose well-meaning recommendations can sometimes be at odds with what clients (mistakenly) believe to be in their best interests.

For the adviser in a fiduciary but *nondiscretionary* relationship, the challenge increases. The advice must still be in the best interests of the client, but the client is the final decision maker. Every recommendation must pass through the client's thicket of emotions and the well-intentioned decision-making shortcuts (heuristics) clients may use to cope with the mass of information with which they are flooded each day. In effect, the difficulty of giving good advice doubles for the fiduciary in a nondiscretionary relationship. The adviser must create a recommendation that is in the best interests of the client and then convince the client that accepting and sticking with the recommendation is, in fact, in the client's best interest.

More and more advisers will face this challenge because the amount of assets in nondiscretionary advisory relationships is expected to increase dramatically. Cerulli Associates (2007) estimates that assets in nondiscretionary advisory accounts will grow from $321 billion in 2007 to $577 billion by 2011.

Behavioral finance has furthered our understanding of the ways in which individuals are prone to make mistakes when making decisions. With this knowledge, an adviser can gain a more accurate picture of

> the cognitive and emotional weaknesses of investors that relate to making investment decisions: their occasionally faulty assessment of their own interests and true wishes, the relevant facts that they tend to ignore, and the limits of their ability to accept advice and to live with the decisions they make. (Kahneman and Riepe 1998, p. 52)

We believe advisers who study behavioral finance and incorporate its insights into their practices will improve the outcomes for their clients by making prudent recommendations in a way that increases the odds that the clients will act upon them.

We address the topic in the following four sections:

- *Establishing the relationship.* This process begins with the first encounter of the adviser and the client in the postsales environment; that is, the "prospect" has become a "client." A relationship has been established in a legal sense, but in reality, the client and the adviser are getting to know each other.

- *Profiling the client.* After the establishment of the relationship comes the process of obtaining a detailed understanding of the client—wants, needs, fears, history, and present circumstances.

- *Making recommendations.* With an understanding of the client in hand, the adviser prepares recommendations for the client. If the relationship is nondiscretionary, the adviser must also determine a strategy for presenting the recommendations to obtain the client's assent before implementation of the strategy.

- *Evaluating performance and renewing the relationship.* This stage encompasses a review, evaluation, and quality assessment of the recommendations that were made earlier in the relationship. It is a time to check in and ensure that expectations are still aligned with strategy, make adjustments if necessary, and deepen the relationship on the basis of increased knowledge (e.g., how the client has reacted to certain situations). After this stage, the cycle ends and begins again.

Within each section, we describe key findings from behavioral finance and make recommendations for how advisers can incorporate these findings into their practice. We do not cover every behavioral finding that has a bearing on the adviser–client relationship. We focus on (1) findings that our experience suggests most frequently impede an effective client–adviser relationship and (2) findings that suggest practical recommendations we can make for advisers to use.

Establishing the Relationship

We believe the adviser–client relationship works best for everyone when the ground rules are established at the beginning. When establishing these sensible rules, the adviser will benefit from understanding four tendencies exhibited by most people—tendencies that can potentially influence all interactions between adviser and client. These tendencies are betrayal aversion, overconfidence, the illusion of control, and optimism.

Betrayal Aversion. Individuals who hire an adviser to manage or consult on the management of their financial affairs are not buying a device or a commodity. They are hiring a person to perform an ongoing service in an area of life that most people find deeply personal and that some people even find scary and/or overwhelming. Individuals entering into such a relationship subject themselves not only to the inherent risk of the financial markets but also to social risk.

Bohnet, Greig, Herrmann, and Zeckhauser (2008) identified social risk as arising in situations in which decisions by other human beings are the primary source of uncertainty. They found that individuals are less willing to take on risk when the source of the risk is driven by the actions of another person as opposed to the source of risk being pure chance. The authors call the tendency to make a special effort to avoid social risk "betrayal aversion."

In an advisory context, this finding means that individuals may be overly cautious in their willingness to accept and endorse investment recommendations made by advisers. Understanding this tendency and addressing it when first establishing the relationship can help clients overcome the aversion.

> Recommendation 1: Establish and communicate an understandable corporate investment philosophy and a disciplined process.

When presenting recommendations to institutional investors, advisers must include in the presentation an extensive discussion of their firm's philosophy and process. Advisers presenting recommendations to individuals too often take the approach of "Trust me; I'm an intelligent, experienced professional." This approach, which emphasizes the adviser as a person, can trigger betrayal aversion.

To mitigate betrayal aversion on the part of the client, we suggest that firms document their investment philosophy and process. The documentation should be in the form of a compelling yet concise description that can be used by all members of the firm who interact with clients and that can be easily understood by unsophisticated clients.

Advisers may be concerned that this approach diminishes them to some extent in the eyes of the client. In fact, we believe it enhances their stature. Individual investors are drawn to organizations that combine commitment to a philosophy with the expertise of professionals who apply that philosophy to the specific circumstances of clients. This combination should be communicated when evaluating an investor's unique needs and circumstances and emphasized as a driving force in the selection of recommendations.

The creation, documentation, and adherence to a philosophy and process also help alleviate concerns clients may have about employee turnover. Discussion of the firm's philosophical grounding can help clients understand that they are dealing with a firm that is more than a collection of individuals. Furthermore, the creation, documentation, and adherence to a philosophy and process can be used to increase employee morale and engagement by providing a common purpose to rally around.

Overconfidence. Confucius is said to have defined knowledge as knowing what we do not know. Unfortunately, most people are not aware of what they do not know and tend to be overconfident when making decisions involving uncertain outcomes.

One reason individuals tend to be overconfident is that they have an inflated sense of their skill when it comes to forecasting. For example, consider this exercise proposed in a Kahneman and Riepe (1998) study: The task was to forecast a price range within which Google's end-of-quarter stock price would fall 98 percent of the time. To establish the range, the forecasters in the study picked a price they were 99 percent confident would be higher than the actual price and a price they were 99 percent confident would be lower than the actual price. The two prices established a 98 percent confidence interval. They repeated this exercise once per quarter and counted the extent to which the actual Google price finished within the range. For a forecaster who was "well calibrated," the actual price would fall within the range about 98 percent of the time; about 1 percent of the time, the actual price would be above the range, and about 1 percent of the time, the actual price would be below the range. Kahneman and Riepe concluded,

> Few people are well-calibrated. A vast amount of research documents a highly systematic bias in subjective confidence intervals; there are far too many surprises, indicating that the intervals were set too tightly. A typical outcome in many studies is a surprise rate of 15–20%, where accurate calibration would yield 2%. Overconfidence has been confirmed even when it is in the best interest of the research subjects to be well-calibrated. (p. 54)

Two types of clients who seek to use the services of an adviser may well be subject to overconfidence: those who believe they could manage their investments but are too busy and those who have total faith that the adviser will succeed.

- *I could do it, but I do not have the time.* Such clients believe they are perfectly capable of managing their own investments. For example, Moore, Kurtzberg, Fox, and Bazerman (1999) conducted what we believe is a realistic trading simulation with MBA candidates at Northwestern University. Nearly two-thirds of the students overestimated their actual past performance, despite being given regular updates as to how they were doing relative to the market.

Individuals of this type choose to retain the services of an investment adviser because they (1) realize they do not have the time to devote to the task of managing their investments and/or (2) do not enjoy the task enough to justify allocating their own time to it. In either case, because they are overconfident in their own abilities, they will use that inflated sense of their own skill as the standard against which to measure the performance of the adviser.

> Recommendation 2: Avoid making overconfident statements to clients.

- *I cannot do it, but you can.* These clients recognize that they lack the requisite skill and/or knowledge to manage money effectively. They have unrealistic expectations about what results are possible in the financial markets, however, and project onto the adviser the mantle of super adviser.

> Recommendation 3: Communicate realistic odds of success.

A key to success in the advisory business is setting realistic expectations and living up to those expectations in clients' eyes. Advisers who project competence through bold pronouncements about what they can accomplish may improve their initial attractiveness to potential clients, but failure to live up to those bold pronouncements will come back to haunt these advisers.

Defining success and setting realistic expectations around achieving that success need to happen in the early stages of the adviser–client relationship. The definition and expectation setting should be comprehensive and cover the investment plan, portfolio, and relationship.

- *Investment plan.* Success of the plan should be defined as progress toward or achievement of a future goal. The goal should be presented in both dollar terms and more personal terms (e.g., what those dollars will help fund). We find that describing how endowments, foundations, or pension plans approach investment strategy with a plan to fund *future liabilities* resonates with clients. The plan should incorporate current asset levels, savings rates, return projections, sustainable withdrawal rates over a given period, and any residual amount the client wants for heirs or gifting.

- *Portfolio.* Success of the portfolio should be discussed in terms of return relative to risk. Many clients view success solely in terms of the rate of return on their money. We have observed that communicating risk control as a measure of success, however, is an effective tactic.

Framing the conversation by comparing the client's portfolio with a benchmark composed of the same asset classes used in the client's portfolio can often be useful. It helps clients conceptualize that the overall success (i.e., return on a diversified portfolio) is linked to the performance of the underlying asset classes. Then, a discussion or graphic showing the vagaries of asset class performance from year to year can prevent the mistaken belief that anyone can successfully predict the best-performing sector of the market in which to invest.

At a more detailed level, describing the number of stocks or funds from a given category that outperformed the benchmark in a given year is often enlightening for individuals. For example, showing funds from a particular category over a 10-year period that were able to be in the top quartile for 1, 2, 3, 4, and so on of those years can illustrate the difficulty of picking the right funds all the time. For U.S. domestic equity mutual funds with a complete 10-year record, 90 percent had at least 1 year with top-quartile performance in the past 10 years. When the hurdle rate is raised to producing top-quartile returns in 6 out of 10 years, however, the percentage of funds drops to 3 percent.[1]

- *Relationship.* Defining a successful relationship that encompasses more than returns can be helpful. A firm usually provides account services, planning functions, and client education as part of a relationship. These benefits lead to overall success and satisfaction but do not show up in short-term returns. Successfully setting and meeting realistic expectations for the relationship over time may go beyond simple satisfaction to become client loyalty. True client loyalty can lead to referrals from and evangelizing by existing clients about what the firm is capable of beyond performance.

Illusion of Control. A golfer stands over a 30-foot putt on a severely undulating green and strikes the ball, and a few seconds later, it eases over the lip of the cup and falls to the bottom. Is the golfer lucky, is the golfer skillful, or is the pleasant result a combination of both? More importantly for purposes of this discussion, is the golfer able to distinguish between luck and skill?

Illusion of control refers to the tendency of individuals to think they have more influence over events than they actually do. One manifestation of this illusion is that people tend to mischaracterize future events as being determined by one's skill rather than chance.

---

[1]The source of this information is a 2008 report from the Schwab Center for Financial Research with data provided by Morningstar. The universe in this study included 1,167 U.S. domestic equity funds with a complete 10-year history from 1998 through 2007.

When thought about in this way, the link between illusion of control and overconfidence is apparent. As noted, overconfidence can be caused by a miscalibration on the part of the individual about the true odds of success. What might cause that miscalibration? One cause is individuals' having an unrealistic perception of the control they exert over the events that affect them.

An example of this trait was uncovered by Strickland, Lewicki, and Katz (1966), who found that study participants were willing to bet more on the outcome of a dice roll before the roll than after the roll but before the outcome of the roll was revealed. This behavior reveals their perception that they could influence the outcome of the dice's roll.

In a comprehensive treatment of the topic, Langer (1975) identified many factors associated with an increase in the illusion of control even when the situation's outcome is driven purely by chance. One hypothesis of Langer's study was that individuals will perceive that they have more control over a situation when they have a choice over some aspect of the situation. In a test of the hypothesis, a group of workers agreed to participate in a lottery at their office. Half of the participants were sold a lottery ticket for $1. The other half were also sold a lottery ticket for $1 but were allowed to pick which ticket they wanted. A week later, on the day of the drawing, each participant was asked the price for which he or she would be willing to sell his or her ticket. The average selling price for those who were randomly assigned a ticket was $1.96. The average selling price for those who picked their ticket was $8.67.

Other factors also were associated with an inappropriately heightened level of perceived control in this study. Subjects believed they had more control even though the results were random when the subjects

- were familiar with a task,

- had spent a great deal of time involved with the task, and

- had a sense of superiority to others engaged in the same task.

Think about the world of investing from the standpoint of a client who is hiring an adviser. The adviser is obviously familiar with investments, spends all day, every day doing it, and makes representations that he is a top-notch professional (superior not only to an amateur but also to many of the other professionals who ply the same trade and compete for the same clients). Given these facts, it is no wonder that clients sometimes gain a perception that advisers have a level of control over outcomes in investing that is unrealistic.

> Recommendation 4: Be clear about what you, as the adviser, do and do not control.

Much of the necessary clarity about what the adviser controls can be accomplished by properly setting expectations, describing the firm's philosophy and process, and using an investment policy statement (see Recommendation 11). Even so, however, clients may need reminding that an adviser has limited control over the outcomes of her recommendations. The market performs in a mostly random pattern, and so will individual portfolios. Disappointments can be avoided by being explicit from the beginning about where the adviser does add value and why delivering that value is within her control. We recommend that the adviser focus on communicating and highlighting the following:

- the benefits of risk control that come from using the firm's philosophy and disciplined process;

- the time, tools, and resources allocated for periodic portfolio reviews to monitor the quality of securities;

- ongoing adjustments to the investment plan and portfolio when they are necessary to reflect changes in the client's personal situation;

- account servicing;

- client education; and

- progress toward a goal.

Optimism. Individuals tend to be optimists. The optimist has at least three qualities that are relevant to the adviser–client relationship. Optimists tend to (1) overestimate their skills, (2) suffer from illusion of control, and (3) underestimate the odds that a bad event will affect them. Optimism interacts with overconfidence and illusion of control to make a bad situation worse as each of the three reinforces the other.

Recommendation 5: Make clients aware of what can go wrong with the recommendations.

To combat overoptimism, the client should be made aware of the downside of the adviser's recommendations. Every recommendation contains a degree of uncertainty. The recommendation may turn out well or poorly as a result of whether various assumptions that underlie it do or do not pan out and whether unanticipated events that occur work in favor of or against the recommendation.

If in laying out the recommendation, the adviser also lays out the basis on which that recommendation is made and the countervailing forces that may work against it, the client probably will not only be more appreciative of the work involved in preparing the recommendations but will also develop a realistic idea about how capital markets work.

For clients who have a long investment horizon, common practice is to show them a graph or table that illustrates how various asset classes have performed over long periods of history. Such graphs and tables serve a useful purpose, but focusing on long-term average returns masks the short-term volatility that investors usually experience to achieve high rates of return. Therefore, we suggest that when an adviser is presenting summarized historical data, he take the time to walk the client through the year-by-year results. The adviser should highlight periods of poor performance and explicitly ask clients how they would feel during the worst years and whether they would be willing to act on the rebalancing recommendations the adviser would suggest at such times. If the adviser has a sense of the client's total portfolio size, the adviser can convert the yearly results to dollars. (We find that clients connect better emotionally with dollars than with percentages.)

> Recommendation 6: Make clients aware of the time frame over which success of a recommendation should be measured.

As part of this education process, the adviser should attach a time frame within which each recommendation is to achieve results. Many advisers who work with individuals suggest investment strategies that are expected to pay off successfully over a few *years* and find they must explain after a few *weeks* why the results are not as expected. We think this misunderstanding often stems from the adviser's failure to communicate in the beginning that the road between recommendation and ultimate results is not linear.

> Recommendation 7: Take special care with clients who are prone to optimism and betrayal aversion.

An adviser with a client who is overly optimistic and who then feels betrayed when her lofty expectations are not met is in a high-risk situation. Such a dangerous combination is one reason we include a section on understanding the client. This often-overlooked step is incredibly valuable to the success of the long-term relationship. We find that overly optimistic clients are often those who want to act the fastest without coming to a common understanding. Slowing them down enough to provide the education and context necessary for them to set realistic expectations can be a challenge. Such clients usually have soured advisory relationships and/or bad investing experiences in their pasts, however, which an adviser can use to gain understanding of the client. For example, advisers can ask the clients what they liked and disliked about past advisory relationships to uncover areas in which concerns need to be addressed and areas in which optimism may need to be reined in and proper expectations set. Asking clients about bad investing experiences will reveal areas in which a little education on the capital markets may cure overly optimistic views.

Profiling the Client

When establishing a relationship, the adviser seeks to demonstrate trustworthiness and expertise and to provide education about the firm's investment philosophy and process. This dialogue introduces the client and adviser to each other and promotes an understanding of the way in which they wish to interact.

In the profiling stage, the adviser seeks to develop a deeper and more personal understanding of the client. What are the client's investing preferences? What past experiences might influence the client's behavior? How does the client make decisions? What influences that decision-making process? What are the nuances among the client's needs that provide the color, flavor, and texture of that particular client's universal investment needs, such as investing savings for retirement?

To gain an accurate and deep understanding of the client during the profiling stage, the adviser will benefit from understanding how behavioral tendencies may influence this step. We suggest keeping projection bias, the availability heuristic, and different performance expectations in mind and using our recommendations to counteract them.

Projection Bias. Projection bias refers to the tendency of individuals to

> understand qualitatively the directions in which their tastes will change, but systematically underestimate the magnitudes of these changes. Hence, they tend to exaggerate the degree to which their future tastes will resemble their current tastes. (Loewenstein, O'Donoghue, and Rabin 2003, p. 1210)

When advising individuals, advisers commonly assess the client's willingness and capacity to bear risk. This task is difficult for many reasons. One reason is that an individual's willingness to take on risk is influenced by recent market performance. Grable, Lytton, O'Neill, Joo, and Klock (2006) placed a financial risk–tolerance survey online and asked respondents to take it while answering a set of control questions that might reasonably be expected to influence risk taking (e.g., age, income, education). When analyzing what variables influenced risk tolerance, they found that price activity in the stock market over the previous week had a positive correlation with the risk assessment score.

Yao, Hanna, and Lindamood (2004) used data from the Federal Reserve Board's Survey of Consumer Finances to perform a similar study. Respondents were asked about their willingness to take on investment risk and were asked a large number of other questions about their financial affairs. Their self-reported willingness to take on risk was correlated with market movements in the years preceding the survey even after the authors controlled for a set of relevant variables.

> Recommendation 8: Be cautious about risk-tolerance assessments performed during or near periods of extreme market movements.

Ideally, an assessment of a client's willingness to bear investment risk will be undertaken several times throughout a client–adviser relationship, with assessments taking place during periods when the market is exhibiting different levels of volatility. If multiple assessments are not practical, we suggest scheduling the single assessment when the market is behaving in a neutral fashion.

Even finding a time of market neutrality in which to assess the client, however, is frequently impractical. So, if the initial assessment takes place during or near a period of extreme market performance (whether the volatility is on the upside or the downside), the adviser should encourage the client to think about periods of time in the past when market performance was different or times in the future when it will be different from recent experience. This process of encouragement could include reviewing portfolios with low levels of risk following large upswings in the market and, conversely, considering portfolios with high levels of risk following severe downturns.

We have no illusions about the ease of this task. Its inherent difficulty leads to our recommendation of interpreting the assessment results with caution. If the adviser maintains frequent dialogues on the subject of risk, then over time, both adviser and client will develop a clear sense of the client's true level of risk tolerance.

Availability Heuristic. Our discussion of projection bias in the context of risk assessment focuses on one aspect of risk (the client's willingness to endure the volatility that comes with stock market exposure). The availability heuristic is the tendency of individuals to base decisions on the evidence and considerations that are most easily accessible. On the one hand, if individuals are subject to the availability heuristic, they are willing to take on more market risk if gains from recent market activity are fresh in their minds. On the other hand, the availability heuristic suggests that individuals who still carry emotional scars from seeing their parents' retirement nest eggs wiped out in the technology wreck of 2000–2002 or from their own losses during the Great Recession of 2007–2009 will ascribe greater weight to capital preservation than growth through risk taking.

Advisers need to be concerned with more than short-term volatility when performing a risk assessment at the beginning of a client relationship. Clients who are saving for retirement will need to consider a broad set of risks—purchasing power risk, longevity risk, timing risk, consumption risk, and health risk:

- *Purchasing power risk.* The risk that inflation will eat away at the purchasing power of the client's portfolio.

- *Longevity risk.* The risk that the client will outlive his portfolio.

- *Timing risk.* The risk that the client will leave the workforce and begin drawing down the portfolio just as the market begins to perform extremely poorly or that the client will enter into an annuity arrangement when interest rates are extremely low.

- *Consumption risk.* The risk that the client will experience unavoidable expenses in retirement that were not anticipated when the client's retirement plan was being assembled.

- *Health risk.* The risk that the client will experience an adverse health event that will accelerate her separation from the workforce or prevent her from returning to the workforce should a return to work be necessary to support her desired standard of living.

These risks are real, and similar lists could be created for clients in any stage of life. Which risks most concern a particular client? In general, because of the availability heuristic, risks that are more important to clients will be those with which they are most familiar and those that are most salient or vivid. Factors that drive familiarity, salience, and vividness include how frequently the experience has occurred in the client's life, how recently it occurred, and whether it was personally experienced (or experienced by a close friend or relative).

> Recommendation 9: Probe the client about risks that the client may not have experienced but should consider.

An important task for the adviser is to have a discussion with the client about each risk and assess the applicability of each risk to the client. Furthermore, the adviser needs to evaluate whether the client's expressed level of concern about each risk is driven by the "availability" of that risk. We think particular attention should be paid to those risks that the adviser, in his professional judgment, believes to be relevant but to which the client gives short shrift because of the availability heuristic; that is, neither the client nor her friends or family members have experienced it. In this way, the adviser must be more than simply a survey taker.

A technique for making legitimate risks more "available" to clients is to archive stories of real clients or acquaintances that have experienced each risk. Preferably, this collection of stories will reflect a wide variety of client types so the adviser can use the type that most closely resembles the client currently being advised. Such stories about "people like me" may shift the real risk from a merely theoretical idea to a real possibility that requires steps to prevent it from happening.

Moreover, individuals can be subject to the availability heuristic with respect to past relationship experiences. In the arena of investment management, this bias can strain the client–adviser relationship and hamper the success of the adviser.

> Recommendation 10: Understand the client's past experiences working with advisers.

Past experiences, good and bad, may influence the client's perception of an adviser's intention or actions. Prospective clients often seek out a new adviser because of a poor relationship with a past adviser. Understanding what worked—and more importantly, what did not—in that relationship will help the adviser set expectations, communicate the asset management process the adviser will follow, and reduce the odds of disappointment down the road.

The adviser should engage in questioning and dialogue that uncover the specifics of client likes and dislikes in adviser behavior and services. We have found that many adviser–client relationships soured because of communication approaches and service expectations, so we recommend expanding the conversation beyond investment approach.

Differing Performance Expectations. At some point in the relationship, the client will ask, "How well am I doing?" The performance discussion is a hornet's nest that reveals a number of biases when broken open. For that reason, the last step in profiling is for the client and adviser to agree on performance expectations and the process for measuring progress.

Advisers tend to think of performance in terms of such gauges as return relative to a benchmark, risk-adjusted return, and absolute return. These measures can be thought of as objective measures of performance. Meeting performance objectives is not easy, but at least the adviser knows the benchmark, can track progress against it, and can declare victory or defeat after some set period of time.

A different perspective on the performance question is found in the literature of psychologists. They suggest that "a person's objective achievements often matter less than how those accomplishments are subjectively construed" (Medvec, Madey, and Gilovich 1995, p. 603). We find that at least three subjective performance benchmarks are relevant to the adviser–client performance discussion. They are as follows:

1. *Performance compared with that experienced by others.* Individuals sometimes talk about the performance of their investments with friends and family. We would not be surprised if the better the performance, the more they talk. If clients hear these conversations, they will naturally wonder how they are doing in comparison and allow the performance stories they hear to guide their expectations of their own investments.

Another source of comparisons is the popular financial press's frequent lionization of successful investors. This acclaim often takes the form of articles entitled something like "Secrets of the Five Best Mutual Fund Managers Alive Today." For at least some individuals, these five managers will be perceived to be a fair standard against which their advisers should be measured; thus, the performance of the five constitutes an expectation of performance.

Why do individuals latch on to the performance of others as a benchmark? One explanation is that this kind of comparison is an example of the availability heuristic at work.

2. *Performance compared with the client's original expectations.* Many financial media outlets periodically survey individuals about, for example, their long-term rate of return forecasts for the U.S. stock market. Our sense is that these forecasts tend to be much higher than appropriate. This result is consistent with the tendency toward optimism discussed earlier.

3. *Performance compared with what might have been.* Imagine an adviser has a young client who inherits a substantial number of shares in the company his father worked for his entire career. The father never sold the shares because of his emotional commitment to the company, and that emotional attachment was passed on to the adviser's client. With the step-up in cost basis upon the father's death, the client has no reason—beyond his emotional attachment—to hold on to the shares, so the adviser recommends a sale of the shares and the reallocation of the proceeds into a more diversified portfolio. In the two years that follow, the shares of the father's stock triple in value while the diversified portfolio beats the S&P 500 Index on an after-fee basis by 200 bps. Is the client content because his adviser has beaten the market, or does he spend his days imagining what he could have done with all his gains had he not diversified?

Wondering about what might have been is an example of "counterfactual thinking," and it can be destructive because it causes clients not to focus on their objective states and whether they are better off now than they were previously but, instead, to compare their current states with a different (nonrealized) state that would have been achieved by following the path not taken. A vivid example of counterfactual thinking is provided by Medvec et al. (1995) in a study of the behavior of Olympic medalists. An analysis of the athletes' behavior on the medal stand indicates that silver medalists appeared to be less happy than bronze medalists. Objectively, silver medalists were better off than the bronze medalists (and nonmedalists), but they appeared to be less satisfied—presumably because they were thinking of the gold medal that got away. The bronze medalists appeared to be happy that at least they had received something for their years of toil.

> Recommendation 11: Prepare an investment policy statement.

The importance of agreeing on and documenting the goal of the client–adviser relationship, the expectations of reaching the goal, and the measures by which progress will be measured cannot be overstated. A great tool for documenting this agreement is the investment policy statement (IPS). Creating and getting the client to agree to an IPS at the beginning of the relationship helps avoid surprises later on (see Recommendation 4).

The IPS allows the adviser to clearly lay out what services the firm provides, what the firm does and does not control, and where the adviser's time, expertise, and resources will thus be spent. Ideally, this information should establish the value and benefits a client gains from the relationship. In addition, the adviser and client can clearly establish in the IPS, before the emotions of the market or stories from others cloud comparisons, the performance expectations, benchmarks, measurement frequency, and gauges of success.

Discussions about the IPS are also an ideal time to highlight the unique needs of the client and how these needs may make the client different from others whom she may be tempted to use as a comparison. For example, an endowment may have an indefinite time horizon that allows it to invest in illiquid investments, but individuals who need money for retirement, college, or an emergency do not have the same flexibility. The adviser can point out the client's specific time horizon, tax situation, liquidity needs, legal or structural issues, and unique preferences.

The IPS should be revisited from time to time, especially if client expectations need to be reset because of market gyrations or changes in client circumstances. The IPS also serves as a place for documentation of and agreement on the rationale for proposed changes to the plan; this process will help avoid comparisons with what might have been. Too often, people view the IPS as only a legalistic document when, in fact, it also helps to address a client's emotional needs.

Making Recommendations

The adviser–client life cycle begins with the establishment of the relationship and then proceeds with an in-depth profile of the client by the adviser. At the conclusion of the profiling process, the adviser and client formulate an IPS. Then, it is time for the adviser to combine his professional expertise in the technical aspects of portfolio management with the knowledge of the client's situation and the IPS and to prepare specific recommendations for the client to act upon.

We think many advisers make a mistake at this phase of the relationship because they approach it as purely a technical problem to be solved. The technical problem is to "make the best recommendations possible." Are the best recommendations those that are technically proficient and demonstrate expertise but go unimplemented because they are not accepted by the client? We believe the goal of the adviser–client relationship is to improve the outcome for the client. Achieving that goal requires that the recommendations be expert but also take into account the likelihood of being enacted.

Ideally, no compromise would need to be made between expert advice and recommendations that can be implemented, but if forced to choose, we would prefer good advice that clients implement over great advice that gathers dust on a shelf. The ideal of not needing to compromise requires that the adviser, when preparing recommendations, be ever mindful of behavioral biases when presenting recommendations to the client. Particular biases to be wary of are regret avoidance, the endowment effect, the focus on unusual events, narrow framing, and mental accounting.

Regret Avoidance. "Eliminate emotion" is a standard prescription in innumerable how-to guides that purport to provide a path to better investing. We agree with those sentiments and have expressed them many times ourselves. We make the unremarkable observation, however, that nothing in our experience suggests that emotion is going away anytime soon. Emotion can, at best, be reduced. Even so-called quants, who delegate their trading decisions to machine-driven algorithms, are buffeted by emotional turmoil when their models do not work and they are asked (or ask themselves) whether they still have "faith" in their models.

Among the emotions that arise in the context of advising individuals on investing, *regret* is a particularly interesting one because of several characteristics:

- *Pervasive.* We would not be surprised if every investor had felt regret's sting—perhaps when she failed to carry out a buy trade and then watched the security's price soar. Even those who pride themselves on their cold-blooded objectivity and discipline have probably remarked at least once, in the face of poor performance, "If only I had ____."

- *Influential in decision making.* If regret were merely a pervasive emotion that individuals tended to deal with effectively, then it would not interest us for purposes of this article. Larrick and Boles (1995) found, however, that when individuals expect to receive feedback on a forgone alternative, they alter their behavior so as to avoid the feedback. In other words, the possibility of being faced with evidence that they would have been better off going down a different path is so painful that individuals take action to block the receipt of the feedback.

- *Frequently misleading.* In some realms of human activity, regret is a good thing. When we look back on decisions we have made, the pain of regret can encourage us to learn from the past and make better decisions in the future. The power of regret as a learning tool works well in a highly predictable world, but it does not work well in a world where randomness rules. Statman (2002) opined that "regret often teaches us the wrong lesson in the stock market, where randomness and luck rule" (p. 8).

- *Painful.* Regret hurts, so individuals who feel regret may naturally try to make it go away by blaming someone else. In the context of the adviser–client relationship, the client may blame the adviser.

The world of investment advice is fruitful ground for generating regret. First of all, investing provides many opportunities for regret. Perfectly reasonable and well-intentioned recommendations go wrong all the time, and each mistake creates regret. Second, clear alternatives exist for each decision. The opportunity for feedback is present in probably all investing decisions. A plausible alternative for each decision is simply not to do it. Thus, each decision evaluated solely on the basis of the rate of return it generated can be compared with a reference point of 0 percent. Or if the investor is choosing between investing in Security A and in Security B, then the security not chosen provides a clear benchmark for comparing results. Finally, in the world of investing, measurement is easy. For regret to influence decision making, the outcome of the decision has to be known; feedback of some form as to the outcome of the decision has to be possible. When it comes to investing, data on the success of alternatives are often easily available to the client.

> Recommendation 12: Make sure the client "buys into" each recommendation.

Recommendation 12 seems ridiculously obvious. After all, in a nondiscretionary relationship, as a matter of law, the adviser is not the decision maker. The client agreement or buy-in that we recommend, however, is something deeper and more meaningful than the type of consent that is usually obtained. We suggest creating a sense of joint ownership by bringing the client close to the decision-making process. Giving clients choices on various product types that may achieve the same goal enables them to make more decisions, which promotes an increased level of client acceptance of recommendations.

We have also found that clients can be resistant in areas with which they have little familiarity. Increasing clients' awareness of the investments being recommended through education can thus help client buy-in, although this approach may take several meetings and explanations.

After expending the energy to present and explain recommendations to a client, an adviser may feel his job is done, but seeking out client objections or questions and addressing them can solidify client buy-in. Therefore, advisers should always take time to check with clients.

We advise against ever talking a client into a recommendation with which the client is not comfortable. It is always better to wait and seek opportunities for more education and dialogue rather than to proceed and risk client regret.

> Recommendation 13: The adviser's recommendations should take into account the client's past investment experiences.

We recommended earlier that investment advisers take an investment history of their clients, just as physicians take a medical history of their patients. In profiling, the motivation for this history is typically to gauge the client's level of sophistication and risk tolerance. An additional reason for collecting this history, however—a reason we think is underappreciated—is that the past history of the client will influence how current recommendations are viewed. Gilovich (1981) explains this process:

> We do not view each new decision or dilemma as entirely novel. Rather, we often liken new dilemmas to past events or decisions from which useful information, strategies, and courses of action can be gleaned. That is, we form associations between existing circumstances and past situations and are influenced by what we consider to be the implications of those past events. . . . This process can greatly benefit effective decision making, because it brings additional information to bear on the decision analysis and thus fills in some of the uncertainty surrounding the decision. However, this process is also fraught with potential costs, since the associations between existing circumstances and past events can sometimes be inappropriate and misleading. (p. 797)

Advisers who want to recommend an investment that is similar to something that was disastrous for the client in the past will have a tough task. But the effect of past experience can also work in favor of the adviser; one approach to creating client buy-in to a recommendation is to review the client's history and couch the recommendation in terms of a successful past investment.

The Endowment Effect. The theory of the endowment effect (proposed by Thaler 1980) posits that simply owning an item causes individuals to value that item more than similar items they do not own. Kahneman, Knetsch, and Thaler (1990) conducted a classic experiment showing this effect. Some individuals in a group were given a mug, and others were not. Those with the mugs were asked how much they were willing to sell the mugs for, and those without the mugs were asked how much they were willing to pay for a mug. In two separate experiments conducted, the median prices for the sellers were $7.12 and $7.00 whereas the median prices for the buyers were $3.12 and $3.50.

This effect is important for advisers to understand because often clients arrive with already existing portfolios—in many cases, portfolios that the client was responsible for creating. The adviser may have difficulty convincing clients to part with these holdings because of the endowment effect.

> Recommendation 14: Understand the ownership history of the client's existing investments.

The adviser needs to understand the ownership history of any existing components of the client's portfolio. One particular facet to focus on is the length of time a security in the portfolio has been owned. In experiments using trivial items such as key chains and mugs, Strahilevitz and Loewenstein (1998) found that length of ownership is positively correlated with the price at which subjects are willing to sell an item. Anecdotal evidence suggests the same applies to investors: The longer a security is held, the more emotionally attached the investor becomes and the less willing the investor is to part with it, irrespective of the investment merits for doing so.

Understanding the ownership history of a portfolio can help advisers plan the delivery of their recommendations. For example, an adviser should be prepared to spend substantial time explaining the rationale for and obtaining client buy-in for a recommended sale of long-held positions. The adviser may want to prepare several approaches for this discussion in case the client has difficulty overcoming the endowment effect. In this area, we find that sharing stories of other clients who have successfully reduced risk, constructed improved portfolios, or had better outcomes by changing their portfolios may help clients visualize a different path and overcome the endowment effect.

One of the large risks related to the endowment effect that we see facing clients is their tendency to have excessively large portions of their portfolios invested in a single stock or industry. This concentration exists not only for wealthy clients (e.g., former company executives) but also for clients with smaller portfolios. For example, the largest asset in 401(k) plans continues to be company stock, despite the well-publicized losses employees experienced at companies such as Enron Corporation, WorldCom, Bear Stearns, and Lehman Brothers.

> Recommendation 15: Trim concentrated positions over time.

If a client holds a large position in a single stock, a recommendation to immediately sell all the shares will often be unsuccessful. The endowment effect can be particularly strong in these situations because the concentration is often a result of past periods of strong stock performance. We recommend breaking the sell decision down into increments for two reasons.

First, this approach will reduce regret. Unloading an entire position at once carries the risk of major regret if the stock performs strongly subsequent to the sale. Unloading through several smaller decisions helps lessen the chance of regret.

Second, spreading the sale out over time lessens the emotional pain of taxes. The prospect of giving up some of the gain by paying taxes can amplify the endowment effect. Smaller sales over time can lessen the tax burden at any given point, and pushing portions of the tax liability into future years can ease the emotional pain of selling.

In addition, we suggest that advisers continue to point out the risks of a concentrated position to dilute the value associated with it. In many cases, the adviser can find examples of similar companies to illustrate this—companies that seemed safe at one time but for some reason (e.g., fraud, mismanagement, technical obsolescence, product replacement) proved very risky.

If we assume that no complicated tax issues exist, is this gradualist approach to reducing concentrated positions at odds with good advice? Stated more harshly, does pandering to the emotional whims of the client compromise the professional standards to which the adviser is held?

Our answer is no. One interpretation of the adviser's job is to maximize long-term wealth subject to considerations of risk. Another interpretation is to maximize *utility*. This latter and more expansive view of the adviser's role requires recognition that

> the long term is not where life is lived. Utility cannot be divorced from emotion, and emotions are triggered by changes. A theory of choice that completely ignores feelings such as the pain of losses and the regret of mistakes is not only descriptively unrealistic, it also leads to prescriptions that do not maximize the utility of outcomes as they are actually experienced. . . . (Kahneman 2003, p. 1457)

Focus on Unusual Events. Advisers want an accurate history of a current portfolio. Typically, however, individuals tend to display a bias toward recalling those events that were the most unusual. Morewedge, Gilbert, and Wilson (2005) asked subway passengers to recall a past occasion when they missed a train and what resulted and also to predict their reaction if they miss a train in the future. Those who chose to recall a single occasion recalled the worst one and predicted their experience would be equally bad if they missed a train in the future.

> Recommendation 16: Do not assume the client's version of the portfolio's history is accurate.

Advisers should always seek to uncover and verify the history that a client remembers. The adviser can probe into the rationale for purchases/sales and specifics on the time period of purchases/sales. Clients may not recall all the facts or time lines, but this questioning can help the adviser develop the proper pattern of facts and clarify the client's recollection. We have seen, for example, a client perceiving a past real estate investment as having worked out well. After further exploration, however, the client recalled that he had overlooked the maintenance and interest costs. When these facts were pointed out, the client's perception changed.

This bias can be a particular problem in situations in which an adviser wishes to recommend an instrument that is perceived by the client to be unusual or exotic and then the investment does not work out over time. It will stick out in the client's mind for a long time and potentially color future interactions between the client and adviser. An adviser might ask the client if a recommendation is similar to some investment strategy the client followed in the past. The client may have a vivid memory of a past experience that could taint her perception—for better or worse—of the current recommendation. To reinforce the benefits of the current recommendation, the adviser should remind the client of the broad context in which past recommendations were made. This approach can improve the client's memory, increase the accuracy of the client's version of history, and shift the focus from an isolated recollection.

Narrow Framing. Tversky and Kahneman (1981) introduced the concept of "framing"—that is, the idea that the context in which a decision is made influences the choice of the decision maker. Kahneman and Lovallo (1993) later introduced the concept of narrow framing, in which an individual faced with a decision evaluates that decision in isolation from other decisions. An example of a narrow frame is the investor who evaluates each trading decision in isolation, without considering the rest of the portfolio. In a broad frame, the investor not only evaluates a trade on its own merits but also takes into account the trade's effect on the rest of the portfolio.

Clients who adopt narrow frames create problems for investment advisers (as well as for themselves if they choose to be self-directed and make their own decisions). The reason is that most advisers prefer to manage at the portfolio level (i.e., they want to be evaluated on how the portfolio as a whole performs in comparison with a relevant benchmark). The client who adopts a narrow frame will tend to evaluate each trade individually and is likely to be unimpressed by the adviser who recommends trades that are primarily motivated by a desire to maintain or enhance diversification in the overall portfolio.

There are competing, but not mutually exclusive, explanations for why individuals exhibit narrow frames. Two that are relevant for our topic are regret avoidance and intuitive decision making.

- *Regret avoidance.* Barberis, Huang, and Thaler (2006) suggested that when the tendency toward regret is high, it can lead to narrow framing. Consider the investor who frets over the performance of each and every security in a portfolio. This individual will naturally be unable, or at least find it difficult, to take a portfolio view.

- *Intuitive decision making.* Kahneman (2003) suggested that narrow framing can arise when individuals make intuitive, spontaneous decisions. The spontaneous decision is influenced by evidence and reasoning processes that are quickly made available to the individual. We believe that the intuition of most people is to look at an investment decision in isolation and to consider its effect on the broader portfolio only after thoughtful deliberation.

> Recommendation 17: Bundle recommendations.

Narrow frames are the enemy of diversification. Bundling recommendations combats narrow frames and benefits the client in two ways.

First, bundling recommendations creates an educational opportunity. Explaining to the client how a set of recommendations works as a unified set is easier when the recommendations are bundled together. Bundling also helps show the client the complexity of the portfolio-building task (see Recommendation 21).

Second, bundling recommendations combats another common bias—the disposition effect. Shefrin and Statman (1985) first documented the reluctance of individual investors to sell securities if the investors would have to recognize a loss on them (thanks to individuals' aversion to losses) and investors' willingness to sell securities that have increased in value. They termed this tendency the "disposition effect." Kumar and Lim (2008), using actual investor data, found that those who grouped trades together were less prone to the disposition effect and built more diversified portfolios.

Mental Accounting. Thaler (1999) defined mental accounting as a "set of cognitive operations used by individuals and households to organize, evaluate, and keep track of financial activities." Mental accounting is relevant in the context of investment management because money is not fungible across accounts. For example, if an individual unexpectedly finds $20 on the sidewalk, he may well be more likely to spend that $20 on a self-indulgent, impetuous expenditure than if the $20 came out of his next paycheck. The sidewalk money can be thought of as being in the "windfall" account, which is governed by different rules from those governing the "serious" account represented by the paycheck.

> Recommendation 18: Segregate "emotional" investments from the rest of the portfolio.

Emotional investments are those to which the client has a strong emotional attachment that biases the client's objectivity. These attachments can develop for many reasons, including inheritance, impact that a company's products have had on the client (e.g., a medical device or treatment that helped a family member), or social welfare. For investments to which the client has an emotional attachment, any discussion of the *merits* of the investment can strain the relationship. Therefore, as long as the amount in the investment is a relatively small percentage of the portfolio and does not put the portfolio at risk, segregating this investment into its own account can often be fruitful. This approach allows the adviser to focus on adding value to areas of the portfolio in which it will be welcomed. The initial segregation should not be used, therefore, as a reason to avoid revisiting the situation and continuing attempts to educate the client.

Evaluating Performance and Renewing the Relationship

Good performance cures a remarkable variety of ills, so if performance were always stellar, many of the emotional pitfalls discussed in the previous sections would not be a cause of concern for the competent adviser. Of course, performance is not always stellar. In fact, periods of poor performance are inevitable. For example, one study of equity mutual funds found that 99 percent of the top-quartile funds for the entire 1998–2007 period had at least one year in which the fund finished in the bottom half of its peer group and 95 percent had at least two years of such performance. In fact, 83 percent had at least one year in which the fund finished in the *bottom quartile.*[2]

The point in the relationship when the client and adviser are evaluating performance and renewing the relationship is a natural time to review some of the assumptions and expectations that were set at the beginning of the relationship. The adviser has learned about the client's background and preferences, and the client has experienced the adviser's process and communication style, as well as seen more of the market's performance. In addition, the client's life situation and circumstances may have changed. This is an appropriate time to

---

[2]Schwab Center for Financial Research.

see if expectations are being met, to reset them if necessary, and to conduct further client profiling, albeit not as extensive as the initial profiling. Continued profiling will help uncover any new information that can be used to deepen the relationship. Clients may fall prey to behavioral traps as time passes even if signs of the biases were not present at the beginning of the relationship. For this reason, the adviser should always be looking for signs of the behavior we have mentioned. Recommendations initially suggested may need to be revisited, or new suggestions may need to be made. In addition to the biases already described, a time of review may reveal hindsight bias, outcome bias, and myopic loss aversion.

Hindsight Bias. Advisers have a difficult job because their performance is judged after the fact and *ex post* evaluations are often clouded by hindsight bias—that is, the tendency for people with knowledge of what happened to have an inappropriately strong belief that they would have predicted that outcome. Hindsight bias can be thought of as an offshoot of the availability heuristic. As the client reviews what has happened since the relationship began, "events that actually occurred are easier to imagine than counterfactual events that did not" (Camerer and Loewenstein 2004, p. 10). That is, clients may think the outcome that occurred was the only possible outcome and should have been foreseen by the adviser.

Because of this selective interpretation of history, Kahneman and Riepe (1998) concluded,

> Events that the best-informed experts did not anticipate often appear almost inevitable after they occur. Financial punditry provides an unending source of examples. Within an hour of the market closing every day, experts can be heard on the radio explaining with high confidence why the market acted as it did. A listener could well draw the incorrect inference that the behavior of the market was so reasonable that it could have been predicted earlier in the day. (p. 55)

Worse for the adviser is the fact that, as shown by experiments by Fischhoff (1975), those influenced by hindsight bias are not even aware it is happening.

Hawkins and Hastie (1990) suggested that hindsight bias is particularly likely in at least two situations that are present in financial advice:

1. *The event has a well-defined alternative outcome.* Whether a client evaluates the adviser against a benchmark, against peers, or on the basis of absolute returns, *ex post* performance is clear cut.

2. *The outcome has emotional or moral significance.* Anyone who has ever worked with an individual investor will attest to the emotion that is often present when making financial decisions and discussing subsequent outcomes.

> Recommendation 19: Convey the complexity of the task.

The market and economic dynamics, together with the multitude of product choices available, create a complex environment with many decision points for an adviser. Popular media and the wide availability of market information have led many investors to minimize the complexity of the investment task. The adviser can convey the complexity of the task by creating an understanding of the current situation and the broad array of alternative choices before making final recommendations to the client. The adviser can illustrate for the client the steps in the analysis used to arrive at the recommendations. The firm philosophy and process (see Recommendation 1) can and should be revisited at this point.

Outcome Bias. A relative of hindsight bias is outcome bias—inappropriately taking the known outcomes of a decision into account when evaluating the quality of the decision. Baron and Hershey (1988) tested for the existence of outcome bias in the realm of laypeople evaluating medical decisions made by doctors. In their experiment, the authors provided subjects with a description of several situations faced by a doctor treating a patient. Each situation was described in two ways. In the first way, the situation was described from the standpoint of what the doctor knew (i.e., the facts and circumstances of the case, the treatment options), the decision made by the doctor, and the fact that the outcome was successful. The second method of description was identical to the first description except that the outcome was described as being a failure. The task assigned to the subjects was to rate the quality of the decision.

In 44 percent of the situations rated by subjects, the "success" version was rated as having been a high-quality decision compared with such a rating in only 9 percent in the "failure" situations. In 46 percent of the situations rated, the subjects saw no difference in decision quality between the "success" and "failure" versions.

What is particularly interesting in this study is that when subjects were asked whether they should have taken into account the outcome when evaluating the decision quality, 88 percent said they should not; yet, an analysis of the subjects showed that 75 percent did take the outcome into account.

> Recommendation 20: Continually reinforce investment philosophy and process.

As clients experience a variety of outcomes in various periods, they may start to second-guess the adviser or lose confidence in the adviser's recommendations. To help counteract this outcome bias, reinforcement of the firm's investment philosophy and process should continue throughout the relationship. The adviser should emphasize the logic of the philosophy and process and how they were developed. The adviser should communicate that the investment approach is designed to work most of the time, shifting the odds in favor of the client over the long term, but that the approach cannot be expected to work in all environments (refer to Recommendation 3).

Myopic Loss Aversion. Loss aversion, first documented by Kahneman and Tversky (1979), is the tendency of individuals to allocate more weight to losses than to gains of an equal magnitude (e.g., losing \$100 hurts more than the pleasure of gaining \$100 is enjoyed). Various studies have estimated that for most people, the pain from a loss of X dollar amount is twice as strong the pleasure of a gain of the same dollar amount (see also Tversky and Kahneman 1992; Kahneman et al. 1990).

Benartzi and Thaler (1995) pioneered the study of *myopic* loss aversion, which is loss aversion combined with a tendency to evaluate results over short time periods. Clients with myopic loss aversion create problems for advisers who recommend a strategic asset allocation tilted toward equities. These clients will tend to evaluate the performance of their equity exposures over inappropriately short periods of time and to prefer more and more conservative investments, which may be inconsistent with what an objective analysis suggests they need.

Thaler, Tversky, Kahneman, and Schwartz (1997) conducted an experiment designed to test these tendencies. Subjects were told they were portfolio managers whose task was to allocate dollars between Fund A and Fund B. Subjects were not told that the return and risk characteristics of Fund A were modeled after the historical performance of five-year bonds and that Fund B was given the characteristics of a capitalization-weighted stock index. Each subject was to invest for 200 periods.

Three groups of subjects were created. In Group 1, each subject made an allocation decision between Funds A and B for each of the 200 periods. In Group 2, the subjects were allowed to make an allocation decision once every 8 periods (i.e., they were told that when they made an allocation decision, they would have to stick with it for 8 periods). In Group 3, subjects had to stick with their allocations for 40 periods.

After each decision, the subjects received feedback on how their portfolios were performing. After all 200 periods had passed, subjects in all three groups were asked to make an allocation decision between Funds A and B that would last for the next 400 periods.

Group 1 subjects (who received the most feedback) allocated roughly twice as much to Fund A, which was modeled after the performance of bonds, compared with subjects in Groups 2 and 3. Group 1 thus exhibited myopic loss aversion. Moreover, analysis revealed that the subjects in Group 1 were not aware of the myopic loss aversion. This finding is consistent with the results of many studies on other types of biases: Individuals committing the error are often unaware that they are doing so.

What is particularly intriguing about myopic loss aversion is that it appears to be hardwired into the human brain. Shiv, Loewenstein, Bechara, Damasio, and Damasio (2005) conducted an experiment similar in spirit to that of Thaler et al. (1997). The innovation of Shiv et al. was to compare the results of 19 individuals who had normal brains with a group of 15 individuals who each had "chronic and stable focal lesions in specific components of a neural circuitry that has been shown to be critical for the processing of emotions" (p. 436).

The experiment consisted of 20 rounds. In each round, the individual faced a decision to invest or to not invest. The optimal strategy was to invest each time.

The brain-damaged individuals invested about 84 percent of the rounds, and this percentage was stable from Round 1 through Round 20. The normal patients invested only about 58 percent of the time overall, and their decision making got steadily more conservative over time.

> Recommendation 21: Adopt broad frames when discussing performance.

Clients with myopic loss aversion and a narrow frame will tend to evaluate performance one security at a time and view performance as simply price sold minus price paid. The adviser can broaden the frame by getting the client to think about performance in more comprehensive ways. For example, for the taxable investor, taking into account after-tax returns is a good idea. Considering taxes justifies the sensible practice of selling some securities at a loss to offset realized gains.

Broadening the frame by including risk and/or risk-adjusted return can also be effective. This approach has the benefit of keeping clients focused on risk, which an adviser has greater ability to influence than return.

Another way to broaden the frame is to define performance not simply as percentage gains and losses but also as growth in dollars toward a goal or an increase in wealth.

Reducing myopic loss aversion while broadening the frame of reference in performance review can also be accomplished by lengthening the evaluation period. This can be done in client reporting or in discussions with clients. Continually reinforcing the need to avoid noise in the marketplace over the short term and refocusing the client on longer, more meaningful periods are part of reducing myopic loss aversion.

Finally, we are often surprised by the number of clients who are not aware of compounding effects or total return. In these cases, some baseline explanations may help, especially for clients who are overly focused on price moves or yield.

Conclusion

The business of advising individuals on their investments is ultimately about improving outcomes for clients. One aspect of "outcome" is risk-adjusted return for the client over the long term. Therefore, of course, an adviser naturally needs expertise in the technical aspects of how to increase the odds of achieving risk-adjusted returns over the long term. The outcome will not be realized, however, unless the advice is acted upon and the client sticks with the advice over time. Advisers who use the findings of behavioral finance to develop a better understanding of the lens through which their efforts are viewed by clients stand a better chance of their clients understanding their strategy and approach, agreeing to implement that approach in a timely manner, and sticking with that approach during the inevitable periods of poor performance.

Bryan Olson, CFA, is senior vice president at Charles Schwab & Co., Boston.

Mark W. Riepe, CFA, is senior vice president at the Schwab Center for Financial Research, Charles Schwab & Co., and president of Charles Schwab Investment Advisory, San Francisco.

REFERENCES

Barberis, Nicholas, Ming Huang, and Richard H. Thaler. 2006. "Individual Preferences, Monetary Gambles, and Stock Market Participation: A Case for Narrow Framing." *American Economic Review*, vol. 96, no. 4 (September):1069–1090.

Baron, Jonathan, and John C. Hershey. 1988. "Outcome Bias in Decision Evaluation." *Journal of Personality and Social Psychology*, vol. 54, no. 4 (April):569–579.

Benartzi, Shlomo, and Richard Thaler. 1995. "Myopic Loss Aversion and the Equity Premium Puzzle." *Quarterly Journal of Economics*, vol. 110, no. 1 (February):73–92.

Bohnet, Iris, Fiona Greig, Benedikt Herrmann, and Richard Zeckhauser. 2008. "Betrayal Aversion: Evidence from Brazil, China, Oman, Switzerland, Turkey, and the United States." *American Economic Review*, vol. 98, no. 1 (March):294–310.

Camerer, Colin F., and George Loewenstein. 2004. "Behavioral Economics: Past, Present, Future." In *Advances in Behavioral Economics*. Edited by Colin F. Camerer, George Loewenstein, and Matthew Rabin. Princeton, NJ: Princeton University Press.

Cerulli Associates. 2007. *Cerulli Quantitative Update: Managed Accounts 2007.* Boston: Cerulli Associates.

Fischhoff, Baruch. 1975. "Hindsight (Not Equal to) Foresight: The Effect of Outcome Knowledge on Judgment under Uncertainty." *Journal of Experimental Psychology: Human Perception and Performance*, vol. 1, no. 3 (August):288–299.

Gilovich, Thomas. 1981. "Seeing the Past in the Present: The Effect of Associations to Familiar Events on Judgments and Decisions." *Journal of Personality and Social Psychology*, vol. 40:797–808.

Grable, John, Ruth H. Lytton, Barbara O'Neill, So-Hyun Joo, and Derek Klock. 2006. "Risk Tolerance, Projection Bias, Vividness, and Equity Prices." *Journal of Investing*, vol. 15, no. 2 (Summer):68–74.

Hawkins, Scott A., and Reid Hastie. 1990. "Hindsight: Biased Judgments of Past Events after the Outcomes Are Known." *Psychological Bulletin*, vol. 107, no. 3 (May):311–327.

Kahneman, Daniel. 2003. "Maps of Bounded Rationality: Psychology for Behavioral Economics." *American Economic Review*, vol. 93, no. 5 (December):1449–1475.

Kahneman, Daniel, and Daniel Lovallo. 1993. "Timid Choices and Bold Forecasts: A Cognitive Perspective on Risk Taking." *Management Science*, vol. 39, no. 1 (January):17–31.

Kahneman, Daniel, and Mark W. Riepe. 1998. "Aspects of Investor Psychology." *Journal of Portfolio Management*, vol. 24, no. 4 (Summer):52–65.

Kahneman, Daniel, and Amos Tversky. 1979. "Prospect Theory: An Analysis of Decisions under Risk." *Econometrica*, vol. 47, no. 2 (March):263–291.

Kahneman, Daniel, Jack L. Knetsch, and Richard H. Thaler. 1990. "Experimental Tests of the Endowment Effect and the Coase Theorem." *Journal of Political Economy*, vol. 98, no. 6 (December):1325–1348.

Kumar, Alok, and Sonya Seongyeon Lim. 2008. "How Do Decision Frames Influence the Stock Investment Choices of Individual Investors?" *Management Science*, vol. 54, no. 6 (June):1052–1064.

Langer, Ellen J. 1975. "The Illusion of Control." *Journal of Personality and Social Psychology*, vol. 32, no. 2 (August):311–328.

Larrick, Richard P., and Terry L. Boles. 1995. "Avoiding Regret in Decisions with Feedback: A Negotiation Example." *Organizational Behavior and Human Decision Processes*, vol. 63, no. 1 (July):87–97.

Loewenstein, George, Ted O'Donoghue, and Matthew Rabin. 2003. "Projection Bias in Predicting Future Utility." *Quarterly Journal of Economics*, vol. 118, no. 4 (November):1209–1248.

Medvec, Victoria Husted, Scott F. Madey, and Thomas Gilovich. 1995. "When Less Is More: Counterfactual Thinking and Satisfaction among Olympic Medalists." *Journal of Personality and Social Psychology*, vol. 69, no. 4 (October):603–610.

Moore, Don A., Terri R. Kurtzberg, Craig R. Fox, and Max H. Bazerman. 1999. "Positive Illusions and Forecasting Errors in Mutual Fund Investment Decisions." *Organizational Behavior and Human Decision Processes*, vol. 79, no. 2 (August):95–114.

Morewedge, Carrie K., Daniel T. Gilbert, and Timothy D. Wilson. 2005. "The Least Likely of Times: How Remembering the Past Biases Forecasts of the Future." *Psychological Science*, vol. 16, no. 8 (August):626–630.

Shefrin, Hersh M., and Meir Statman. 1985. "The Disposition to Sell Winners Too Early and Ride Losers Too Long." *Journal of Finance*, vol. 40, no. 3 (July):777–790.

Shiv, Baba, George Loewenstein, Antoine Bechara, Hanna Damasio, and Antonio R. Damasio. 2005. "Investment Behavior and the Negative Side of Emotion." *Psychological Science*, vol. 16, no. 6 (June):435–439.

Statman, Meir. 2002. "Financial Physicians." In *Investment Counseling for Private Clients IV*. Charlottesville, VA: Association for Investment Management and Research.

Strahilevitz, Michal A., and George Loewenstein. 1998. "The Effect of Ownership History on the Valuation of Objects." *Journal of Consumer Research*, vol. 25, no. 3 (December):276–289.

Strickland, Lloyd H., Roy J. Lewicki, and Arnold M. Katz. 1966. "Temporal Orientation and Perceived Control as Determinants of Risk-Taking." *Journal of Experimental Social Psychology*, vol. 2, no. 2 (April):143–151.

Thaler, Richard H. 1980. "Toward a Positive Theory of Consumer Choice." *Journal of Economic Behavior & Organization*, vol. 1, no. 1:39–60.

———. 1999. "Mental Accounting Matters." *Journal of Behavioral Decision Making*, vol. 12, no. 3 (September):183–206.

Thaler, Richard, Amos Tversky, Daniel Kahneman, and Alan Schwartz. 1997. "The Effect of Myopia and Loss Aversion on Risk Taking: An Experimental Test." *Quarterly Journal of Economics*, vol. 112, no. 2 (May):647–661.

Tversky, Amos, and Daniel Kahneman. 1981. "The Framing of Decisions and the Psychology of Choice." *Science*, vol. 211, no. 4481 (January):453–458.

———. 1992. "Advances in Prospect Theory: Cumulative Representation of Uncertainty." *Journal of Risk and Uncertainty*, vol. 5, no. 4 (October):297–323.

Yao, Rui, Sherman D. Hanna, and Suzanne Lindamood. 2004. "Changes in Financial Risk Tolerance, 1983–2001." *Financial Services Review*, vol. 13, no. 4 (Winter):249–266.

The Sociology of Markets

Michael J. Mauboussin

I have titled this presentation "The Sociology of Markets" to express the idea that the rise and fall of financial institutions leave an indelible imprint on asset prices. I will expand on this conclusion by breaking the discussion into three parts.

First, I will ask the question, Do financial institutions matter? Interestingly, the theoretical answer is no, but of course, I will argue that the practical answer is yes. Second, I will provide three specific case studies to show how institutions have mattered in the past. Finally, and I think most importantly, I will consider where we might go from here—that is, where the money flows are, what the incentives look like, and what those two things may mean for future asset prices.

Do Financial Institutions Matter?

In Franklin Allen's presidential address to the American Finance Association in 2001, he pointed out what he thought was a puzzling dichotomy: In corporate finance, the idea of agency theory is well understood and has been explored quite extensively for about 75 years, beginning with Berle and Means (1932) and certainly well codified with Jensen and Meckling (1976). Yet, agency theory is nearly absent in asset-pricing theory. Although a few recent papers have been written on the topic (Allen 2001; Cornell and Roll 2005), they are overwhelmed by the number of papers that assume away the role of institutions and asset pricing.

Putting It in Context

What triggered you to write this piece? And how do you think it should be helpful to professional investment practitioners?

Classic finance theory suggests that the demand curve for stocks is nearly horizontal, and hence financial institutions do not matter. But what we observe from the real world is that demand curves are downward sloping and that institutions do matter. This assertion is backed by three case studies, each of which shows that demand by a specific group of institutions (large mutual fund companies, Asian central banks, and hedge funds) had an impact on asset returns and valuation.

This article is helpful for investors because it underscores the importance of understanding who has the money, how their incentives drive where they invest, and what that means for asset prices. Classic theory overlooks this very real-world consideration.

This presentation comes from the Next Generation Asset Management conference held in Washington, DC, on 12–13 June 2008.

Reprinted with permission from CFA Institute Conference Proceedings Quarterly, *vol. 26, no. 1 (March 2009):21–28.*

Importantly, a handful of individuals, including John Bogle, Charles Ellis, and David Swensen, have been vocal in pointing out that agents, professional money managers and others, have incentives that may have led to some questionable behaviors, but to the best of my knowledge, none of them has discussed specifically the role and implications of agents on asset pricing.

So, the question is: Why haven't financial institutions and related agency cost issues been central to asset-pricing theory? Several very good reasons can be found. The first reason is that until fairly recently, no principal–agent problem existed. As recently as 1980, individuals owned almost three-quarters of all stocks in the United States. Only recently have institutions come to own a majority of that asset class. When asset-pricing theory was being developed in the 1950s and 1960s, individuals absolutely dominated agents. Agency theory was not in the asset-pricing models because agents basically were not in the picture.

The existence of efficient markets, or the acceptance of the efficient market hypothesis (EMH), can be explained in two standard ways. The first is mean–variance efficiency. Rational investors understand their preferences and the distribution of asset prices. They rationally trade off risk and reward. Most academics and practitioners, however, do not strictly believe the assumptions of the EMH, so the second way to explain it is to recognize the absence of arbitrage opportunities, which allows one to relax the assumption of investor rationality. All that is really needed to achieve market efficiency is a handful of smart arbitrageurs who can find price-to-value gaps and then close those gaps and generate some small returns in the process. But it is believed that the benefits they enjoy are roughly equal to the costs they incur.

Both of these approaches lead to efficient asset pricing. Almost all the literature in asset pricing—the capital asset pricing model, Black–Scholes options pricing, the Modigliani and Miller invariance proposition—uses one or the other of these approaches as a foundation for their arguments. And note that under these models, agents do not matter.

But times change. First, agency theory is relevant because agents now control the market, and not surprisingly, agents have very different incentives in many cases from the ones the principals have. And because the investment management business is close to a zero-sum game, the more the agent extracts, the lower the return for the principal. Second, as is well known, a number of challenges have been raised against classical theory, some going so far as to question the practical usefulness of some of these approaches.

Taken together, these two factors argue that financial institutions absolutely do matter, just as Allen argued in his speech in 2001. As a result, one needs to understand where the money is, who will invest it, and what the incentives look like all around.

Case Studies

Before I delve into the case studies, I need to spend a moment on theory. One of the crucial implications of mean–variance analysis and the absence of arbitrage opportunities is a nearly horizontal demand curve for stocks. The rationale is very straightforward from a theoretical perspective: For a stock, price equals the present value of future cash flows. If price deviates from that value, arbitrageurs will step in and bring it back into line. In the real world, however, demand curves are downward sloping. The key point is that if demand curves are downward sloping, then demand shocks will change asset prices. In fact, importantly, they may lead to asset prices that are different from the present value of future cash flows.

Case 1. The first case study is the story of large institutions and large-capitalization stocks. Early 1980s research showed that from 1926 to 1979, small-cap stocks outperformed large-cap stocks by about 400 bps annually (Banz 1981). This was the first in-depth research showing that small caps outperformed large caps. This finding, of course, did not hold for the 1980s or the 1990s; large-cap stocks trounced small-cap stocks during those two decades. Gompers and Metrick (2001) noted a large increase of flows into mutual funds beginning in the early to mid-1980s. Between 1980 and 2000, large institutions effectively doubled their market share.

How did the large institutions invest the money? Not surprisingly, they showed a preference for large-cap stocks that were liquid. In addition, large-cap stocks were cheap in the early 1980s. Large institutions realized that investment management is a scalable business. In fact, estimates suggest that large fund groups have expense-to-asset ratios that are roughly 40 percent lower than those of smaller funds. Gompers and Metrick argued that these institutions created a demand shock that, combined with this downward-sloping demand curve for stocks, drove the prices of large-cap stocks higher. For the 20 years ended 1999, large-cap stocks outperformed small-cap stocks by about 430 bps (17.6 percent versus 13.3 percent) annually. The Gompers and Metrick analysis suggests that up to 230 bps of that outperformance is attributable to that flow into large institutions.

Not surprisingly, this asset price performance also had very clear implications for valuation. The forward P/E for the large-cap-dominated S&P 500 Index ended the 1990s at a multiple roughly four times higher than where it started in 1980 and more than two times the average multiple over that same period, as shown in **Figure 1**. Said differently, a substantial part of the total return of large caps in the 1980s and 1990s is attributable to multiple expansion.

Figure 1.   Value Line Median and S&P 500 Forward P/E, 1980–2000

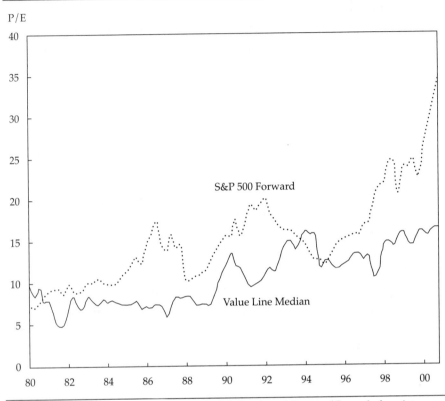

Sources: Based on data from Value Line, Standard & Poor's, and Raymond James & Associates.

Meanwhile, the small- and mid-cap universe, represented in the figure by the Value Line median multiple, ended the two decades with a P/E multiple about 30–40 percent higher than where it started, which is not bad but certainly is not as dramatic as for large caps. At the peak of the NASDAQ in March 2000, the S&P 500 forward-looking multiple was about 26, but the Value Line median P/E in March 2000 was just 12.7. Thus, of the 1,700 Value Line companies with earnings, about 850 companies had a multiple of 12.7 or lower. At that point, it was truly a tale of two markets.

Case 2. If the 1980s and 1990s were the decades of the mutual fund, the 2000s have certainly been the decade of the hedge fund. Hedge fund assets have exploded from about a half trillion dollars in the year 2000 to nearly $2 trillion today. And because hedge funds use leverage, their purchasing power is quite a bit larger than the assets under management may suggest. In fact, some estimates suggest the aggregate purchasing power of hedge funds today is close to $6 trillion. To provide some sense of the purchasing power of hedge funds, consider that they represent only about 3 percent of global equity assets but about 30–40 percent of the trading volume of the average Wall Street trading desk. To be clear, not all this capital is dedicated to equities. Still, equities represent a very large, if not the largest, component of hedge fund assets.

Seeing the large-cap/small-cap valuation disparity in 2000, and being generally much smaller than large institutions, hedge funds gravitated toward the logical part of the market for them, small- and mid-cap stocks. As shown in Panel A of **Figure 2**, hedge funds have a much higher percentage of their assets in small- to mid-cap stocks than mutual funds do. Furthermore, as Panel B shows, hedge funds have a much smaller percentage of their assets under management in large-cap stocks than mutual funds do. So, the hedge fund move into small caps again created a meaningful demand shock for that group, paving the way for small-cap returns. Indeed, small caps have trounced large caps in the 2000s, providing 710 bps (8.8 percent versus 1.7 percent) of annual outperformance. Estimates suggest that roughly one-third of that outperformance, or 250 bps, is attributable to hedge fund demand.

Once again, one can see a large demand increase leaving its footprint on valuation. After spending the vast majority of the time in the 1980s and 1990s at a P/E multiple less than that of the S&P 500, the Value Line P/E now has risen consistently above the S&P 500 since 2003. The massive valuation

Figure 2. Aggregate Assets for Hedge Funds and Mutual Funds, 2001 and 2008

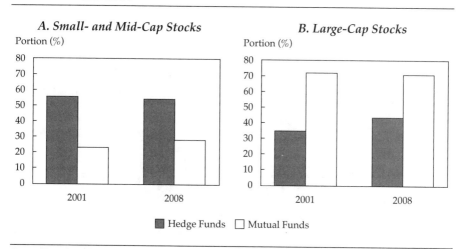

Source: Based on data from *Hedge Fund Trend Monitor*, Goldman Sachs Research (20 May 2008).

disparity of March 2000 is certainly a distant memory at this point. Where we go from here, of course, would be anybody's guess, but it is probably fair to say that the market for large-cap stocks has atoned for its valuation sins of the late 1990s by delivering, in this decade, returns below the returns on T-bills.

Case 3. This last case study is from the world of fixed income and addresses Alan Greenspan's interest rate conundrum. During the 2003–04 period, as the U.S. Federal Reserve was raising short-term rates, long-term interest rates went down. So, the question was: Why did long-term rates come down as short-term rates were going up? The answer again is demand. The source of that demand was foreign central banks, most notably from Asia, and in particular from China. At that time, China followed a mercantilist strategy, which typically has three components. One is a strong export strategy, which resulted in large trade deficits with the United States. The second aspect is a pegged and undervalued currency. The third is low-cost labor. So, a natural outgrowth of China's policy was a surge in foreign exchange reserves, as shown in **Figure 3**. As can be seen, Chinese foreign exchange reserves nearly doubled from 2001 to 2003 and effectively doubled again from 2003 to 2005. In fact, from 2005 to mid-2008, they have effectively doubled once again, to about US$1.5 trillion.

Figure 3. Chinese Foreign Exchange Reserves, 1995–2005

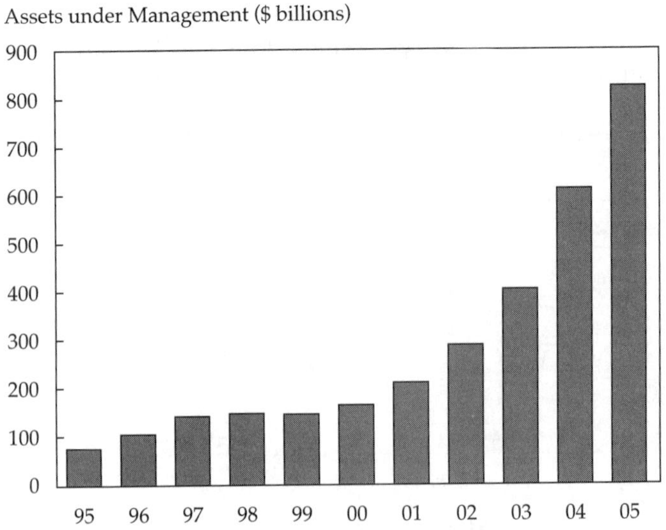

Source: Based on data from Chinability.com.

China is not the only country in this story, but it is the most significant one. The Chinese government and others invested in U.S. Treasuries to manage foreign exchange risk and to shelter against shocks. This demand was not insignificant. Foreign ownership of U.S. Treasuries basically doubled from US$1 trillion in 2001 to US$2 trillion at the end of 2005. Put differently, foreign ownership of U.S. debt rose from 17 percent in 2001 to about 25 percent in 2005. Although this analysis is not without controversy, it has been estimated that strong foreign demand dampened the yield on the 10-year Treasury note by 50–150 bps. In the absence of that large demand, instead of the 4.1 percent yield that prevailed in the spring of 2005, it would have been between 4.6 and 5.6 percent—once again a very material impact that also played a central role in encouraging leverage in the United States.

Summary. The same pattern can be seen in every one of these cases. First, a certain set of conditions creates a flow of money. Second, the beneficiaries of those flows have incentives to invest that money in a certain way. Third, the money and the incentives combine to create a demand shock, which finally leads to asset price performance and, in many cases, asset price revaluation. Although none of these case studies included commodities, this approach is a reasonable way to assess the activity in the commodity markets as well.

Where Do We Go from Here?

In October 2007, the McKinsey Global Institute published a fascinating report titled "The New Power Brokers" (Farrell, Lund, Gerlemann, and Seeburger). That report quite logically points to four power brokers. Two of them—Asian central banks and holders of petrodollars—can be thought of as sources of capital, and two others—hedge funds and private equity—as agents or intermediaries that will invest the money. How big a factor might these power brokers be?

I will start with the sources of capital. Asian central banks today represent more than US$4 trillion of capital, with China and Japan representing the majority of that total. Estimates suggest this sum will swell to US$5 trillion to US$7 trillion in the next five years, depending on what scenario unfolds. The petrodollar inflows are even more impressive. From its current US$4.5 trillion base, forecasts suggest these assets may surge to US$6 trillion to US$8 trillion over the next five years. The bulk of that change, not surprisingly, will flow to Gulf countries, such as Saudi Arabia and Kuwait, but other countries, such as Norway and Russia, will be large beneficiaries as well. Currently, the United States sends US$1 billion a day overseas to pay for petroleum.

Who will invest this money? McKinsey points to continued growth in hedge funds and private equity. Hedge funds currently have about US$1.9 trillion of assets under management. Projections suggest that this amount will grow to US$3.5 trillion to US$4.5 trillion in the next five years. Private equity today is much smaller, about US$700 billion, but estimates here call for a doubling or perhaps even a tripling of assets under management over the next five years. Also, both hedge funds and private equity use a substantial amount of leverage, which will amplify their impact.

Even if the current account surpluses of Asian economies moderate, which many economists anticipate, reserves will continue to grow. Although Asian central banks have historically invested quite conservatively, evidence suggests that Asian governments are starting to seek much higher returns. This shift in asset appetite could have very important implications for markets. In his book *When Markets Collide*, El-Erian (2008) describes a four-step process for countries as they evolve. The first phase is what the author calls "benign neglect," which suggests that most countries are slow to recognize the change in their external accounts. But in phase two, what he calls "sterilization," countries start to realize that they have this money and elect to invest it in safe assets to manage their exchange rate risk and protect against shocks. This mentality has translated into buying high-quality securities, such as U.S. Treasuries.

Step three is what he calls "liability and asset management," which takes some of these excess reserves and invests them in riskier assets or uses them to refinance government debt on more favorable terms. The final step is what he calls "embracing change," which encourages more domestic demand. Large Asian central banks are probably somewhere between stage two, the sterilization phase, and stage three, the liability and asset management phase, right now. But each transition will have a big impact on world markets.

Naturally, the petrodollar flow story hinges largely on the price of oil, and under almost any price scenario, the dollar sums are very large. According to McKinsey's calculations, US$70 a barrel roughly equals US$3 trillion of petrodollars available to be invested over the next five years. At US$90 a barrel, that figure rises to US$4 trillion. Every additional US$20 a barrel change is roughly another US$250 billion in annual net capital inflows. Although predicting the price of oil is extremely difficult, as the last few years have shown, it is hard to see a scenario over the next 5–10 years in which petrodollar capital flows will not be extremely material to the world.

An important item to consider at this point is the return demands of U.S. pension funds. Many large corporations try to strike a balance between provisioning for their future liabilities and maximizing short-term earnings. But when the provisioning and the short-term earnings meet head to head, it is often the provisioning that loses. In his 2007 letter to shareholders, Warren

Buffett noted that the 363 S&P 500 companies with pension funds had about an 8 percent rate of return assumption for those funds. With 28 percent of their assets invested in cash or fixed income with an estimated 5 percent rate of return, the other 72 percent has to earn a 9 percent rate of return to get to the overall 8 percent return assumption. Not surprisingly, this dynamic has led to a meaningful move into alternatives, including hedge funds, private equity, and most recently, commodities. Rightly or wrongly, many pension managers are looking to these alternatives to help solve their liability problem. Many pension funds expect high—in some cases, double-digit—returns from some of these alternative asset classes. According to a Greenwich Associates survey, roughly 45 percent of pension funds indicate that they expect to substantially increase their asset allocation to hedge funds and private equity. At the same time, about 20 percent expect to substantially decrease their allocation to U.S. equities and about 10 percent expect to substantially decrease their fixed-income allocation.

As I mentioned earlier, evidence clearly shows that both central banks and petrodollar countries are shifting away from conservative investments and moving toward more risky assets. These funds are going to be big enough to move the needle. Sovereign wealth funds today are estimated to be US$3.7 trillion, and some projections suggest they could get as large as US$12 trillion by the year 2015. Also, U.S. pension funds seem to be looking for higher returns to satisfy their liabilities. One could argue that hedge funds and private equity stand to benefit from these trends.

What does all this mean for asset prices? Following is a concrete estimate of the impact that sovereign wealth funds may have. Morgan Stanley economists Miles and Jen (2007) argued that as sovereign wealth funds shift their asset allocation away from bonds more toward equity, they are going to express lower risk aversion (i.e., be more tolerant of risk). This lower risk aversion will dampen the equity risk premium and ultimately increase valuation multiples. If true, this analysis suggests an upward repricing and would be fairly constructive for global equities.

What about the intermediaries? Although the lure of hedge funds is certainly undeniable, it remains to be seen whether they will deliver the market-beating returns that investors want. After all, there are about 7,500 hedge funds. And because of the rapid growth in assets under management, concentration has increased. Estimates suggest that the top 100 funds today control 70 percent of the assets, up from 55 percent of the assets just a few years ago. Concentration also forces the large funds to invest more heavily in large-cap stocks. As a result, they may look more like the market, be more correlated with the S&P 500, and as a result, not achieve the return objectives they set out to reach. In private equity, currently, the buyout business has, of course, quieted greatly since the credit crisis started. But these firms are still capital rich and will certainly be opportunistic, as evidenced by the number of distressed funds being started.

Another aspect of opportunism is the recognition that it is a very big world out there. Although the United States still has a dominant share of the global equity market, most economists believe that the U.S. share will decline in years to come. In this context, I recommend Zakaria's book *The Post American World* (2008). His argument is not that the United States is in decline but, rather, that the rest of the world is in ascent, which is a very different dynamic. Jeremy Siegel's (2008) work, as shown in **Figure 4**, suggests that the United States will dip well below 20 percent of the global equity market cap by the middle of the century and China and the rest of the world will grow sharply.

In thinking about where future returns may come from, it is instructive to look at recent performance, shown in **Figure 5**. For return data, mean reversion is the concept that asset classes that are in vogue, that have fared well recently, will tend to cool and those that are unloved, that have been sluggish, will tend to do better over time. This figure shows 10 years of returns in a few selected asset classes. The globalization theme is evident, as seen in the returns of emerging markets and commodities. At the same time, the excesses of the 1990s put a damper on the returns of U.S. large-cap equities. The combination of large pools of capital to be invested, a growing appetite for risk, and a greater concentration in the favored investment vehicles (hedge funds and private equity) suggests that the future for large-cap equities could be brighter.

Conclusion

First, financial institutions/agents do matter. Interestingly, this reality has not seeped into the asset-pricing literature yet, which is a divergence between the real world and theory.

Second, new power brokers are emerging. Intellectually, most people know this, but the numbers are probably bigger than they realize. The foundation is clearly in place for the Asian central banks and petrodollar pools to play a major role in markets, at least for the next three to five years.

Third, money flows can alter asset prices. Demand curves, unlike in theory, are not horizontal for equities, as my examples showed. This perspective may also be relevant for today's commodity markets given the increasing role of indexing in commodity markets.

Finally, I will conclude with the key point of the sociology of markets: Follow the money and consider the role of incentives.

Michael J. Mauboussin is a chief investment strategist at Legg Mason Capital Management, Baltimore.

**Figure 4.   Characteristics of World Equity,
              2007 and 2050**

A. 2007 World Equity

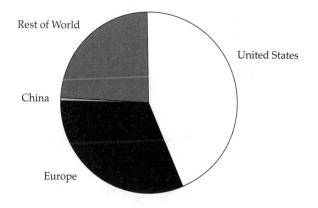

B. 2050 World Equity

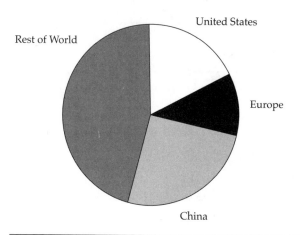

Sources: Based on data from Siegel (2008), MSCI Blue Book, and author estimates.

Figure 5.   Annual Return by Asset Class, 1998–2007

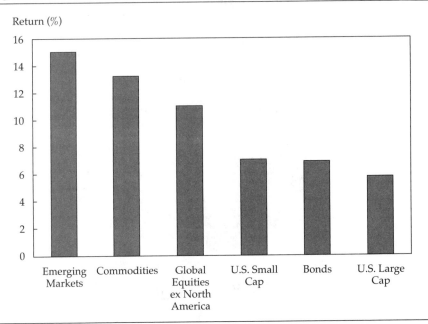

Sources: Based on data from Callan Associates and Bloomberg.

REFERENCES

Allen, Franklin. 2001. "Do Financial Institutions Matter?" *Journal of Finance*, vol. 56, no. 4 (August):1165–1175.

Banz, Rolf W. 1981. "The Relationship between Return and Market Value of Common Stocks." *Journal of Financial Economics*, vol. 9, no. 1 (March):3–18.

Berle, Adolf A., and Gardiner C. Means. 1932. *The Modern Corporation and Private Property*. New York: Harcourt, Brace & World.

Cornell, Bradford, and Richard Roll. 2005. "A Delegated-Agent Asset-Pricing Model." *Financial Analysts Journal*, vol. 61, no. 1 (January/February):57–69.

El-Erian, Mohamed. 2008. *When Markets Collide: Investment Strategies for the Age of Global Economic Change*. New York: McGraw-Hill.

Farrell, Diana, Susan Lund, Eva Gerlemann, and Peter Seeburger. 2007. "The New Power Brokers: How Oil, Asia, Hedge Funds, and Private Equity Are Shaping Global Capital Markets." Executive summary, McKinsey Global Institute (October).

Gompers, Paul A., and Andrew Metrick. 2001. "Institutional Investors and Equity Prices." *Quarterly Journal of Economics*, vol. 116, no. 1 (February):229–259.

Jensen, William H., and Michael C. Meckling. 1976. "Theory of the Firm: Managerial Behavior, Agency Costs, and Capital Structure." *Journal of Financial Economics*, vol. 3, no. 4 (October):305–360.

Miles, David K., and Stephen Jen. 2007. "Sovereign Wealth Funds and Bond and Equity Prices." Morgan Stanley Research (31 May).

Siegel, Jeremy J. 2008. *Stocks for the Long Run*. 4th ed. New York: McGraw-Hill.

Zakaria, Fareed. 2008. *The Post American World*. New York: W.W. Norton.

Question and Answer Session
Michael J. Mauboussin

Question: How will these institutional flows play out?

Mauboussin: The problem is that it gets very crowded very fast. The most applicable example today is commodities. Demand growth in the rest of the world has led to legitimately higher prices. At the same time, studies have supported investing in commodities as an asset class because of their attractive and uncorrelated returns. But the conditions that prevailed in the past in commodity markets (such as the backwardation in market prices) are not the conditions that prevail today. Instead, speculators have been an important reason for the price swings in commodities, in general, and oil, in particular.

The problem is that markets tend to be efficient when there is a diversity of opinion operating. When diversity breaks down, markets become inefficient. I think it would be fair to say we have diversity breakdowns in some commodity markets.

Question: How "smartly" do you think sovereign wealth funds are being run?

Mauboussin: I suspect that the managers of sovereign wealth funds are following a learning curve. At present, I believe there is a wide range of sophistication in sovereign wealth fund managers. In many respects, it is not unlike winning the lottery. In a short time, one goes from modest resources to an abundance of them. As a result, most do not have a premeditated game plan for how to proceed.

Question: What are the implications for stock pickers if stocks are not fairly priced based on their fundamentals?

Mauboussin: I believe that over long periods of time, stock markets are basically efficient. But for markets to be efficient, there must be diversity of opinion and properly functioning incentives. If this is not the case, markets can be mispriced for substantial periods of time, perhaps even years, before fundamentals come back into line.

The only answer I can offer is to maintain a long-term orientation without too much leverage, and have a lot of patience. Ultimately, I believe that price and value tend to converge.